# DOWN SYNDROME

*Birth to Adulthood*

Giving Families an EDGE

## JOHN E. RYNDERS
*University of Minnesota*

## J. MARGARET HORROBIN
*Pediatrician, HealthPartners of Minneapolis*

## LOVE PUBLISHING COMPANY®
Denver · London · Sydney

Library of Congress Catalog Card Number 94-76444

Copyright © 1996 Love Publishing Company
Printed in the U.S.A.
ISBN 0-89108-236-0

# ONTENTS

# 7 THE SCHOOL YEARS: BECOMING LITERATE 163 AND SOCIALIZED

*John Rynders*

# 8 ONE FOOT IN SCHOOL, ONE IN 193 A COMMUNITY RECREATION SETTING

*John E. Rynders, Stuart J. Schleien,
and Shannon L. Matson*

# 9 ONE HAND ON THE SCHOOL DOOR, 213 ONE ON THE DOOR TO WORK AND INDEPENDENT LIVING

*Alan Fletcher*

*10* **M**AINTAINING HEALTH INTO ADULTHOOD **239**

*Margaret Horrobin*

*11* **L**OOKING BACK, LOOKING AHEAD    **257**

*John Rynders*

*12* **G**IVING VOICE: YOUNG ADULTS'    **281**
PERSPECTIVES ON THEIR LIVES

*I. Karon Sherarts*

# OREWORD

small book appeared in 1974 bearing the title *To Give an EDGE*. That book was an outgrowth of a federally funded early intervention study called Project EDGE that we co-directed. The project provided family-based early intervention designed to improve the language capabilities of children with Down syndrome, as well as whole family development in general, beginning when the children were born.

We wrote the 1974 book because we felt that all parents who had a child with Down syndrome needed strong but realistic encouragement, tips on helpful child-rearing strategies, and accurate information regarding which types of programming looked promising and which did not. While the 1974 book was not a comprehensive how-to manual, it did provide accurate, in-depth information in areas we believed were key to assisting families in their efforts to achieve a more satisfying life. Most importantly, the *EDGE* book of 20 years ago served as a vehicle for parent-to-parent communication, support, and learning.

The desire for attractively presented, accurate, practical, research-based, cutting-edge information remains strong among parents who have a child with Down syndrome and the professionals who serve them. We know this is so because requests for the original *EDGE* book have continued to come in at a relatively high and constant rate. (More than 40,000 copies of the original book have been purchased in the last 20 years, even though it has never been advertised except by word of mouth.) Nevertheless, realizing that the 1974 book was in need of major updating and upgrading, we decided to do a new one. Moreover, we had a very exciting possibility at hand: We and the EDGE parents had an opportunity to write a book that would not only be of immediate help to parents with a newborn child with Down syndrome, but it would also let new parents know what children with Down syndrome can accomplish *across the entire age span of birth to adulthood!* EDGE parents could share—through words and pictures—what 20 years of life with a son or daughter who has Down syndrome has been like. In addition, the exciting possibility of encouraging the EDGE young adults with Down syndrome to speak for themselves now existed. Thus, in Chapter 11, parents and brothers and sisters share their feelings about life with a sibling who has Down syndrome. Then, in Chapter 12, persons with Down syndrome offer their own perspective on school, work, friends, fun, and becoming more independent. They also share their feelings about having Down syndrome.

We wish to note that this book cannot possibly "speak" for all persons with Down syndrome and their families. Although the EDGE group in the Twin Cities included a black child (who, sadly, died early in life), all of the Twin Cities parents are of Caucasian extraction. Furthermore, while EDGE parents in the Twin Cities represent a relatively broad cross-section of socio-economic status, they tend to represent middle- to upper-middle-income Americans. Such a "selection bias" was inevitable to a large extent because the parents in the Twin Cities and the parents in the Chicago area who served as a contrast group (we are eternally grateful for their cooperation) volunteered for study inclusion through ads placed in parent organization newsletters. Since dues are required to belong to these organizations and to receive the organizations' newsletter, the parents tend to be reasonably well-off economically.

It's a new day for individuals with Down syndrome and their families. The practices prevalent 20 years ago, such as advising parents to place their child in an institution for a lifetime, excluding people with Down syndrome from meaningful academic and vocational training, and sometimes from schooling and employment itself, have now given way. Currently, early institutionalization is almost unheard of. Academic and vocational training is now not only functionally oriented, but prepares the individual for a satisfying community life. A sizeable number of opportunities, offering a large measure of independence for persons with Down syndrome and their family members, are available in 1995. Not that everything is ideal, but at least there are many more options and resources available today for people with Down syndrome and their families than there were in even the recent past. We trust that parents and professionals, working together, will create opportunities for people with Down syndrome in the next century that are now hard to imagine. We expect, also, that persons with Down syndrome will become increasingly more able to advocate in their own behalf.

JR & MH

# $\mathcal{A}$CKNOWLEDGMENTS

$\mathcal{T}$his book is dedicated to parents of children who have Down syndrome, to individuals with Down syndrome, and to their sisters and brothers. It is especially dedicated to parents and their children with Down syndrome in Project EDGE,* who challenge us continuously with their capabilities, resiliency, and courage. In Minnesota they are:

Richard and Margaret Bauman, and David
Eugene and Lorraine Byland, and Karen
David and Char Colwell, and Holly
Don and Kathy Finnerty, and Tim
Wayne and Judy Fleming, and Richard
Alan and Judy Fletcher, and Amy
Charles and Bettye Grigsby, and Bryan**
William and Joan Krippner, and Wayne
Phillip and Barbara Lindblad, and Alexander
John and Wanda Nightengale, and Andrew
Harold and Joan Opat, and Tom
Ted and Karon Sherarts, and Eric
Ray and Barbara Thomes, and Brian
Lowell and Phyllis Wheeler, and Eric
Richard and Shirley Woodard, and Robert
Tibor and Olga Zoltai, and Lillian

The authors wish to acknowledge the contribution of several individuals and agencies for their support in the development, production, and distribution of this book:

David Colwell and the Colwell Press, Inc. for their generosity in printing and distributing the original EDGE booklet in 1974, and to David's niece, Meg, for distributing the original book over the last 10 years through Viking Press, Inc.

David Wangsness for some of the excellent photographs in this book.

Cheryl Morgan, Laura Lafrenz, and Lori Mack for their outstanding work in typing the manuscript.

The University of Minnesota Rehabilitation Research and Training Center on Community Integration of Persons with Mental Retardation, funded through the National Institute on Disability and Rehabilitation Research under Cooperative Agreement No. 133B80048, for supporting the development of portions of the manuscript for this book.

No contributor to the book, including its two authors, receives royalties from its sale. Royalties earned are all donated to nonprofit parent-professional organizations that support people with Down syndrome and their families.

---

* Project EDGE (*E*xpanding *D*evelopmental *G*rowth through *E*ducation) was a five-year early intervention project to promote the development of young children with Down syndrome. Project EDGE was supported by Grant No. OEG-09-332189-4533(032) from the United States Office of Education and was administered through the University of Minnesota's Research, Development and Demonstration Center in Education of Handicapped Persons. EDGE was directed by Drs. John Rynders and Margaret Horrobin.

The project currently is in a follow-through phase. Portions of the follow-through phase are supported by the Rehabilitation Research and Training Center on Improving Community Integration for Persons with Mental Retardation, U.S. Department of Education (Grant No. H133830072), NIDRR. Support for the development of this book came, in part, from this grant. The opinions expressed in this document do not necessarily reflect official federal policy and/or philosophy.

** Child is deceased.

~*1*~

# *A* VIEW OF LIFE AS A JOURNEY

John Rynders

very person is a time traveler, on a journey through the places, times, opportunities, and events of a lifetime. Each will mark his or her progress, based, perhaps, on passing successfully through age-related events (school graduation, getting and holding a job). Some will gauge their success in terms of attaining certain personal goals (building a cabin in the wilderness, winning a blue ribbon at the state fair). Every person's journey will be influenced by the era in which she or he lives (cold war, hot war; depression, prosperity; before TV, after TV), the geographic area in which he or she grows up (urban ghetto versus affluent suburb), the individual's health and temperament, and a myriad of other factors. For children, the ability and motivation of their parents will likely play a very large part in their attaining many of life's goals.

In most parents' journey through life, having a baby is a landmark event. Not only do prospective parents usually have a deep-seated biological urge to pass on their genes, but expectant parents also dream about what their baby will grow up to be. Moreover, expectant parents dream about what living with a new son or daughter will be like. Some of the dreams are unrealistic, of course. Dreaming about the baby's arrival, however, is an enjoyable thing to do.

But what happens when the new baby does not fit into the parents' dream because the baby has a disability? Although most prospective parents think briefly about the possibility of having a baby with Down syndrome, they dismiss these thoughts quickly as a "bad dream that won't happen to me." What, then, if the "bad dream" is suddenly thrust upon them? Because they usually are totally unprepared for having a baby with a disability (unless a prenatal diagnosis has prepared them for it), their dreams of having a normal baby and the personal expectations that go with that dream are shattered abruptly, replaced perhaps by frightening images of "mongoloids." For most, the dream reconstruction period soon begins, based in part on factual information about Down syndrome they will gather. More important than facts, however, their reconstructed dreams will be built on information from other parents who have a child with Down syndrome: information about their happy times and sad ones, their fears and the ways they tried to conquer them, the techniques they developed to overcome problems.* Relating their own experiences, seasoned parents help new parents rebuild their dreams.

To illustrate the significance of dream building and then rebuilding, we turn to an inspiring "journey report" written by Emily Kingsley, a mother whose son, Jason, has Down syndrome.

## ELCOME TO HOLLAND

*by Emily Perl Kingsley***

I am often asked to describe the experience of raising a child with a disability—to try to help people who have not shared that unique experience to understand it, to imagine how it would feel. It's like this....

When you're going to have a baby, it's like planning a fabulous vacation trip—to Italy. You buy a bunch of guide books and make your wonderful plans. The Coliseum. The Michelangelo David. The gondolas in Venice. You may learn some handy phrases in Italian. It's all very exciting.

After months of eager anticipation, the day finally arrives. You pack your bags and off you go. Several hours later, the plane lands. The stewardess comes in and says, "Welcome to Holland."

"*Holland?*" you exclaim. "What do you mean, Holland? I signed up for Italy! I'm supposed to be in Italy. All my life I've dreamed of going to Italy."

But there's been a change in the flight plan. They've landed in Holland, and there you must stay.

The important thing is that they haven't taken you to a horrible, disgusting, filthy place, full of pestilence, famine, and disease. It's just a different place.

So you must go out and buy new guide books. And you must learn a whole new language. And you will meet a whole new group of people you never would have met.

It's just a *different* place. It's slower-paced than Italy, less flashy than Italy. But after you've been there a while and you catch your breath, you

---

\* See Chapter 3 for a full discussion of what new parents experience during the newborn period of life.

\*\* We thank Emily Kingsley for allowing us to reprint this wonderfully insightful piece.

look around, and you begin to notice that Holland has windmills, Holland has tulips, Holland even has Rembrandts.

But everyone you know is busy coming and going from Italy, and they're all bragging about what a wonderful time they had there. For the rest of your life, you will say, "Yes, that's where I was supposed to go. That's what I had planned."

And the pain of that will never ever, ever, ever, go away, because the loss of that dream is a significant loss.

But if you spend your life mourning the fact that you didn't get to Italy, you never may be free to enjoy the very special, the very lovely things about Holland.

---

Just as each individual in a family goes on a lifetime developmental journey, *families* composed of individuals interacting with each other and influenced by all sorts of external events have a distinctive developmental journey, too. Indeed, families have journeying experiences that are every bit as distinctive as individual journeys. Thus, this book will take a *family* focus throughout its pages.

Rearing a child with Down syndrome has a significant impact on a family's journey—no question about that. Often, though, what is far from clear is the specific nature of the impact and its long-term consequences. Is the impact of raising a child with Down syndrome largely negative, as some have suggested? Are the long-term consequences inevitably crippling to family harmony and disruptive to parents' and siblings' goals, as some have alleged? Or might some children with Down syndrome learn to speak intelligibly and even learn to read? Might some live relatively independently and hold a job? Might some (dare we think it) become an asset, even a joy, to their parents?

The goal of this book is to address these questions. In doing so, we will draw extensively from the personal experiences of fifteen parents who have a child with Down syndrome, parents who have been together as a group ever since their babies with Down syndrome were born, journeying together because of their involvement in an early education research project called EDGE (*E*xpanding *D*evelopmental *G*rowth through *E*ducation), which began in 1968. In the pages that follow, we will blend in our research findings from EDGE and summarize relevant findings from many other studies. Readers of this book, then, will receive not only an in-depth view of the personal journeying experiences of fifteen families but also a composite view of at least parts of the journeys of hundreds of families around the USA and, in some cases, beyond.

We will begin by describing the time in which the fifteen EDGE families lived over the last 25 years. A family journey beginning in 1968 is vastly

## TABLE I

Contrasting a family journey beginning in 1994 with one that began in 1968.

| 1968* | 1994** |
|---|---|
| ■ *Child with Down syndrome is born:* Parents typically are given two options:<br>1. Immediate placement of child in a state residential institution.<br>2. Take your baby home; "good luck"—you're on your own.<br>Focus of service is on the *child*, not on the whole family. | ■ *Child with Down syndrome is born:* Parents typically are encouraged to take their baby home; residential placement at birth is rare. Parents receive early intervention services, beginning at birth in most states, including attention to health needs, whole-family social support, early education. If possible, services are provided without financial cost to parents. Focus of service is on the *family*, with the child as part of the family. |
| ■ *Child with Down syndrome is preschooler:* Self-contained (segregated) preschool program is the rule, not the exception. | ■ *Child with Down syndrome is preschooler:* Mainstream preschool program is becoming the rule, with the self-contained (segregated) program becoming the exception to the rule. |
| ■ *Child with Down syndrome is school age:* Mainstreamed (integrated) education is rare. Special schools and special classes are commonly accepted. Academic instruction is extremely limited; emphasis is on self-care. Class placement is usually in a class labeled "trainable" rather than "educable." | ■ *Child with Down syndrome is school age:* Mainstreamed (integrated) education, at least for part of the day, is common and often takes place in the regular neighborhood school. Academic instruction is provided. Class placement usually is in a class labeled "educable" or "regular" rather than "trainable." |
| ■ *Child with Down syndrome is approaching high school graduation:* Education occurs mainly in the special class. Emphasis is placed on classroom simulations of living in the community. | ■ *Child with Down syndrome is approaching high school graduation:* Education occurs at least as much in the community as it does in the school classroom, whether it's a regular class or a special class. Emphasis is on skills needed to live successfully in the community, which then are practiced in the community prior to graduation. |
| ■ *Person with Down syndrome graduates:* If living at home, stays at home until parents cannot care for him or her any longer; then the individual is placed in a state institution. Employment opportunities are limited or nonexistent. | ■ *Person with Down syndrome graduates:* May live at home for a while but often moves gradually into a supported living and working environment in the community. A guardian or trustee is appointed to tend to the person's needs when natural parents are no longer able to do so. A variety of employment opportunities are available. |

*When EDGE project began.  ** EDGE children are now young adults.

different from a journey beginning in 1994, as Table 1 shows. Let's meet two of the fifteen families and their sons and daughters with Down syndrome from the EDGE project. The montages that follow were created from photos contributed by individuals with Down syndrome and their parents. These mini family photo albums cut across three age periods—infancy, school years, young adult—and highlight a few events and activities that influenced family life.*

---

* Mini family albums are inserted throughout the book in alphabetical order, except for the Fletcher and Sherarts families; their family photos were placed in the chapters they contributed.

## ℬAUMAN FAMILY

Dad: Dick
Mom: Margaret
Sister: Melissa
Brother: J. R.
Brother with Down
    syndrome: David

Future sports stars.

Do you see a family resemblance? (People with Down syndrome don't "all look alike.")

Gaining some independence.

# 𝓑AUMAN FAMILY (continued)

Trick or treat.

Ready to take the plunge.

Do a good deed every day.

A proud moment for a young adult.

# ℬYLAND FAMILY

Dad: Eugene
Mom: Lorraine
Brother: Eugene
Brother: Jeffrey
Sister: Judy (Osterndorf)
Sister: Jacqueline (Hannasch)
Sister with Down syndrome:
   Karen

Every day is fun when
you are three years old!

Hairstyles may change over the years, but families are *eternal*.

## $\mathcal{B}$YLAND FAMILY (continued)

*Some* boys are o.k.

Growing up.

Dancing is great!

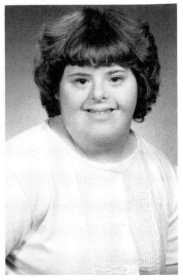

Grown up.

# ~2~

# $\mathcal{B}$EGINNING THE JOURNEY

John Rynders

$\mathcal{D}$r. King, a pediatrician, has just told Joyce and Frank Blakely that their newborn son, Rob, has Down syndrome.* At that moment, having only a vague idea of what the term *Down syndrome* means but a great deal of anxiety about what it *might* mean, Joyce and Frank begin to pick up pieces of emotionally charged historical "baggage" to begin their journey. This baggage was created more than a hundred years ago and becomes the exclusive burden of parents who have a child with Down syndrome. Indeed, at the moment of their child's birth (before, if prenatal diagnosis was done), parents who have a child with Down syndrome begin their journey weighted down with baggage that no parent with a normal baby has to pick up. What is this baggage? Misperceptions, folklore, and half-truths about the condition of Down syndrome which create barriers to their child's and their own developmental progress.

Reflecting their anxiety, the parents pour out a flood of questions for Dr. King: "What is Down syndrome? What causes it? Whose fault is it? Could it have been prevented? How can you, our doctor, be certain that our child has it? Will it happen again if we have another child? How serious is it? Should we take our baby home or not?"

## $\mathcal{C}$HROMOSOMAL MAKE-UP

Dr. King explains that Down syndrome is a chromosomal disorder. Children with the condition have an extra chromosome in their cells, the result of faulty cell division in the egg or sperm before conception, or the result of an error in cell division after the ovum is fertilized and begins to divide. Dr. King

---

* "Syndrome" means a cluster of specific symptoms. "Down" is the name of the physician credited with describing Down syndrome in a formal manner for the first time.

explains that chromosomes are biochemical strands somewhat like complex "zippers," with each "tooth" of the zipper representing a gene, a coded portion of the whole zipper. Each gene carries a different piece of information and is a complex biochemical structure in its own right. Although chromosomes can be seen through powerful magnification techniques, genes are too small to be seen even with the most powerful microscopes.

Each form of life has its own genetic code and special set of chromosomes, which differ from life form to life form in terms of chromosome size, shape, number per cell, and other characteristics. The typical nondisabled person has forty-six chromosomes in each cell. People with Down syndrome have one extra chromosome in each of their cells, for a total of forty-seven. How does this happen? In humans, the mother and father ordinarily contribute twenty-three chromosomes each at conception, creating the normal complement of forty-six per cell. Sometimes, however, the chromosomes, from father or mother, do not "unzip" properly, do not divide in half as they should before conception, and one extra chromosome is carried into the new cells that become an embryo. This is called *chromosomal nondisjunction*, or failure to disjoin. Hence, eventually, all cells in the baby will have forty-seven chromosomes instead of the typical forty-six.

Each chromosome has different characteristics, such as differences in size, shape, and combination of various genes. Down syndrome occurs when certain, identifiable chromosomes (those designated as number 21 in a charting system called a karyotype) stick together, creating a tripleting of chromosomes rather than the normal pairing (see Figure 1). If a tripleting had occurred in some other pair of chromosomes—for example, the pair designated as number 13 on the figure—the child would have a specific syndrome but not Down syndrome.

Unfortunately, medical researchers have not discovered why this error in cell division happens, although scientists know it can be of either maternal or paternal origin. In at least 5 percent of live births of babies with Down syndrome, the father can be identified as contributing the extra chromosome. Down syndrome is correlated with the aging of either parent, with the clearest correlation related to maternal age. Other than that, it seems to occur by chance, except in some rare instances in which one parent may be a carrier for the translocation form of Down syndrome. If a husband or wife has a relative with Down syndrome, the couple may want to seek professional genetic counseling before having children to find out whether either is a carrier for the translocation type of Down syndrome. Other than seeking genetic counseling, scientists know of nothing that the wife or husband could have done to prevent Down syndrome, short of preventing conception itself.

Down syndrome occurs in approximately one of 1,000 live births (four

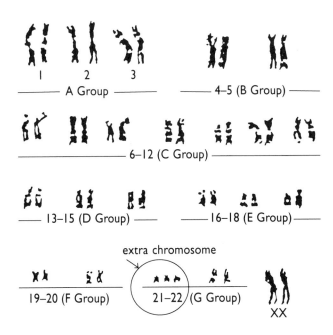

## 𝓕IGURE 1

Chromosomes (karyotype) of a female with Down syndrome.

Based on a photo of a karyotype in a pamphlet, *Down Syndrome*, published by the National Down Syndrome Congress.

of five fetuses with Down syndrome are aborted spontaneously) during a woman's prime childbearing years (usually the mid-20s). Though women in their later years of fertility should realize that their chances of having a child with Down syndrome increase with each year after their mid-20s, the chances are only about one in forty live births in their late 40s or even early 50s.

Running laboratory tests on a sample of a child's blood shows whether the child has Down syndrome. To do this test, a blood sample is drawn and then cultured under special laboratory conditions to enable the cells to divide. At the point of cell division, cells are killed, treated with chemicals to make certain features of the chromosomes stand out, and photographed under conditions of high magnification so the photos of individual chromosomes can be cut out and arranged in accord with the chromosome charting system.

Nondisjunction is responsible for about 95 percent of Down syndrome cases. In the other 5 percent of cases, the extra chromosome is attached to another chromosome, rather than floating free. This is the rare condition called *translocation*, mentioned earlier. In other equally rare circumstances, a child will have a type of Down syndrome called *mosaicism*. Mosaicism means that some, but not all, of the cells in the child's body contain an extra chromosome. Children with the mosaic form of Down syndrome seem to be less affected, on the average, in terms of their functioning, as compared with children with the other two forms of the syndrome, but there seems to be little or no relation between the percentage of normal cells and the child's functioning ability. Currently, scientists do not know what causes chromosomal nondisjunction, translocation, and mosaicism, but they are convinced that the mystery of abnormal chromosome division will be solved early in the next century, if not sooner.

New parents should know that the extra chromosome that produces Down syndrome is a perfectly *normal* number 21 chromosome, which comes directly from the mother or the father. It is not a chromosome from somewhere else or someone else, nor is it defective, "bad," or unhealthy. Also of importance to know is that, because the two parents personally contributed the chromosome material, their new child with Down syndrome will resemble them and other members of their family. Their child, just as distinctive as every human being is, also will be uniquely like them.

Clues that a child might have Down syndrome often are obvious during an infant's first days of life. Noticing that a baby has a slightly "Oriental" appearance (which spawned the term *mongolism,* an erroneous racial association, as true Oriental people and people with Down syndrome show clear facial dissimilarities), hospital personnel will examine the child to see if certain physical characteristics that often, though not always, accompany the syndrome are present.

They will look to see if the child has almond-shaped eyes with a fold of skin at each inner corner, a flat nasal bridge and flattened cheeks, short ears, "floppiness" of muscle tone (hypotonia), inward-turned, shortened, little fingers, abundant neck skin, or absence of the Moro reflex (a reflex appearing in a normal baby when body support is carefully and suddenly withdrawn, whereupon the baby's muscles tighten). None of these signs, or even clusters of signs taken together, can definitely confirm a diagnosis of Down syndrome because no child who has this syndrome will show all of the signs (there are more than fifty of them), and any single so-called critical sign observed in confirmed cases of Down syndrome also can be found in normal children. Confirmation comes only by examining the chromosomes of a child suspected of having the condition.

Regarding the seriousness of Down syndrome, Dr. King tells the Blakelys that several types of chromosomal conditions are far more devastating to a child's development than Down syndrome. Even so, the condition certainly is not to be taken lightly.

# *D*EVELOPMENTAL CHARACTERISTICS

Table 2 should be helpful to new parents as they attempt to judge what type of physical, language, social, and self-help development to expect of their child at a given age. Although young children with Down syndrome tend to be delayed in every area of development as compared with normal children, notice that individual children with the condition vary a great deal. Their developmental prospects are highly individualistic. Furthermore, research findings gathered over the last twenty years show that children with Down syndrome, particularly those who have received early education, often func-

# ᴛABLE 2

## Children's Developmental Achievements: A Comparison

| | Young Children Who Have Down Syndrome | | Young Nondisabled Children | |
|---|---|---|---|---|
| | Average Age | Age Range | Average Age | Age Range |
| *Gross Motor* | | | | |
| Sits | 10 months | 6–24 months | 7 months | 5–9 months |
| Crawls | 13 months | 7½–21½ months | 8½ months | 6–11½ months |
| Stands | 15 months | 11-35½ months | 11 months | 8–16½ months |
| Walks | 23 months | 12–46½ months | 13½ months | 8½–18 months |
| *Language* | | | | |
| First Word | 23 months | 1–4 years | 12 months | 8–23 months |
| Two-Word Phrases | 36 months | 2–7½ years | 2 years | 15–32 months |
| *Social* | | | | |
| Responsive Smile | 3 months | 1½–5 months | 1½ months | 1–3 months |
| *Self-Help* | | | | |
| Finger Feeding | 15 months | 9–24 months | 9 months | 6–15 months |
| Drinks from Cup (Unassisted) | 23 months | 12–32 months | 13 months | 9–17 months |
| Uses Spoon | 29 months | 13–39 months | 14 months | 12–20 months |
| Bladder Control | 48 months | 20–95 months | 32 months | 18–60 months |
| Bowel Control | 43½ months | 26–87 months | 26 months | 16–44 months |
| Undressing | 40 months | 29–72 months | 32 months | 22–42 months |
| Dresses Self (Not Doing Fasteners) | 7¼ years | 3½–8¼ years | 4 years | 3¼–5 years |

Contents of this table are based on developmental achievements as described in *Down Syndrome: The Facts* by M. Selikowitz (New York: Oxford University Press, 1990) and *A Parent's Guide to Down Syndrome* by S. Pueschel (Baltimore: Paul H. Brookes, 1990). Achievement descriptors in the two sources were combined in some instances, and age-equivalents were averaged in some cases to create the present table.

tion at the educable level in school, have productive hobbies, are contributing members of their families, and are well-received in their communities. Indeed, their stereotyped portrayal as uneducable, unskilled, and unproductive is unfortunate and unrealistic.

In the area of intellectual ability, expectations are frequently erroneous. Although most school-age children with Down syndrome have mild-to-moderate, not severe, intellectual impairments, their classmates, their teachers, and sometimes even their parents often underestimate their potential. That is unfortunate because people with Down syndrome today are achieving success in education, vocation, and self-sufficiency, especially if they received long-term stimulation and support of a high quality.

We have considerable reason for optimism, even though the condition will not go away. Children who have forty-seven chromosomes in their cells at birth will have that number in their cells for their entire lives. Even if one were able somehow to remove the extra twenty-first chromosome from each cell, the manifestations of Down syndrome would not disappear. They were laid down in the early stages of embryonic development. Even though Down syndrome cannot be prevented in a primary way, enhancing the child's developmental potential can be pursued with positive results.

Regarding the seriousness of the chromosome problem, new parents of a child with Down syndrome often have glaring misconceptions about the condition, stemming from outdated, distorted statements in books and magazines, many of which imply that their child will be grossly abnormal. Depressing expressions such as "mongolian type of idiocy," "unfinished children," and "monster" have appeared throughout the past hundred years in reference to Down syndrome.

Sooner or later parents will need to deal with their feelings at the deepest, and perhaps most troubling, levels of thought. Some parents even feel that God is punishing them with a child with Down syndrome because of some sin they have committed. They should stop to consider that even highly religious and loving parents can have a child with Down syndrome. As deep feelings are bared—a process that often takes considerable time, and often the assistance of someone skilled in counseling in matters such as these— parents also will need to receive factual information that will help them decide whether they will be able to cope successfully with their child's condition.

Regarding the question, "Should we take our newborn child home?" Dr. King advises the Blakelys that most parents adjust to the characteristics of Down syndrome and grow to love their child deeply. Occasionally, though, parents are unable to love their new child with Down syndrome genuinely even after the initial shock and depression have passed. To force them to rear a child whom they clearly and completely reject is not a good idea. It is psychologically unhealthy for them and for their child. In many cases of "rejection," however, a counselor observes that parents, though reluctant at first to keep their baby at home, may be receptive to this possibility once they are educated on how to cope successfully with rearing the child on a long-term basis.

Having supplied a few basic facts about the cause of Down syndrome, Dr. King tells the Blakelys that sometimes people, even today, refer to a child with Down syndrome as a "mongoloid." This label becomes the Blakely's first piece of baggage, a trunk full of misperceptions and folklore that have been accumulating for more than a hundred years.

# HE BAGGAGE

In 1866 Dr. John Langdon Down provided the first formal published description of Down syndrome, a condition he called "mongolism."[1] He said that people with this condition (whom we now refer to as having Down syndrome) represent a genetic mutation of the "Mongolian family," a result of ethnic and racial degeneracy. We will trace the history of Down syndrome from 1866 to the present because parents need to be aware of what professionals have said about children with Down syndrome as they acted in their behalf, sometimes with disastrous results.

J. Langdon Down's article stands as a landmark document in the written history of Down syndrome. In attempting to classify the various forms of "feeblemindedness" he had observed, and probably influenced strongly by Charles Darwin's thoughts on evolution, which were popular at that time, Down concluded that individuals with mental retardation belonged to various ethnic classifications, including the "Ethiopian and Malay varieties." His description of people he believed to belong to the "Mongolian family" is of particular interest. He wrote:

> The great Mongolian family has numerous representatives, and it is to this division, I wish, in this paper, to call special attention. A very large number of congenital idiots [not a derogatory term at that time] are typical Mongols. So marked is this that, when placed side by side, it is difficult to believe that the specimens [people] compared are not children of the same parents. The number of idiots [persons with mental retardation] who arrange themselves around the Mongolian type is so great, and they present such a close resemblance to one another in mental power, that I shall describe an idiot member of this racial division, selected from the large number that have fallen under my observation.
> The hair is not black, as the real Mongol, but of a brownish color, straight

and scanty. The face is flat and broad, and destitute of prominence. The cheeks are roundish, and extended laterally. The eyes are obliquely placed, and the internal canthi more than normally distant from one another.... The lips are large and thick with transverse fissures. The tongue is long, thick, and is much roughened. The nose is small. The skin has a slightly dirty yellowish tinge, and is deficient in elasticity, giving the appearance of being too large for the body.

The boy's aspect is such that it is difficult to realize that he is the child of Europeans, but so frequently are these characters presented that there can be no doubt that these ethnic features are the result of degeneration.[2]

In light of the era of racial elitism in which he lived, it is remarkable that Dr. Down did not portray the developmental prospects of "mongols" (persons with Down syndrome) as devoid of hope. To the contrary, near the end of his historic article in *Clinical Lectures and Reports*, he wrote: "They are cases which very much repay judicious treatment..." (p. 261). Moreover, he seemed to draw away from the European superiority notion that was popular in his time, saying at the end of his article: "These examples of the result of degeneracy among mankind appear to me to furnish some arguments in favor of the unity of the human species" (p. 262).

Approximately sixty years after Dr. Down's paper, Crookshank made an assertion so incredible (and so wrong) that J. Langdon Down's hypothesis of ethnic degeneracy seemed pale by comparison. In 1924 Crookshank concluded that people with Down syndrome represent a regression to a nonhuman species.[3]

From more recent times there is the story of the well-known theologian, Joseph Fletcher, who attempted to comfort a bereaved parent, Bernard Bard. After an emotional struggle, this father had concluded that he must institutionalize his child with Down syndrome. Fletcher, too, went far beyond the notion of degeneracy when he wrote:

> People in the Bards' situation have no reason to feel guilty about putting a Down's syndrome baby away, whether it's "put away" in the sense of hidden in a sanitarium or in a more responsible lethal sense. It is sad, yes. Dreadful. But it carries no guilt. True guilt arises only from an offense against a person, and *a Down's is not a person* [emphasis added].[4]

Fortunately, this incredible assertion was met with a storm of protests by parents and professionals alike. Nevertheless, the notion that people who have Down syndrome may not be fully human persists to this day.

## A MAGIC CURE?

Interestingly, in addition to hypothesizing that "mongolism" was a manifestation of ethnic degeneracy, Dr. Down suggested that the degeneracy itself stemmed from tuberculosis in the parents. Though Down was incorrect, the search for a biological or chemical "cure" has been pursued actively since 1866.

Many drug treatments have been attempted to improve the functioning ability of people with Down syndrome. We review only a few examples of this work here, examples that have been popularized in one way or another, often by the originators of the treatments.

None of the large number of drug related therapies tried since 1866 has proven to be a "magic potion." Administering thyroid and pituitary extracts, glutamic acid, combinations of vitamins, minerals, and enzymes, dimethyl sulfoxide, and brain cell transmitter substances such as tryptophan compounds have all proven to be ineffectual. Some of these therapies have produced serious negative effects. For example, sicca cell therapy (material prepared from embryonic animal organs and then injected into the child) has raised concern that the injection (shown not to be helpful to the child) may transmit fatal slow virus infections.

Turkel's "U-series," a megadose vitamin-mineral combination, aroused great optimism when it was first introduced, because of claims about its intellectual and even physical benefits. Optimism was replaced by disappointment, however, when the mixture was subjected to a double-blind study.[5]

A diet known as the Feingold diet, designed originally for children with "hyperactivity," excludes foods that contain specific artificial coloring agents and food substances present naturally in fruits and certain other foods. Many experimental trials revealed that, though the diet may produce some behavior improvement in a small proportion of children, improvement is slight. Nevertheless, because the diet is sound nutritionally (although vitamin C might be reduced too much), if the parent thinks the child's behavior has improved, this diet may be okay.[6]

While we're on the subject of hyperactivity (also termed attention deficit disorder), some stimulants, such as Ritalin and Dexedrine, slow down certain hyperactive children. Unfortunately, these medications sometimes are overused. They are looked upon as *the* intervention, the only one needed. Parenthetically, loss of appetite, lessening of growth, and change in mood can be serious side effects of these medications. For a select few children with Down syndrome, those few who exhibit serious behavior control problems out of proportion to their performance expectations, a properly prescribed and carefully monitored dosage of these medications may be beneficial.[7]

A controversial treatment that bridges medical and psychological realms is plastic surgery. This treatment has been proposed for (a) reducing physical stigmata that often accompany Down syndrome—for example, almond shaping of the eyes, flattened nasal bridge; (b) improving speech and language through tongue reduction followed by speech therapy; or (c) both of these.

This treatment, requiring radical surgical techniques, must be approached with extreme caution because of the physical and psychological risks to the child ("Why are you doing this to me? Didn't you love me the way I looked before?"). Moreover, parents need to examine their own motives carefully to avoid a heavy load of guilt if "miracles" don't happen. Nevertheless, a few children with Down syndrome may benefit from the surgery, particularly those who (a) have the intellectual ability (or ability potential) to live with normalized expectations of peers, (b) have devalued themselves because of their perceptions of their appearance, (c) have environmental supports, particularly parents who are motivated by loving aspirations, and (d) receive extensive speech and language therapy. Parents should realize from the outset, however, that no convincing research findings are available to substantiate its effectiveness. (This topic is discussed further in Chapter 10.)

A few popular treatments are not actually medically related but have an aura of biomedical intervention about them. Among these is the Doman-Delacato method. Premised on establishing which hemisphere of the brain is dominant (and that it has not been established sufficiently in some children), proponents of the program put the child through a series of physical manipulations. These consist of moving the child's limbs passively (not voluntarily by the child) under the assumption that this movement ("patterning") will cause the brain to undergo neuronal change (hemispheric dominance).

This process requires parents to accept a regimen of exercise and other therapies. The program often is expensive and can be extremely draining from both an emotional and a physical standpoint—not only for parents but for the child as well. It requires parents to virtually change their home into a "gymnasium" and recruit droves of volunteers who will move the child's limbs in a reciprocal movement pattern for many hours a day. This can be hard on a marriage and on siblings' mental health.

Parents' unfounded (and often highly unrealistic) expectation of a "cure" for their child's intellectual and physical disabilities (a cure that does not exist, according to the findings of a number of well-controlled studies) leads eventually to extreme disappointment and guilt at putting the child through such an intense routine. This risk has led the American Academy on Pediatrics to issue a formal statement advising against passive movement exercise.

Parenthetically, in the early childhood years, parents may consider the possibility of embracing a program called "A Chance to Grow," based on the premises of the Doman-Delacato regime. Here, as with the traditional Doman-Delacato program, parents of young children with Down syndrome might be attracted to the program because so much is promised, and the methods have high appeal because they are so "hands on." As with Doman-Delacato programming, however, parents need to be extremely wary of taking on what can be a radical, time-consuming, energy-draining, often expensive "cure-promising" program that has not been tested under adequate experimental conditions.

Finally, we offer a word of caution about chiropractic treatments for children with Down syndrome. The instability of the spinal joints in some children with Down syndrome makes them susceptible to spinal cord injury during spine manipulation. Paralysis or death may follow.[8]

In summary, parents of children with Down syndrome need to be extremely skeptical of promises of "miracle cures." Certainly, under a physician's care, vitamins, thyroid medication, and other nonradical drug therapies, if needed, can be helpful in treating children with Down syndrome. (More will be said about appropriate medical treatment and physical care in Chapter 4).

## THE EUGENICS SCARE

The movement to build large, state-operated, residential institutions for people with mental retardation seems to have received its impetus from the thoughts of Johann Guggenbuhl, thirty years before Dr. Down wrote about "mongols." In 1836 Guggenbuhl founded a small community (a colony of cottages) on a mountainside in Switzerland with the intent of curing cretinism (a generic term often used in the 1800s to refer to many types of conditions, including Down syndrome).

Unfortunately, Guggenbuhl's idyllic plan for creating an intimate community of cottages to protect people with mental retardation from society was seized upon in the eugenics scare period (the late 1800s and early 1900s) as a way to protect society from people with mental retardation. Ironically, because of irrational societal fears about all people with mental retardation, "cottages" on state institution grounds often took the form of huge dormitories that became human warehouses. The colony idea, adopted by designers of institutions, also lost its originally intended orientation as being a supportive, intimate community. Instead, it became a geographically isolated, fenced-in set of facilities that often were operated in a highly regimented manner.

The eugenics scare was premised on the erroneous notion that mental retardation (at least the form often termed "cultural-familial retardation," which does *not* relate to the cause of Down syndrome) was inherited. It was alleged that society's gene pool would be ruined by people with mental retardation, who were believed to be sexually promiscuous and, therefore, would breed rampantly and indiscriminately. This fueled a worldwide frenzy to build large institutions. Sounding the alarm, Goddard, a former superintendent of Vineland Training School, a large residential institution in the eastern United States, wrote in 1912:

Feeblemindedness [mental retardation] is hereditary and transmitted as surely as any other character. We cannot successfully cope with these conditions until we recognize feeblemindedness and its hereditary nature, recognize it early, and take care of it. In considering the question of care, *segregation through colonization* [emphasis added] seems in the present state of our knowledge to be the ideal and perfectly satisfactory method.[9]

Goddard's ideas, accepted virtually without challenge in the early 1900s, led to the building of institutions in every state in the USA, passage of permissive sterilization laws for residents of these institutions, and the promotion of a policy favoring lifelong institutional segregation for people with mental retardation. Individuals with Down syndrome, although they did not belong to the group of individuals termed cultural-familial retarded, became one of the largest subpopulations within these residential facilities. It would take the atrocities against the "unfit" propagated by Hitler during World War II to show society the horrors of unbridled prejudice. The Nazis not only murdered millions of Jewish people and other "undesirables," but Hitler ordered the killing of thousands of people with disabilities, including many with Down syndrome.

## THE BABY DOE CASE

In 1982, Baby Doe, a newborn child with Down syndrome, was nearing death from starvation because his parents refused to allow routine surgery to correct an incomplete esophagus. As death approached, several organizations representing citizens with disabilities, including the National Down Syndrome Congress, sought feverishly to find legal means to save his life. A number of parents, some of whom already had a child with Down syndrome, offered to adopt him. All advocacy efforts were to no avail.

Following Baby Doe's death, a lawyer representing the child's parents said, "There would have been horrific trauma—trauma to the child who would never have enjoyed a quality of life of any sort, trauma to the family, trauma to society...."[10] In his column reacting to the lawyer's statement, George Will wrote, "The task of convincing communities to provide services and human sympathy for the retarded is difficult enough without incoherent lawyers laying down the law about whose life does and does not have 'meaning.' "

# *L*IGHTENING THE LOAD

## THE DISCOVERY OF A CHROMOSOMAL DISORDER

Until 1956, textbooks on human development and medical genetics reported that human cells normally have forty-eight chromosomes. In the mid-1950s, new cytogenetic (gene study) techniques (use of special chemicals, advancements in electron microscope technology) allowed researchers to visualize chromosomes in metaphase (separation) preparations as never before. Thus, in 1956, Tjio and Levan were able to demonstrate clearly that normal human cells had forty-six, not forty-eight, chromosomes. Then, in 1958, Lejeune, a French geneticist, confirmed that the cells of a child with Down syndrome had an additional chromosome. Lejeune and his co-workers studied two more individuals before reporting that individuals with Down syndrome have an extra chromosome in the G group (see the chromosome charting system example in Figure 1). Shortly thereafter, other investigators found that some people with Down syndrome have a chromosomal translocation or mosaicism.

## DEINSTITUTIONALIZATION

The general mood of the 1970s was conducive to the deinstitutionalization movement, in which people institutionalized for mental and emotional disabilities were released from institutional settings. Indeed, the movement to establish rights for people with disabilities was consistent with the public's greater sensitivity to establishing equal rights for other minority groups such as African-Americans and Native Americans.

In this change-oriented atmosphere parents and professionals had expanding opportunities to move children with Down syndrome from large state institutions to community settings. A key opportunity for opening regular education programs to children with Down syndrome came in 1972 with the landmark case *Pennsylvania Association for Retarded Children* v. *Commonwealth of Pennsylvania,* known as the PARC case. In that case the judge ruled that every child, regardless of mental ability, has the right to a free, appropriate public program of education.

## A FREE, PUBLIC EDUCATION

Before 1975, parents of school-age children with Down syndrome could not require public school officials in most states to provide an education for their children. Instead, the families had to rely totally on the good will of school officials to accept their children, a situation that often forced families into a supplicant role. With the passage of the Education for All Handicapped Children Act (Public Law 94–142), often referred to as the "mainstreaming act," the U.S. Congress gave parents of children with Down syndrome a guarantee of a free public education for their children in the least restrictive appropriate schooling environment possible. Also mandated were the writing of individualized education programs (IEPs), which were to include measurable objectives, and the right to due process hearings if parents were dissatisfied with their child's educational plans or services.

How successful has this law been? It has been highly successful in guaranteeing a free public education for children with Down syndrome. The legal process assures that. Not yet totally clear, however, is what a "least restrictive," "appropriate" environment contains or should contain. Part of the problem is that educational researchers have not been able to fully validate several major assumptions about the effectiveness of educating children with disabilities in the mainstream. There is a problem in approaching mainstreaming in an overly simplistic manner.

Simply arranging for handicapped and nondisabled students to be in physical proximity with one another does not ensure that positive interactions and interpersonal attraction will result. Some evidence indicates that nondisabled students, when integrated casually, sometimes develop feelings of rejection toward peers with disabilities.[11] This is particularly true when an educational situation is created without deliberate planning for promoting positive child-to-child interactions. Nondisabled peers' rejection or acceptance of students with Down syndrome depends extensively on the way the teacher structures learning goals and rewards. Evidence is accumulating that properly structured cooperative experiences result in a greater number of positive interactions between students without disabilities and students who have disabilities.[12]

A second problem in providing educational opportunities in regular schools is that school officials might be reluctant to have students with Down syndrome in a program that emphasizes "the three Rs." A low educational expectation for school-age children with Down syndrome poses serious difficulties for parents. Sadly, few specific attempts have been made to promote academic achievement in school-age children with Down syndrome. Advocacy "ammunition" is in short supply. Fortunately, a few researchers have provided evidence that many children with Down syndrome, given sound instruction, can learn basic and sometimes relatively sophisticated academic skills, including skills in reading with comprehension at a functional literacy level. (More will be said about mainstreaming and academic learning opportunities in Chapter 7.)

## HEAD START AND THE EARLY EDUCATION MOVEMENT

Spawned by President Lyndon Johnson's War on Poverty, Head Start was designed to prevent mental retardation in young disadvantaged children (minority children living in slum areas). Gradually, Head Start–type programs began to serve young children with biological and physical disabilities, such as those with serious brain damage, congenital hearing and vision impairment, and Down syndrome.

During the late 1960s, new laws such as the Handicapped Children's

Early Education Program (HCEEP), Public Law 90–538, generated funding for an array of research and demonstration projects specifically for infants and preschool children with disabilities. By then, it was becoming obvious that "quick-fix" Head Start programs, such as summer-only programs, could not produce the sustained, whole-family, lifelong achievement increases desired. Subsequently, the federal government passed legislation guaranteeing free, public educational services for children with disabilities down to the age of three years (Public Law 99–457) with permissive legislation allowing free public educational intervention down to the newborn period. Today, babies with Down syndrome receive early intervention services routinely, often beginning at birth, in most states.

## NATIONAL ORGANIZATIONS ON DOWN SYNDROME

During the 1940s and 1950s, parents of children with many types of mental retardation formed parent-professional groups such as the National Association for Retarded Children (now the Association for Retarded Citizens of the United States). In the 1970s, parents of children with Down syndrome began to organize. In 1973, the Down's Syndrome Congress was formed, following a national meeting of parents of children with Down syndrome, held in Anaheim, California, in October 1972. Eleven years later, the membership voted to drop the possessive from "Down's" (because Dr. Down did not "own" the condition). Because of its growing national status, that organization voted to become the National Down Syndrome Congress (NDSC).

NDSC accomplishments since that time include:

—helping to bring about the 1984 presidential proclamation on Down syndrome and the 1985 public law designating October as National Down Syndrome Month.

—fostering public awareness of the value of people with Down syndrome through TV and other media.

—publishing a journal for parents and professionals, the *Down Syndrome News*.

—coordinating a national parent group network and offering parent group leadership seminars annually.

—providing a national convention each year and sponsoring several international conventions.

The NDSC has been joined by several other national organizations including the National Down Syndrome Society and the Canadian Down Syndrome Society. Today, parents have strong support group resources, as well as a stronger voice in national and state lobbying.

## MAJOR ADULT-FOCUSED LEGISLATION

Several pieces of federal legislation opened up community living opportunities for people with Down syndrome. For example, the Rehabilitation Act of 1973 (Public Law 93–112), Sections 503 and 504, prescribed far-reaching civil rights protections for people with disabilities, leading to independent living and job opportunities.

In 1991, the Americans with Disabilities Act (ADA) was passed. This legislation contains wide-sweeping inclusionary specifications for individuals with disabilities. For instance, it specifies that no person shall be denied a job based on physical or sensory impairments if the workplace can be made more accommodative without unusual expense. The accommodative intent extends into the area of leisure and recreation as well.

In a real sense, then, the road on which new parents of a child with Down syndrome are journeying has improved dramatically since the EDGE parents began their journey 25 years ago.

# OTES

1. J. L. H. Down, "Observations on an Ethnic Classification of Idiots," *London Hospital, Clinical Lectures and Reports* 3 (1866): 259–262.
2. Down, pp. 260–261.
3. F. Crookshank, *The Mongol in Our Midst* (London: Kegan Paul, Trench and Trubner Ltd., 1924).
4. B. Bard and J. Fletcher, "A Right to Die," *Atlantic Monthly* 3 (1968): 59–64.
5. T. S. Bumbalo, H. V. Morelewicz, and D. L. Berens, "Treatment of Down's Syndrome with the "U" Series of Drugs," *Journal of the American Medical Association* 5 (1964): 187.
6. M. Selikowitz, *Down Syndrome: The Facts* (New York: Oxford University Press, 1990).
7. Selikowitz.
8. Selikowitz.

9. H. Goddard, *Feeble-mindedness, Its Causes and Consequences* (New York: Macmillan, 1914), pp. 260–261. Cited in L. Kanner, "A Miniature Textbook of Feeblemindedness," *Child Care Monographs*, No. 1 (New York: Child Care Publications, 1949), p. 132.

10. Cited by George Will, "If the Baby's Not 'Meaningful,' Kill It," editorial, in *Minneapolis Star and Tribune*, April 22, 1982 (reprinted from *Washington Post*).

11. H. Goodman, J. Gottlieb, and R. Harrison, "Social Acceptance of EMR's Integrated into a Nongraded Elementary School," *American Journal of Mental Deficiency* 76 (1972): 412–417.

12. L. Martino and D. W. Johnson, "Cooperative and Individualistic Experiences Among Disabled and Normal Children," *Journal of Social Psychology* 107 (1979): 177–183; J. Rynders, R. Johnson, D. W. Johnson, and B. Schmidt, "Effects of Cooperative Goal Structuring in Producing Positive Interaction Between Down's Syndrome and Nonhandicapped Teenagers: Implications for Mainstreaming," *American Journal of Mental Deficiency* 85 (1980): 268–273.

## $\mathcal{C}$OLWELL FAMILY

Dad: Dave
Mom: Char
Brother: Charlie
Sister with Down syndrome:
    Holly

Who says people
with Down
syndrome don't
have distinct
personalities!?

Big treats coming.

In costume for a show.

## $\mathscr{C}$OLWELL FAMILY (continued)

Prom night.

Athletes stick together.

Figure skating exhibition.

A champion at 21.

# ~*3*~

# Unfolding OF THE NEW BABY'S LIFE WITHIN THE FAMILY

Janet Sophie Thayer

*U*sually the birth of a baby is an event touched with great joy and a bit of sadness. Parents begin the process of parenting before their baby is even born. Several authors[1] have described at least three psychological phases of adjustment (described mainly in terms of the mother's psychological adjustment) in the prenatal period—phases that most parents go through in accepting a new life into their lives.

## *P*RENATAL PSYCHOLOGICAL PHASES _____

When a woman first discovers she is pregnant, she usually feels somewhat ambiguous, even when the baby is very much wanted. The ambiguity arises from her feelings of joy at the discovery that she is pregnant and her sadness over the loss of a way of life that she had before becoming pregnant. Even as she feels elated over the news, a small doubt is there. This phase corresponds to the period of "break up" that Joann O'Leary has described.[2] In a sense, the woman recognizes that her past way of life is about to end, sensing that she will have many responsibilities she never has had before, particularly that she will be responsible for the care and nurturing of another human being. This realization is sobering for any woman.

The physiological changes taking place within the mother's body correspond to the psychological changes that take place in the relationship with the prospective father. The old relationship is breaking up, and both partners must begin to redefine their roles to include "mother" and "father" in addition to "partner." As O'Leary pointed out, "Becoming a mother or a father means taking on a new identity, which involves a complete rethinking and redefining of oneself."[3]

From fertilization to twelve weeks' gestation, the baby is going through a period of rapid development. By the end of this period, most of the internal organs have formed, and the fetus shows behaviors such as swallowing and hiccoughing. As the mother and baby move into the "sorting out" phase of development, the mother begins to direct her energies inward toward her baby. She has sorted out some of the ambiguity she felt during the first phase and begins to merge her identity with her baby's. During this phase the mother begins to feel her baby's movements, giving rise to the realization that this baby is *real*. The fetus at this stage has a growing repertoire of behaviors such as sucking, rooting, grasping, and yawning.

By the third stage of prenatal development (6–9 months), the mother (and father) begins to feel that the developing baby is a real person, an "other." During this phase the baby's brain is developing rapidly, and movements within the womb have decreased. Researchers have identified distinct states of fetal consciousness in this later stage of development, states of alternating movement and quiet that correspond to those seen after the baby is born.[4] The fetus can hear in the uterus. Even just a few hours after birth, a baby will turn to the sound of the mother's or father's voice over that of another adult voice.

During this final, "inwardizing" phase of "prenatal parenting,"[5] parents begin to dream and fantasize about their baby. They wonder who the baby will look like and what kind of temperament the baby will have. They may dream of giving their baby all they were denied as children, of being perfect parents (as perhaps their own parents were not). Past relationships are brought to bear in a very real way in this phase of development, because they color parents' expectations of *what the baby will be* and also *how they will be with the baby*.

Perhaps the mother fears she will be like her own mother, who didn't nurture her very well. Maybe the father fears he will be distant from this child as his own father was distant from him. Parents hope their daughter or son will be smart, good looking, sociable, and kind. In some sense, they are sure their baby will be all these things. These dreams, fears, and fantasies are a normal part of the final stage of prenatal parenting: They heighten the excitement and anticipation of the baby's birth.

Labor and delivery are the culmination of this anticipation. With the birth of a "normal" baby, many of the parents' fears disappear. Under normal circumstances parents do a fairly good job of accepting their baby as "just this baby" and no one else, even though most will occasionally be haunted by what Selma Fraiberg called "ghosts in the nursery,"[6] patterns of past relationships that come back to haunt us now and then.

# $\mathcal{T}$HE UNEXPECTED OUTCOME

What happens, though, when these dreams are shattered in the delivery room or shortly afterward by an unexpected outcome of the pregnancy? The parents have been parenting this baby for nine months, and by the time of delivery, they have a special bond with their baby. They already know the baby in a real sense and are ready to welcome that baby into their world. When the outcome is unexpected, such as the birth of a baby with Down syndrome, parents often report feeling that the baby they expected died and they were forced to accept another baby—one they did not at all expect—in its place, all in the matter of a few moments!

Sometimes parents do know before the baby's birth that the baby has Down syndrome and therefore are spared the shock in the delivery room. In any case, the parents are faced with both the loss of the baby they thought they were going to have and the realization that the baby they did have is less than perfect. Parents often go into a period of deep mourning for the baby they fantasized and dreamed about and *who was not born*. One mother, in a book she wrote about her family's experience following the birth of her daughter, Sophie, born with Down syndrome, tells about writing a memorial service for the daughter she lost.[7]

This initial mourning for the lost child is made all the more difficult by the sadness most parents feel when they think about the reality of the baby with Down syndrome who *was* born. Parents have reported that this sadness never goes away, even after coming to terms with the fact that their baby has Down syndrome. Some parents cannot get past their grief, cannot bear to bring home this "other" baby because the burden of sadness is just too great. Even though taking home a baby with Down syndrome has become common, not all parents can do this. Some do decide to put their baby up for adoption. This decision is a personal one, not easily made, and the feelings of those parents must be respected just like the feelings of parents who do take their baby home.

# $\mathcal{E}$DGE FOLLOW-UP

Parents in the EDGE project were asked at two different points if they could recall their saddest memories when they thought of their child as a baby. This question was first posed when their children were one and one-half to three years of age. Their responses are reported in an earlier book.[8]

The parents reported that they were shocked to learn their baby had

Down syndrome. They also reported feelings of disbelief, hopelessness, and isolation. Some parents reported feeling scared and anxious for the future of their baby. Some said that lack of information on what Down syndrome meant heightened their feelings of isolation and anxiety. Although some parents received emotional support from the physician and hospital staff, others recalled being told about the condition of their baby in an abrupt manner and then being left to deal with the news all by themselves.

These memories are still clear after a time span of eighteen years. When we asked EDGE parents this question in our recent interview, their children were around 21 years of age. Yet, these same themes were sounded again. That parents could recall their earliest feelings after so long a time had passed may seem surprising, but other researchers, too, have indicated that "the feeling of loss of control over one's fate, the dependency and vulnerability, are often felt most strongly by parents."[9] Thus, EDGE parents could look back across the years and recall vividly their feeling of sadness.

These feelings tend to revolve around two major themes. The first has to do with the diagnosis of Down syndrome. This unexpected outcome led to a great deal of confusion for all parents. The EDGE parents were trying to work through their own shock and denial and, at the same time, worried about what other people, including their own relatives, would think and say. They echoed the theme of isolation. Many said the hospital staff, because it also was unprepared for this outcome, was not able to give them much support. Some recall that their doctors advised them not to take their babies home. Others were told that if they did take the baby home, they should not expect much. Relatives sent mixed messages as well. Some relatives told the parents that their baby was a gift from God; others implied that the baby was a punishment for some of their past sins.

Parents indicated that it was hard to tell others about the diagnosis because they were struggling with it themselves. Parents also recalled that it was hard for them to accept the diagnosis (and in some cases to hear their doctors' dire predictions about the future of their baby). To have any positive expectations at all for the baby seemed out of reach. Some parents even reported receiving sympathy cards!

Another theme that emerged in both our former and recent EDGE parent interviews had to do with the emotional strain surrounding health issues with which some parents had to deal. Some of the children had to be hospitalized frequently in their early years, giving rise to parents' uncertainty as to whether the child would come home. The first two years of life are a time when babies form special attachments to their parents, a time when separations are especially difficult. These parents and infants had to face repeated separations as a result of hospitalizations, necessitating many readjustments to each other and heightening parents' anxiety about their infants' very survival.

The overwhelming feeling these parents recalled was of being alone. Not much information or support was available to them until they were enrolled in the EDGE early intervention program, so they felt they had to "go it alone." Nowadays, parents of older children with Down syndrome often visit new parents in the hospital or at home to tell them they are not alone, that other parents are out there ready to support them. This support is often the greatest source of comfort for new parents of a baby with Down syndrome. When we recently asked parents from the EDGE project what they would advise new parents of a baby with Down syndrome to do to get the parents and baby off to a good start, all replied that parents should get the best information possible about Down syndrome and that they should seek out support from other parents. They said that sorting out the feelings that are a normal part of adjusting to the reality of having a baby with Down syndrome is far easier when others understand firsthand what those feelings are.

We should recognize that virtually all parents of newborns have anxieties and misgivings about parenthood. A new baby means change and adaptation on the part of the parents (and on the baby's part as well!). During the first few weeks after bringing their baby home, many parents wonder if they made a mistake in becoming parents. They report feeling that their lives are so disrupted during this time that they sometimes wish the baby never had been born. These feelings are perfectly normal and are expressed by parents who have children without disabilities. Yet, parents of children with a disability such as Down syndrome often deny themselves permission to experience these feelings. They report feeling that, because their baby is especially vulnerable and so in need of all the love and care that can be given, to allow themselves to feel anything but overwhelming love and concern would be horrible, that to do so would mean they somehow were not "good enough" parents for this baby. *Parents of infants with Down syndrome need to give themselves permission to wish the baby away without feeling guilty*, just as parents of "normal" infants do.

## INITIAL TASKS OF BABY AND PARENT

When parents bring their baby home from the hospital, they begin a period of "neurotic fitting together."[10] It is a time when parents and baby have to make tremendous adjustments to the baby's life outside the womb. Parents find they must alter their daily routines and sleep patterns, adjusting these to the sleep-wake patterns of their baby. They learn, *because the baby teaches them*, to anticipate when the baby will be hungry; what sounds the baby likes; what visual stimulation the baby prefers; how much intervention is needed when the baby is crying.

Infants come into the world equipped with the dual ability to respond to their new environment and to elicit responses from it. This ability is governed largely by the baby's states of consciousness. The baby uses its six states of consciousness to regulate the amount of stimulation she or he can handle.[11] In addition, the baby regulates the behavior of his or her caregivers by the states that are available. These states are:

—deep sleep
—light sleep
—drowsy awake
—awake and alert
—irritable fussing
—crying

The baby's first task is *homeostasis*, maintaining balance in the face of internal and external stimuli. The baby uses the states of consciousness to try to maintain this balance.

For example, when a baby is distressed because of hunger or gas (sensations the baby did not experience in the womb), the baby signals this distress to the caregiver by crying. Parents, in turn, learn strategies for helping their baby maintain homeostasis by responding to their baby's signals. Thus, parents move to comfort the baby by feeding, burping, or holding, depending upon their interpretation of the reasons for the baby's crying.

In their research on attachment patterns of young infants, Mary Ainsworth and her colleagues discovered that infants whose crying was responded to more or less immediately by their caregivers in the early months of life tended to cry less in the latter part of the first year.[12] When parents respond in this way, babies learn to trust that their signals to the caregiver will be answered appropriately. These examples illustrate that more than growth and development of the *infant* is taking place in the early months of life; the roots of the development of the *parent-infant relationship* also are being formed.[13]

When the infant is able, by about 2 months of age, to get state under control and maintain homeostasis in the face of internal and external stimulation, the infant is ready to engage in what are termed *reciprocal interactions*. He or she is ready for social exchanges that involve eye gaze, turn taking with regard to vocalizations, visual exploration, and smiling. Parents learn to read the baby's signals that tell them the baby is able to give sustained attention to social stimulation. Much has been written about what researchers term *synchrony* in these interactions. This term refers to the fact that both infants and parents are learning to read and *interpret* each others' signals.

This can best be illustrated with some examples from the research literature. Researchers long ago discovered that very young infants prefer the human face (especially the mother's) over other forms of visual objects, and that they can imitate facial expressions of emotion. In addition, infants respond from birth to the human voice and seem to perceive emotional feelings conveyed by voice. We know that shortly after birth an infant prefers the mother's or father's voice to a competing adult voice, supporting the thought that infants learn to recognize familiar human voices *in utero*. Also, infants can identify their mother's face soon after birth, perhaps because they associate her face with her voice, which they have identified before birth.

Infants also learn quickly to identify the mother by her smell, as evidenced by the fact that they appear more relaxed when the mother picks them up in the dark and in silence than when another woman does. These inborn abilities to identify the mother by voice, face, and smell are evidence of *imprinting* to her, and this imprinting serves "to establish immediately after birth a unique motivational relationship to that committed person, a relationship that will serve future mental development."[14] Brazelton and others argue that infants even younger than three months can interpret their parents' facial and vocal expressions in terms of the emotional significance of those expressions.

To test the theory that young infants are sensitive to their mothers' emotional availability, researchers have conducted some interesting experiments. These were designed to examine how infants younger than three months interpret and respond to emotionally colored situations with their mothers. The results of these experiments indicate that, very early in life, babies are able to interpret their mothers' behavior and *attempt to alter it by their own behavior*.

An illustration of a typical interaction between a mother and her baby may help in understanding the importance of this research. Suppose the infant cries and the mother responds to the crying by picking up and soothing the baby with a gentle voice. The baby responds by alerting and gazing at the mother. The mother smiles at the baby and talks to him or her, and as she does so, the infant moves his or her arms and legs in response. The parent then gazes at the baby and talks some more, but now the infant looks away. The mother either (correctly) interprets her infant's behavior as taking time out from stimulation (the baby is regulating the interaction, and his or her own state), or the mother may interpret it (incorrectly) as the baby's purposely avoiding or rejecting her and may end the interaction. If the mother interprets the situation correctly, she will allow the infant time out to recover energy, letting the baby lead the way in resuming the interaction. If the interpretation is incorrect (if the mother interprets the baby's glance away as a sign of rejection), she may lose interest or she may become more intrusive and overload the baby with too much stimulation.

Because infants with Down syndrome typically are slower to come to the alert state necessary for sustained interactions, the mother may try harder to stimulate her infant, overloading the infant. An infant has the ability to shut out too much stimulation, so he or she may appear even more unresponsive! If parents give their baby with Down syndrome the chance to lead the way, extending their tolerance for the baby's disengagement, parents may become less anxious and less intrusive. Satisfactory interactions then can be maintained.

## CHARACTERISTICS OF INFANTS WITH DOWN SYNDROME

All parents and infants come to the relationship with their own unique characteristics. Infant characteristics include things such as temperament and biological state regulation, as well as the capacity to elicit their parents' nurturing behavior. Parents bring to the relationship their ideas about parenthood, their socioeconomic status, their personalities, and the amount of emotional support they receive when they are stressed. All of these elements affect how the parent and infant relate to each other socially and emotionally. Researchers have found that the interactions between infants with Down syndrome and their parents tend to be a bit more difficult to establish satisfactorily than those between nonhandicapped infants and their parents, at least initially. One of these authors has argued that the characteristics of infants with Down syndrome may influence these interactions to a greater degree than characteristics of nonhandicapped infants.[15]

Much of the information we have on interactions between infants with Down syndrome and their mothers has been summarized by Jiri Berger, who noted that infants with Down syndrome smile later than nonhandicapped infants do, and that their smiles are not as bright or inviting, probably because of the lower tone in facial muscles.[16] Also, infants with Down syndrome are slower to make eye contact, but they are likely to fixate on the parent's eyes for a longer period of their development. They tend not to explore the parent's face as nonhandicapped infants do. This tendency for less visual exploration carries over to other aspects of the infant's environment (such as toy play) as well.

With regard to vocal exchanges in the interactions, infants with Down syndrome have been found to be slower to vocalize than nonhandicapped infants, but they seem to catch up by around 4 months of age. In contrast to nonhandicapped infants of this age, however, infants with Down syndrome tend to increase their vocalizations, giving their mothers less time to have a turn. At the same time, mothers seem to want to match the amount of vocalization by their infants. Mothers vocalize more often, giving rise to frequent clashes in the exchanges (mother and baby both "talking" at once). Researchers theorize that mothers may be trying to compensate for their babies' apparent less frequent initiations of interactions as well as their less intense facial expressions and lack of visual exploration.

Researchers also have noted that infants with Down syndrome are slower to process information than normal infants are. They take longer to perceive *meaning* from their environment, and thus longer to respond to stimuli from the environment. This may be one reason for their "dampened affect," why they do not visually explore their environment (including faces) as actively; why they are slower to smile and laugh; and why they may not understand as early as nonhandicapped infants do the mutual pleasure of give and take, or turn taking, in interactions with their caregivers. When researchers looked at ratings of infant temperament by mothers of infants with Down syndrome and mothers of nonhandicapped infants, mothers of infants with Down syndrome reported that their infants were slower to smile and laugh, had less vocal activity, and were slower in their motor development than the nonhandicapped infants.[17]

These characteristics of infants with Down syndrome may contribute to initial difficulties in parent-infant interactions. All of this illustrates what Arnold Sameroff has called the *transactional nature of relationships*.[18] The infant's behavior affects the parent's behavior, which in turn affects the infant's behavior. The characteristics of infants with Down syndrome may exert a greater influence on the caregiver's behavior than characteristics of nonhandicapped infants do.

Infants with Down syndrome may not respond in these early face-to-face interactions with as much intensity or rapidity as nonhandicapped infants do. They take longer to respond and, when they do, it may be in a way that appears less alert or less bright. When this happens, parents may interpret the baby's seeming lack of interest as rejection and may pull away from the baby. Or parents may attempt to overcompensate for what they perceive as the baby's lack of interest by "moving in" more forcefully, trying harder to stimulate the baby. The baby might react to this by pulling away from the parents—tuning them out, so to speak.

In Berger and Cunningham's investigations into the interactions of infants with Down syndrome and their mothers, when mothers were asked to wait for their babies to initiate behaviors such as vocalizing or smiling and then imitate those behaviors, the babies laughed and vocalized more than when the mothers tried to get the babies to imitate *them*.[19] These investigations can show parents that, if given enough opportunity to initiate interactions, babies with Down syndrome learn the fun of eliciting responses from their caregivers. Parents, in turn, can see that, by giving their infant "more room" to initiate these interactions, they become more pleasurable for all involved.

## ATTACHMENT

All of the infant behaviors discussed, and the parents' responses to them, lay the groundwork for what has been termed *attachment*. Stated simply, attachment is the emotional tie between the infant and his or her primary caregiver (usually the mother). It is an emotional relationship that researchers in this area believe is the prototype for future relationships.[20] Through this relationship the baby comes to learn whether the world is safe, whether his or her needs will be met by a caring person, and it even is thought to affect how the infant comes to think of his or her own competence.

The construct of attachment can be assessed by a laboratory experiment called the "Strange Situation."[21] The baby's organization of behavior toward the mother is assessed in a series of separations and reunions. Babies react to the separations and reunions in a variety of ways. Most babies ("securely attached" infants) respond to the separations from their mothers with varying degrees of distress. Upon the mothers' return (after three minutes, or before if the baby is highly upset), these babies react with some sort of "proximity seeking"; they reestablish contact with their mothers by looking, smiling, or indicating their need to be held and comforted. After contact with the mother has been reestablished, the babies tend to settle and then continue to explore the toys in the room.

The way these babies organize their behavior is an indication of the emotional attachment between the baby and the mother. It also illustrates how babies use their mothers as a secure base from which to explore the environment as well as a safe haven to return to when the baby perceives the environment to be threatening (as in the case of the separations). It is difficult for some babies to take comfort from the mother upon reunion even though they may be very distressed by the separations. Some babies ignore the mother. Others seek her out and at the same time resist her ministrations. Although these examples are oversimplified, they illustrate the organization of infant behavior assessed by the Strange Situation as "anxious avoidant" or "anxious resistant."

Most babies do organize their behavior in a way that indicates they have a secure attachment relationship with their mothers. They have learned from their early interactions with her that they can trust her to be there for them to provide comfort and security. The mother represents, in a sense, the baby's world, and thus the baby's *image of the world*. What the baby thinks of the world and how he or she interacts with the world depends to a large extent upon this first relationship. The patterns of attachment of infants with Down syndrome do not differ from those of "normal" infants. Most of them have been found to be securely attached.[22] These examples support the premise that infants with Down syndrome and their parents, after some early difficulties in getting to know each other, can learn to adapt to each other rather well, and they proceed to do so.

## $\mathscr{S}$EPARATION AND AUTONOMY

From the earliest face-to-face interactions with the infant, parents must "listen" to the baby, let the baby teach the parents when to move in and when to back off, when to initiate and when to follow. This type of "listening" continues to be important in late infancy and toddlerhood, when the issues of autonomy and separation arise. If difficulties emerge at this stage of the child's development, they may have to do with the child's growing *self-awareness* and with the issues that surround *separations*.[23]

In the first instance the child may begin to test the limits the parents set. This is one way for the child to establish his or her autonomy, a time when the child recognizes his or her own existence separate from everyone else. The parent's task is to decide which limits are important and, at the same time, encourage the child's independent behavior. This may be especially difficult for parents of a child with Down syndrome. Parents may be so concerned about their child's limitations that they may not see the child's emerging strengths and thus may discourage the child's striving for autonomy.[24] They may try to do too much for their child in the belief that they are protecting the child from the frustration of making mistakes. On the other hand, some parents, because of a desire to have their child be independent and accepted by society, may push the child into activities that are too difficult for the child to master, leading to a great deal of frustration for the child (and for the parents).

Issues that surround separation can crop up at any stage of the child's development. For example, if the mother is working outside the home, she may have to return to her job soon after the baby is born. This is an exceptionally difficult task for many mothers, one that may be laden initially with some guilt and anxiety. The mother may wonder if anyone else can care for her baby well enough. She may worry that the baby will become attached to the new caregiver and not to her. (Research has shown that babies do have attachments to other people, but that the primary attachment figure is the mother or mothering figure.)

In addition, quality out-of-home care often is hard to find. The difficulty may be compounded for infants with disabilities. Many larger cities have resources available to help parents of infants with disabilities find good out-of-home care, but it remains a major concern for many parents. In one form or another, it is often a lifetime concern.

Some parents of infants with Down syndrome hesitate to leave their baby with a babysitter. They may worry that the baby will not be cared for properly, or that something will happen if they are not there all the time to take care of the baby. This poses the danger that they will sacrifice their social life and a part of their own spousal relationship, believing that they are the only ones capable of taking care of their infant. When parents realize that the baby needs to be able to tolerate even brief separations so he or she can "call up" the relationship and rely on its constancy, they are much better prepared to plan for even longer separations. As Hanson and Krentz pointed out, "Each partner must be able to tolerate increased separations from the other and must have enough sense of positive experiences with the other partner so as to sustain separations without negative results."[25]

## EARLY INTERVENTION SUPPORTIVE OF FAMILIES _____

Many states offer early intervention services to infants and toddlers with disabilities and their families through Public Law 99–457, Part H, enacted in 1986. This law heralded the shift from child-focused to family-focused

delivery of services in early intervention. The law states that each family of an infant or toddler determined to be eligible for services (eligibility criteria vary from state to state) is entitled to an *individualized family service plan* (IFSP) in which parents must be offered an active role if the intent of the law is to be carried out.

Early intervention programs now emphasize supporting the *parent-child relationship*, helping parents of infants with Down syndrome to recognize and respond to their babies' signals so that mutually satisfying interactions can take place. This does not mean that parents cannot do this on their own. As Donald Winnicott pointed out, mothers identify with the baby from the last months of pregnancy through the first weeks and months after birth, and this "primary maternal preoccupation," as he called it, enables the mother "to meet the baby's needs in a way that...no teaching can reach." But, he continued, "no one must be expected to succeed always,"[26] and this is why the support from early intervention programs, as well as from other parents, is so important.

When asked what things they would advise new parents of a baby with Down syndrome to do to get the parents and baby off to a good start, parents in the EDGE project offered some insightful tips. They advised parents to seek out information about Down syndrome and to find support from other parents. The theme of parent support is evident throughout all of our recent interviews with the EDGE parents. Because the support for each other has been so important to these families, they all recommended that new parents find a parent group so they will feel less isolated.

In addition to seeking information and support, they advised, "Don't treat this child any differently (or much differently) from the way you treat your other children. Enjoy and love this baby, and don't let the disabilities be all that you see. Try to maintain a balance between your expectations and the child's limitations by setting reasonable goals. Incorporate this baby into normal family life. Take the baby places, read to and play with the baby, *have fun with the baby!*" "Be kind to yourselves," they said. "Realize that getting used to having a baby with Down syndrome takes time. As you take this time, incorporate the baby into the family and find support for yourselves."

In her book, *Bittersweet Baby*, Jolie Kanat said that in parenting, "you stay in the game no matter which cards you are dealt. The best you can do is keep throwing in nickels, practice the perfect poker face, and know that in this particular deck the aces truly do outnumber the crummy hands. You may just have to wait a while for a royal flush."[27]

## THE IMPORTANCE OF HOPE

After some initial difficulty in establishing and maintaining mutually satisfying interactions, parents and their infants with Down syndrome do seem to adjust and adapt to each other in a way that is rewarding for all. Once they realize the unique characteristics of the baby, once they accept the baby's capabilities as well as limitations, parents can move ahead on the journey, enjoying the unfolding of their baby's development within the family. Equally important, as they celebrate each milestone their baby achieves, they can look to the next with *hope*. Eleanor Szanton eloquently addressed the subject of hope.

> Hope does not get discussed much by social scientists or practitioners. Professionals are much more comfortable with words such as "etiology," "observable behavior," "probability," and "expectable outcomes." This is not surprising. One way of looking at the history of science is to note its slow progression toward reliance on what can be "empirically" detected over and above what one thought one should see or wanted to see. The "etiology" of a particular set of problems is exhaustively recorded and analyzed by a clinician. Present observable behavior will be checked and tested from many

angles. Even the future is clothed in terms of the "prognosis," based on past experience with similar cases.

Parents have a very different perspective—one which is not consulted frequently enough. This was particularly striking to me once when I attended a meeting of fifteen or twenty parents of infants and toddlers with disabling conditions. By way of introduction, each parent described her child's condition, when this had become known, what had been the history of her experience with this condition. The cumulative impact of the fifteen stories, each told as if the mother were reading from her child's medical chart, was almost overwhelming.

Luckily, at some point in the introductions, each mother began to circulate a snapshot of her child, which she had been asked to bring. The cumulative impact of the photos went entirely the other way. This was a bunch of buoyant, *hopeful* children! For those children, the reality of that hope— those expectations transmitted in some miraculous way from generation to generation—was every bit as strong as the reality of the medical charts....

In an era when it is fashionable to support the family, preserve the family, hold up the family as an institution which would have to be reinvented if it did not exist, this miracle of *hope*, of focus on "when you group up," is not at all well understood. However, it must be nurtured and cultivated by those who work with parents and young children. When we allow so many families to sink into situations in which hope fails for parents and children alike, we have destroyed a piece of our hopes for America.[28]

The presence of hope is illustrated by the recollections of the EDGE parents when we asked them recently to recall their happiest memories of their child as a baby. Their recollections are excerpted here.

*Mother:*  He was always delightful, always fun to play with, from day one. Always responsive, cheerful—just a delight.

*Mother:*  The first time he could walk, or the first time he could talk. The other kids say he's spoiled, but I don't think he is!

*Mother:*  I'm not a morning person, and [my son] is. He always was. So, not really wanting to get up, there's this wonderful smiling face, greeting me! I think his learning to walk was pretty exciting. We were at his grandmother's house, and he would walk a little bit, and then he would plop. He would just purposely plop down, and he'd giggle! He seemed to be getting all these Christmas wrapping bows stuck on his butt, and then he would bat at them and laugh and plop down again. It was very funny. His first birthday was pretty funny too. I made him a big strawberry pie for his first birthday, and he had just his diaper on because we knew he would be a mess when he fell into this strawberry pie!

*Mother:* He was a very happy baby, a delightful child. We've got some wonderful pictures that have captured the mischief in him...a real sparkling little child, and that wonderful little face of his, just wonderful.

*Mother:* I guess the happiest times were when you could see that all the stimulation you've been feeding in was finally coming out. He was always a smiley, happy kid, and he responded.

*Mother:* He was just a really neat baby, he really was. My memories are so wrapped up in all the accomplishments, the delight, all the fun we had. The baby part was wonderful, it really was.

*Mother:* It was just a wonderful experience to see how our other children have loved, and helped, her. They were very protective of her.

*Mother:* Watching the gains he made. When he was tested at seven months, he was only one month under his normal peers. I was so excited, and I remember calling one of the EDGE staff because I was so excited about how well he tested. And he was always a happy little guy. And once he could start moving around, he was just constant motion—perpetual motion! I think one of our best memories was when somebody was graduating from the EDGE project, and the kids put on a little talent show, and they put a tutu on [our son] and turned on the music. And that kid, it was like somebody turned on a switch and he did this dance. I just sat there and laughed until the tears rolled down my face! He wasn't really a baby then. He was a toddler.

*Mother:* How the children related to her. They always loved her dearly.
*Father:* Her brothers and sisters loved her so much. She was a sweet little gal.

*Mother:* One of the first things I remember, when they brought her in, was that she had the prettiest eyebrows and prettiest fingernails I've ever seen. And she was always happy!

*Father:*  I guess we had envisioned him not being able to do anything. But there was so much delight at what he *could* do! When he took his first step, and when he did speak.... Oh, he did lots of things that I never expected he would ever do, things he learned to do so well!

*Mother:*  I guess how the other kids accepted him. He seemed to fit right in, and there weren't any doubts that he belonged in our home.

*Mother:*  She was a fun baby to play with. She responded. She was a very happy, *fun* baby!

*Mother:*  We have a lot of happy memories. He was a real good baby, a very happy baby. Every roadmark was wonderful. We had the advantage of older kids who gave him a lot of help, and he is so close to his siblings. Those were happy times, when he was a little baby. I think the happiest were when we met the other people in the EDGE project and we could all compare notes—and we didn't feel that we were so odd because we knew other people who were in the same situation. People need to know that their child isn't that much different.

*Mother:*  When he started to do some things, it was such a great thing! It seemed like we'd waited so long that when it really happened, it was so exciting. I still remember how little he was his first year. I thought he was so cute!

# OTES

I would like to thank the EDGE parents, who long ago taught me how important the family is in early intervention, and with whom I have recently had the good fortune to re-connect. The writing of this chapter was supported by a grant to the University of Minnesota, Department of Educational Psychology (USDE H209D20082, Susan C. Hupp and Mary E. McEvoy, Co-Principal Investigators). I am most grateful for that support.

1. See, for example, J. Raphael-Leff, *Psychological Processes of Childbearing* (London: Chapman and Hall, 1991).
2. J. O'Leary, "The Parenting Process in the Prenatal Period: A Developmental Theory," *Pre- and Perinatal Psychology Journal* 7(2) (1992): 113–123.
3. O'Leary, p. 114.
4. D. Arduini, G. Rizzo, C. Giorlandino, A. Vizzone, S. Nava, S. Dell Aqua, H. Valensise, and C. Romanini, "The Fetal Behavioral States: An Ultrasonic Study,"

*Prenatal Diagnosis* 5(1985): 269–276; J. deVries, G. Visser, and H. Prechtl, "The Emergence of Fetal Behavior: I. Qualitative Aspects," *Early Human Development* 7 (1982): 301–322.

5. O'Leary.
6. S. Fraiberg, "Ghosts in the Nursery." Chapter 4 in *Selected Writings of Selma Fraiberg*, edited by L. Fraiberg (Columbus, OH: Ohio State University Press, 1987).
7. J. Kanat, *Bittersweet Baby* (Minneapolis: CompCare, 1987).
8. J. Rynders and J. M. Horrobin, *To Give an EDGE: A Guide for New Parents of Children with Down's Syndrome* (Minneapolis: Colwell/North Central, 1974).
9. R. Halpern and F. Parker-Crawford, "Young Handicapped Children and Their Families: Patterns of Interaction with Human Service Institutions," *Infant Mental Health Journal* 3 (1982): 51–63.
10. O'Leary.
11. T. B. Brazelton, "Behavioral Competence of the Newborn Infant," *Seminars in Perinatology* 3 (1979): 35–44.
12. M. Ainsworth, S. Bell, and D. Stayton, "Infant-Mother Attachment and Social Development: 'Socialization' as a Product of Responsiveness to Signals," in *The Integration of the Child into a Social World*, edited by M. Richards (Cambridge, U.K.: Cambridge University Press, 1974).
13. R. Emde, Forward to *Selected Writings of Selma Fraiberg*, edited by L. Fraiberg (Columbus, OH: Ohio State University Press, 1987).
14. J. Murray and C. Trevarthen, "Emotional Regulation of Interactions Between Two-Month-Olds and Their Mothers," in *Social Perception in Infants*, edited by T. Field and N. Fox (Norwood, NJ: Ablex, 1985), p. 180.
15. N. Richard, "Interaction Between Mothers and Infants with Down Syndrome: Infant Characteristics," *Topics in Early Childhood Special Education* 6(3) (1986): 54–71.
16. J. Berger, "Interaction Between Parents and Their Children with Down Syndrome," Chapter 4 in *Children with Down Syndrome: A Developmental Perspective*, edited by D. Cicchetti and M. Beeghly (Cambridge, U.K.: Cambridge University Press, 1990).
17. M. Rothbart and M. Hanson, "A Caregiver Report Comparison of Temperamental Characteristics of Down Syndrome and Normal Infants," *Developmental Psychology* 19 (1983): 766–769.
18. A. Sameroff, "Transactional Models in Early Social Relations," *Human Development* 18 (1975): 65–79.
19. Berger.
20. L. A. Sroufe, "Attachment as an Organizational Construct," *Child Development* 48 (1977): 1184–1199.
21. M. Ainsworth, S. Bell, and D. Stayton, "Individual Differences in Strange Situation Behavior of One-Year-Olds, in *The Origins of Human Social Relations*, edited by H. Schaffer (London: Academic Press, 1971).
22. P. B. Gunn and R. Andrews, "Behavior of Down Syndrome Infants in a Strange Situation," *American Journal of Mental Deficiency* 85(3) (1980): 213–218; F.

Serafica and D. Cicchetti, "Down's Syndrome Children in a Strange Situation: Attachment and Exploration Behaviors," *Merrill-Palmer Quarterly* 22(2) (1976): 137–150.

23. M. Hanson and M. Krentz, *Supporting Parent-Infant Interactions: A Guide for Early Intervention Program Personnel* (San Francisco: San Francisco State University, 1986).
24. Hanson and Krenz.
25. Hanson and Krenz, p. 13.
26. *Babies and Their Mothers*, edited by C. Winnicott, R. Shepherd, and M. Davis (Reading, MA: Addison-Wesley, 1987), p. 36.
27. Kanat, p. 146.
28. "National Center Notes," *Zero to Three* 12(4) (1992): 29.

*Janet Sophie Thayer* has her doctorate in educational psychology and special education from the University of Minnesota. She taught in the EDGE Project's preschool and in a child-family preschool setting serving children with developmental delays in St. Paul. Dr. Thayer is certified to administer and interpret the Brazelton Neonatal Behavioral Assessment Scale, utilizing its findings to promote child-family growth and development.

## $\mathscr{F}$INNERTY FAMILY

Dad: Don
Mom: Kathy
Brother: John
Brother: Mike
Sister: Therese (Mileti)
Brother with Down
   syndrome: Tim

Flying to Duluth.

A sister can be a very special friend.

Check out all those ribbons.

## $\mathcal{F}$INNERTY FAMILY (continued)

Brothers need to trust each other!

Relaxing in the sun.

The Epcott Center was a blast.

# ~4~

# HEALTH PROMOTION DURING THE EARLY YEARS

Margaret Horrobin

hildren with Down syndrome need the same basic health care that children without disabilities receive. This includes routine well-child check-ups and immunizations. During the early years parents' concerns focus on physical growth, intellectual development, and physical health problems. As the child grows and matures, these concerns change, giving way to issues of sexuality and reproduction, and "social health," such as friendships, integration into the community, work, and recreational opportunities. Eventually, concerns about aging, including Alzheimer's disease, predominate.

To date, no proven medical treatments for Down syndrome itself are available, although medical conditions commonly found in people with Down syndrome can be treated. The doctor can provide good medical care through prompt diagnosis and treatment of associated medical problems. This, plus early education tailored more and more to the individual child's needs, are the best we can offer.

Many attempts have been made through the years to find medical treatments that would substantially improve the functioning ability of people with Down syndrome. These have included, either alone or in combination, various hormones, minerals, vitamins (in normal doses and megadoses), and enzymes. None of these treatments, when carefully evaluated, has borne out the claims of its proponents. (This topic is covered more fully in Chapter 2.)

Because a number of health problems can be associated with Down syndrome, families should be aware of these. Parents are their children's best advocates, and physicians cannot be expected to know everything about every condition. To help parents and physicians, a checklist for routine health care has been developed and is updated periodically (see Table 3). The child's growth can be plotted on curves specifically developed for children with Down syndrome rather than on the standard growth curves (see Figures 2–6, at the end of this chapter).

# ABLE 3

## Down Syndrome Preventive Medical Checklist

At certain ages or developmental periods in everyone's life, specific medical and lifestyle issues usually need to be addressed. This holds true for individuals with Down syndrome. The following is a list of medical, social, educational and vocational issues of which families, individuals with Down syndrome, and professionals need to be aware and address for individuals with Down syndrome to reach their fullest potential and lead happy and healthy lives. These are recommendations for screening asymptomatic individuals.

### INFANT (BIRTH–12 MONTHS)

HISTORY
Prenatal diagnosis of Down syndrome
Pregnancy
Labor
Delivery
Feeding and caloric intake
Stooling pattern and constipation
Review parental concerns
Metabolic screening as required by state law
Respiratory and other infections

PHYSICAL EXAM
General infant exam
Cyanosis
Irregular heart rate
Heart murmur
Cataracts—*must see red reflex*
Intact hearing
Dislocated hips
Fontanelles
Neurological exam
Musculoskeletal exam
Visualize tympanic membranes

LAB AND CONSULTS
Chromosomal karyotype
TSH (thyroid test)

ECHOCARDIOGRAM (ECHO)
Cardiology—even in the absence of a murmur
Genetic counseling
Feeding specialist (lactation nurse or occupational therapist)

AUDITORY BRAINSTEM RESPONSE TEST (ABR) (2–6 months)
Motor evaluation by physical therapist (by 3 months)
Developmental evaluation (by 3 months)
Ear, nose, and throat exam (by 3 months)
Ophthalmology exam (by 3 months)

DEVELOPMENTAL
Discuss early intervention and refer to local program

RECOMMENDATIONS
Appointment at a Down Syndrome Center
Parent (family) support
Compile an information log including the following:
  medical and educational information; deductible expenses such as: mileage, parking, meals, lodging, and related medical care
Reinforce the need for subacute bacterial endocarditis prophylaxis in susceptible children with cardiac disease
Enrollment with Social Security Income (SSI) and Medical Assistance, depending on income
Enrollment with a Mental Health/Mental Retardation agency
Consider a will, trust, and custody arrangements

### CHILDHOOD (1YR–12YRS)

HISTORY
Review interval medical history
Respiratory and other infections
Ear, nose, and throat problems
Constipation
Review parental concerns
Review educational program
Monitor for behavior problems
Review current level of functioning
Sleep problems (snoring; obstructive sleep apnea)
Review audiologic and thyroid function tests
Review ophthalmology and dental care

PHYSICAL EXAM
General childhood exam
Neurological exam—regarding atlanto-axial instability

*continued*

*Checklist continued*

LAB AND CONSULTS
TSH (thyroid test) (annually)
Auditory testing (ages 1–3 annually; ages 3–
13 every 2 years)
Cervical spine x-ray, lateral view in flexion,
extension, and neutral (at 3–4 yrs and 12
yrs); measure atlanto-dens distance
Ear, nose, and throat exam every 2 years
Ophthalmology exam every 2 years
Dental exam at 2 years of age with 6-month
follow-ups

DEVELOPMENTAL
Enrollment in developmental or educational
program
Complete annual educational assessments
Evaluation by a speech/language pathologist
Consider referral for augmentative commu-
nication device

RECOMMENDATIONS
Appointment at a Down Syndrome Center
Twice daily teeth brushing
Total caloric intake below RDA for children
of similar age and height
Enrollment with Social Security Income (SSI)
and Medical Assistance depending on income
Enrollment with a Mental Health/Mental
Retardation agency
Consider a will, trust, and custody arrange-
ments
Well-balanced, high-fiber diet and healthy
eating patterns
Regular exercise program
Respite care
Parent (family) support
Recreational programs
Begin to acquire good self-care, grooming,
dressing, and housekeeping skills, as well
as money handling skills
Continue to compile an information log
Reinforce the need for subacute bacterial
endocarditis prophylaxis in susceptible
children with cardiac disease

## ADOLESCENCE (12–18YRS)
HISTORY
Review interval medical history
Respiratory and other infections
Symptoms of hypothyroidism
History of seizures

Parental concerns
Educational program
Behavior problems
Vision and hearing problems
Dermatologic problems
Immunizations
Address sexuality issues

PHYSICAL EXAM
General adolescent exam: gynecologic exam
ages 17–20
Monitor for obesity by plotting height for
weight
Neurological exam—regarding atlanto-axial
instability

LAB AND CONSULTS
TSH (thyroid test) (annually)
Auditory testing every 2 years
Ophthalmology evaluation every 2 years
Cervical spine x-ray, lateral view in flexion,
extension, and neutral (at 12 yrs and 18
yrs); measure atlanto-dens distance
ECHOCARDIOGRAM FOR MITRAL
VALVE PROLAPSE (ECHO)
Adolescent medicine consult for sexuality
Dental examination twice yearly

DEVELOPMENTAL
Continue speech and language therapy
Consider referral for augmentative commu-
nication device
Psychoeducational evaluations annually as
part of IEP
Transition planning (14–16 years)
Vocational training and planning (17–21
years)

RECOMMENDATIONS
Appointment at a Down Syndrome Center
Discuss plan for future living arrangement
Update will, trust, and custody arrangements
Encourage social and recreational programs
with friends
Register to vote and for the Selective Ser-
vice at age 18
Refine good self-care, grooming, dressing,
and housekeeping skills, as well as refining
money and banking skills
Enrollment with Social Security Income
(SSI) and Medical Assistance depending on
income

*continued*

*Checklist continued*

Twice daily teeth brushing
Low-calorie, well-balanced, high-fiber diet
Health, abuse prevention, and sex education
Smoking, drug, and alcohol education
Parent (family) support
Regular exercise program
Continue to compile an information log
Continued involvement in a Mental Health/
Mental Retardation agency
Reinforce the need for subacute bacterial
endocarditis prophylaxis in susceptible in-
dividuals with cardiac disease

## ADULTHOOD (OVER 18YRS)
### HISTORY
Review interval medical history
Respiratory and other infections
Thyroid imbalances
Seizures
Family/community living arrangement con-
cerns
Loss of independence in living skills
Symptoms of dementia
Behavior problems/mental health problems
Vision/hearing loss
### PHYSICAL EXAM
General adult physical
Gynecology exam (ages 17–20): Pap smear,
testicular exam, breast exam
Monitor for obesity by plotting height for
weight
Neurological exam—regarding atlanto-axial
instability
### LAB AND CONSULTS
TSH (thyroid test) (annually)
Auditory testing every 2 years
Ophthalmology evaluation every 2 years
Cervical spine x-ray, lateral view in flexion,
extension, and neutral (at 30 yrs and as
needed); measure atlanto-dens distance
### ECHOCARDIOGRAM FOR MITRAL
VALVE PROLAPSE (ECHO)
Pap smear annually, if sexually active

Baseline mammogram (at 35 years); follow-
up mammogram (after 35) based on
physical exam and family history
Dental examination twice yearly
Neurological or psychiatric referral for
early dementia and behavior problems
### DEVELOPMENTAL
Continue speech and language therapy
Consider referral for augmentative commu-
nication device
Continue vocational training to improve
skills and train for more advanced jobs
Continue adult educational programs
### RECOMMENDATIONS
Appointment at a Down Syndrome Center
Discuss plan for future living arrangement
Update will, trust, and custody arrangements
Encourage social and recreational programs
with friends
Register to vote and for the Selective Ser-
vice at age 18
Refine good self-care, grooming, dressing,
and housekeeping skills, as well as refining
money and banking skills
Enrollment with Social Security Income
(SSI) and Medical Assistance depending on
income
Bereavement counseling for individuals who
have experienced the death of an impor-
tant person in their lives
Twice daily teeth brushing
Low-calorie, well-balanced, high-fiber diet
Health, abuse prevention, and sex education
Smoking, drug, and alcohol education
Parent (family) support
Regular exercise program
Continue to compile an information log
Continued involvement in a Mental Health/
Mental Retardation agency
Reinforce the need for subacute bacterial
endocarditis prophylaxis in susceptible in-
dividuals with cardiac disease

Compiled by Down Syndrome Center of Western Pennsylvania, Children's Hospital of Pittsburgh, 3750 Fifth Ave., Pittsburgh, PA 15213, 412/692-7963, on behalf of the Ohio/Western Pennsylvania Down Syndrome Network, June 1992. Used by permission.

# EART DISEASE

After you have been told that your baby has Down syndrome and the chromosome tests have confirmed this, one of the first questions should be: Does my baby have heart disease? About 40 percent of babies with Down syndrome have some form of congenital heart disease.[1] A physician usually detects this by hearing a heart murmur, but sometimes the murmur is not present at birth even when heart disease is present. Therefore, an echocardiogram should be administered to detect silent heart problems. This should be done under the supervision of a cardiologist, preferably a pediatric cardiologist. It is reliable in picking up heart problems that otherwise might have been undetected.

The most common problems are ventricular septal defect (a hole between the two lower chambers of the heart) and atrioventricular canal (holes between the upper chambers and between the lower chambers). Not every heart has to be repaired surgically. Some ventricular septal defects close themselves or are small enough so they do not have a harmful effect. Thanks to medical and technological advances, almost every heart that needs it can be fixed now, including heart defects that only a few years ago were regarded as inoperable and caused early death.

# GASTROINTESTINAL CONDITIONS

In the newborn period gastrointestinal malformations are second in frequency to heart defects.[2] They occur in about 8 percent of babies with Down syndrome. Most common is an obstruction of the duodenum, the first part of the small intestine. This constitutes a surgical emergency in the newborn, but results of surgery are generally excellent. This condition is detected in the prenatal period with increasing frequency. Ultrasound examinations during pregnancy often detect this blockage and allow surgery to be done promptly after the baby's birth.

Although obstructions like this usually come to light in the newborn period, partial obstructions also may be present, and may not be diagnosed until much later, especially if symptoms are intermittent. Recurrent bouts of abdominal pain and vomiting are a clue to detecting partial obstructions.

*Gastroesophageal reflux* (GER) is a condition in which the sphincter muscle at the lower end of the esophagus ( food pipe) does not close tightly enough to prevent the stomach contents from flowing back up the esophagus. This condition usually causes excessive spitting up. It may be only a nuisance that will resolve itself when the child is eating thicker foods and is mostly in the upright position rather than lying or sitting. In severe cases, however, the child may vomit and fail to thrive. Another potentially serious problem arises if the regurgitated food spills over into the windpipe, where it may cause irritation and even pneumonia. Certain medicines may be of value for severe cases, and surgery is undertaken in extremely severe cases.

Constipation, a common problem, does not refer primarily to the infrequency of passing a stool but, rather, to the nature of the stool and the difficulty in passing it. A baby who passes a stool of normal consistency every several days without difficulty is not constipated. A dry, hard stool that is painful to pass defines constipation. It probably reflects low muscle tone in the bowel and should be treated vigorously because it can cause pain, abdominal distention, and overflow incontinence of stools, in which small liquid stools flow past a large mass of hard stool, mimicking diarrhea. The best treatment is to take dietary measures—more fluids and fiber in the diet and avoid constipating foods. Stool softeners may be required also.

Constipation is a common symptom of the lack of thyroid hormone, which should be ruled out. Occasionally, severe constipation with abdominal distention is caused by Hirschsprung's disease, a condition in which a small segment of the lower bowel lacks the normal nerves. This prevents the normal muscular contractions that propel the stool through the bowel. This condition requires surgery and, though uncommon in general, is slightly more common in Down syndrome.

Sometimes mechanical problems in the newborn period make babies with Down syndrome hard to feed. These babies may have trouble with the mechanics of sucking and swallowing, and expert help from an oral-motor therapist may be needed. Sometimes, making the transition from milk to solid foods is difficult. Chewing and figuring out how to eat foods of different textures may require a good deal of work.

Breast feeding is encouraged for babies with Down syndrome, not only because of the mother/baby satisfaction but also because breast milk is the ideal food for infants and breast-fed children tend to be somewhat leaner than bottle-fed children. Breast feeding also provides some measure of protection against infection, which may be particularly valuable to children with Down syndrome. If the baby has trouble with sucking and swallowing, breast feeding is not always easy to establish. The services of a lactation consultant may be most helpful at this time.

After infancy the diet of a child with Down syndrome should be somewhat lower in calories than generally is recommended for children of the same age and height. Children with Down syndrome tend to have major problems with obesity as they get older.

# $\mathcal{R}$ESPIRATORY DISORDERS

Recurring respiratory infections are a problem for many, but not all, children with Down syndrome. Some have no more colds or ear infections than their brothers and sisters who do not have Down syndrome. Most children with Down syndrome, however, do have frequent upper respiratory infections, which may lead to secondary infections, such as pneumonia and ear infections. With day-care comes increased exposure to infection. However, given the economic realities of life, there may not be a choice about being in day-care. From the health viewpoint, small home day-care is preferable to large day-care centers.

Ear infections (*otitis media*) often follow upper respiratory infections. These infections require appropriate treatment and follow-up. If fluid is retained behind the eardrum for several weeks, it may affect hearing. Hearing loss from that cause is seen often in children with Down syndrome and can impose an added handicap to the acquisition of language. Unfortunately, many babies with Down syndrome have such tiny ear canals that the eardrums cannot be seen. If this is the case, your baby's doctor sometimes may have to guess, based on symptoms, whether your baby has an ear infection and how to proceed. In these circumstances, the baby should be seen regularly by an ear, nose, and throat specialist.

Regular hearing tests should be part of routine health care for all children with Down syndrome, starting in the first months of life. Certain methods of testing a baby's hearing do not require the baby's cooperation. Even if the baby is found to have normal hearing, the baby should be tested once a year, more frequently if he or she has ear infections. Some children are kept on small doses of preventive antibiotics during the winter in an attempt to prevent ear infections. If children have had fluid behind the eardrum for a long time, ventilation tubes might be placed through the eardrum to get rid of the fluid, allowing the middle ear to return to normal and to restore hearing.

Babies with Down syndrome may be noisy, snorty breathers, because of mucus in the very small nasal passages. Salt water nosedrops with gentle suction may relieve this condition. Decongestant nose drops are not recommended, except occasionally, because of their tendency to cause rebound congestion that becomes more of a problem than the original stuffiness.

Noisy breathing at night, with snoring and sometimes choking sounds, is observed frequently in children with Down syndrome. In one sleep study, 80 percent of children with Down syndrome showed some evidence of *obstructive sleep apnea*, a condition in which breathing may stop briefly because of obstruction and then resume, often with a noisy gasp.[3] If the tonsils and adenoids are found to be overly large, removing them may alleviate the problem, though for many children this is not completely curative. Adenoidectomy always must be undertaken with care, as some children may show changes in voice and speech afterward, because of interference with the function of the palate.

# YE PROBLEMS

By young adulthood almost everyone with Down syndrome is, or perhaps should be, wearing glasses because of refractive errors. The most common of these is *nearsightedness*.

Infants with Down syndrome often have *nystagmus*, a horizontal dancing movement of the eyes. Though it tends to become less apparent in older children, it usually does not go away completely. It may interfere with clear vision.

*Cataracts* are seen at any age from birth on. They become more likely, however, as children get older.

*Stabismus*, an imbalance of the eye muscles so the eyes do not appear straight, should be treated promptly to avoid loss of vision in the affected eye. In the early weeks of life, treatment usually is not needed as the eye turning may resolve by itself. Persistence of eye turning beyond the first several weeks, however, warrants careful assessment by an ophthalmologist, an eye specialist who is a medical doctor. Patching the stronger eye, special lenses, or surgery may be required.

*Chronic blepharitis*, thickening and redness of the eyelid margins, caused by persistent low grade infections, often is seen, as is a tendency to *conjunctivitis*, better known as pinkeye. Eye ointments or drops usually can keep these problems in control, though they do tend to recur.

Because Down syndrome carries with it many potential eye problems, these children should be evaluated regularly. A visit to an ophthalmologist about once a year is recommended.

# NDOCRINE DISORDERS

The endocrine glands produce hormones. For people with Down syndrome, the most frequent endocrine problem by far is malfunction of the thyroid gland.[4] Overproduction and underproduction of thyroid hormone—*hyperthyroidism* and *hypothyroidism*, respectively—are seen, though underproduction accounts for 90 percent of the thyroid problems.

In hypothyroidism the metabolism slows down and the individual may become more sluggish, mentally slower, have a disproportionate increase in weight, drier skin, more problems with constipation, and a slower rate of growth in height. From this list of symptoms, you can see that recognizing this promptly may be difficult in a child who already tends to be consti- pated, is a little overweight, is short, and has dry skin. For this reason, regu- lar thyroid testing should be done. Hypothyroidism increases with age, and an estimated 25 percent of adults with Down syndrome have it to some ex- tent, although it also can occur in early childhood.

A yearly test in the absence of symptoms seems appropriate. Two tests may be done: a TSH (thyroid stimulating hormone) and a T4. TSH, produced by the pituitary gland, stimulates the thyroid gland to produce its hormone, T4. As the thyroid gland slows down, the pituitary gland tries harder to stimulate it. Thus, in the early stages of hypothyroidism, TSH increases before the T4 falls. A fall in T4 indicates that the thyroid gland is not able to produce enough hormone. Yearly screening with TSH is adequate to alert the physician to the potential problem, but, because some children may have an elevated TSH and never develop a low T4, I generally do not start to supplement with thy- roid hormone until the T4 is falling. Hypothyroidism can be easily corrected with oral medication.

*Diabetes*, caused by failure of the pancreas to produce enough of the hormone insulin, also occurs more often in persons who have Down syn- drome. Though it may be treated successfully with diet alone or diet with oral medication in adults, it requires the use of insulin in children. Diabetes typically presents itself with increased thirst, increased urination, and weight loss. As a rule, children developing diabetes get sick relatively quickly, looking quite ill with vomiting and weight loss. Older people may go quite a long time with increased thirst and urination without being particularly ill.

These endocrine disorders seem to be the result of what is called an *autoimmune process*, in which the body starts to produce antibodies to its own organs. Antithyroid antibodies and antibodies against the islet cells of the pancreas, which produce insulin, can be measured. They may be found to be very high in these conditions.

# EUKEMIA

Leukemia is a well-known, but uncommon, disease, with several different types. The type known as acute lymphoblastic leukemia is 15 to 20 times more common in children who have Down syndrome. Despite this incidence, the disease still is uncommon in children with Down syndrome because the incidence in the general community is so small. The most likely age of occurrence is between one and two years of age. Treatment of this formerly uniformly fatal disease has improved remarkably, and the outlook is much more favorable now. Most children probably can be cured.

In the newborn period a baby with Down syndrome may have a blood count that looks much like leukemia. This is known as a *leukemoid reaction* and generally resolves spontaneously, though it may cause some anxiety. Yearly blood counts to look for leukemia used to be recommended but, because the chance of finding it on a random blood count in an otherwise healthy child is small, this probably is not a cost-effective procedure.

Interestingly, other malignancies (cancers) do not seem to occur with more frequency in Down syndrome.

#  GROWTH

Children's growth should be plotted on Down syndrome curves because their rate of growth is much slower than that of other children.[5] The growth rate, especially at the younger ages, does not necessarily progress smoothly. In fact, an individual child may show wide variation on the growth chart. The growth of children with significant heart disease may be affected adversely in addition to the effect of Down syndrome.

At 18 years of age, the average young man with Down syndrome is 9 inches shorter than the average 18-year-old American male. Figure 3 shows a normal male growth curve with the Down syndrome 50th percentile superimposed. The average young woman with Down syndrome is 7 inches shorter than the average American female.

Some have questioned whether growth hormone should be given to young people with Down syndrome to try to improve their ultimate height. Although some children respond to growth hormone, they do not benefit as much as otherwise normal children who have growth hormone deficiency.[6] Although it may speed growth temporarily, it is doubtful if ultimate height can be changed substantially. At the present time there is not widespread enthusiasm for this extremely expensive treatment.

#  BONES AND JOINTS

Children with Down syndrome have what people often call *double-jointedness*. There is no such thing as a double joint. What this refers to is a wide range of motion at the joint, attributable to general looseness of the ligaments that bind the bones together at the joints.

This laxity may lead to problems. In the newborn period, for instance, after a baby has been folded up in the womb for a long time, the hips may be easily dislocatable. This should be checked as part of a normal newborn examination. The infant who is learning to get into the sitting position sometimes may do this by bringing the legs full circle so he or she goes from a prone lying position to a jackknife position from which he or she may sit up and then do exactly the opposite to lie down again or get into a crawling position. To prevent this excessive rotation at the hips, physical therapists sometimes recommend a band around the thighs.

When a child starts to put weight on his or her feet, the feet may be flattened out with an inward rolling at the ankles so the weight is borne almost entirely on the inside surface of the foot and ankle. If the condition is mild, it can be controlled nicely with a firm hightop shoe, but excessive rotation may be treated better with a small, molded insert placed inside the shoe, individually designed to hold the foot and ankle in a better position. Trying to improve the foot position is more than just a cosmetic procedure. It may alleviate foot problems in adult life, which are a major problem for many adults who have Down syndrome, and one more barrier to active exercise.

# ATLANTOAXIAL INSTABILITY

The first neck vertebra is called the atlas, and part of it consists of a bony ring. The second vertebra, the axis, has a bony peg that fits into the ring of the atlas. This configuration permits us to swivel our heads. The joint between the first and second vertebrae is the atlantoaxial joint. In some young people with Down syndrome, the play between the peg and the ring is excessive, which may create pressure on the spinal cord and, in the most extreme cases, paralysis. From an x-ray a radiologist (x-ray specialist) can measure the distance between the ring and the peg. Currently a 5-millimeter or greater distance is regarded as abnormal, and the individual is said to have atlantoaxial instability even though the person may show no actual symptoms.[7]

Approximately 15 percent of young people with Down syndrome have this condition. X-rays should be taken at about three years of age to look for it. Parents of a child with this condition are advised to modify the child's activity to avoid excessive backward and forward movement of the head, as well as direct forces applied to the head. This means that activities such as tumbling, somersaulting, trampolining, diving, and some contact sports should not be permitted—an easy recommendation to give but a difficult one to follow, especially when we encourage children to be physically active.

Only a minority of children who theoretically are at risk for developing a problem actually do. In those cases surgery is performed to fuse the neck bones and thus prevent movement that would press on the nerves.

All children with a positive neck x-ray should be followed carefully, looking for development of specific signs and symptoms, which include gait or postural changes (such as holding the head in a crooked position), bowel and bladder symptoms, changes in the reflexes, changes in sensation, or complaints of pain.

Some people have argued persuasively that because a positive neck x-ray does not call for active treatment but does cause a lot of anxiety to families, and because x-rays may change over time both for better and for worse, routine neck x-rays should not be done. Every child should be followed carefully and, if signs or symptoms develop suggesting atlantoaxial instability, the appropriate x-ray studies should be done, followed by active treatment. At the present time in the United States, children participating in the Special Olympics events are required to have had the neck x-ray. If the neck x-ray is normal, no restrictions whatever should be placed on activity but the x-ray should be repeated about every ten years.

# $\mathcal{N}$EUROLOGICAL PROBLEMS

## SEIZURES

Seizures occur more often in people who have Down syndrome than those who do not. Of the several types of seizure, infants with Down syndrome do seem to have a particular predilection for the type known as infantile spasms, or *hypsarhythmia*. This type of seizure usually occurs in the first year of life. The child suddenly drops his or her head, often with a hugging type of arm movement, a brief lapse of awareness, and sometimes a short cry. These seizures are regarded generally as quite harmful. Many babies subsequently have a serious setback in development, and the previous rate of developmental progress may never be regained.

An EEG (electroencephalogram) is required to make the specific diagnosis, as it shows a characteristic pattern. A course of injections of ACTH (adrenocorticotrophic hormone) is administered, often with a dramatic effect in bringing these seizures to an end, following which other seizure medication may be required.

## ATTENTION DEFICIT HYPERACTIVITY DISORDER (ADHD)

This condition, seen in about 5 percent of nondisabled school children, cannot be diagnosed before school age because so many of the symptoms—

such as inability to sustain attention, inability to sit still, or inability to re-main focused on a task—are normal characteristics of young children. Be-fore this diagnosis can be made in a child with Down syndrome, his or her developmental level has to be taken into account. A child of age 6 with a developmental age of perhaps 3 to 4 may well have some of these character-istics, which will stand out if he or she is in an integrated classroom with normal 6-year-old children. It may not mean that the child truly has ADHD.

Accurate incidence statistics are hard to come by, but ADHD probably is no more and no less common in children with Down syndrome than in other children, meaning that approximately 5 percent of school-age children with Down syndrome may have this disorder.

If the diagnosis can be made with some confidence, the child should be treated in an appropriate school setting with an educational management plan and family counseling. Last, medication should be given if appropriate, though it is never the first approach and is not required in many instances.

## SKIN

Though the skin of the newborn baby with Down syndrome tends to be very soft, dry skin frequently is a problem as children grow older. The skin may thicken, and in cold climates winter chapping is troublesome. A small amount of mild soap should be used for washing, and the skin should be lubricated with emollient creams.

*Cutis marmorata*, a lacy-appearing mottling of the skin, is seen in many young children who have Down syndrome, but it gradually disappears. It is of no medical significance.

*Vitiligo* is a condition in which pigment changes appear in patches on the skin. Some areas are entirely depigmented and look pale in contrast to adjacent areas, which appear more pigmented. This condition is not com-mon but is somewhat more so in individuals with Down syndrome. *Vitiligo* has no curative treatment. Although it can be unsightly, it is harmless. It is thought to express a deficiency in the functioning of the immune system.

*Alopecia* occurs in as many as 6 percent of children with Down syn-drome, according to some surveys. In this condition completely bald patches appear on the scalp. These may be quite small. In some children this condi-tion will resolve but almost half of the children progress to total hair loss. This condition, like vitiligo, is associated with immune system dysfunc-tion, and a quarter of the children with alopecia have antibodies to thy-roid tissue.

# 𝒯HE EDGE PROGRAM: MEDICAL STATUS _____

The information in this chapter, although sobering, need not create a pessimistic outlook in new parents. Indeed, when the parents of our young people in the EDGE program were surveyed recently, 87 percent of them regarded their sons and daughters, now in their early twenties, as "healthy" or "very healthy." The other 13 percent were judged to be "fairly healthy." This positive regard by EDGE parents should be considered in light of the fact that the current group is composed of individuals with Down syndrome who have survived more than twenty years (because of the lack of effective treatment at that time, children with known heart disease were excluded). Three of the children in the EDGE group died before age seven and, thus, are not represented in our current findings.

Of fifteen young people, eight have some degree of hearing loss, though in most it is slight; twelve have corrective lenses; one has nystagmus; none have cataracts to this date; one has seizures; three require thyroid supplements; one has atlantoaxial instability; and twelve are overweight. In Chapter 10, covering health concerns that arise at an older age, some of this information will be referred to again, and other conditions also will be discussed.

# 𝓗EALTH PROMOTION IN DAILY FAMILY LIFE _____

The child should always be considered in the context of the family, to promote well-being and to avoid focusing primarily on ill health. Establishing routines from the start helps to bring a sense of order and perhaps calmness into family life, to minimize the stress of a new baby with a diagnosis that brings with it uncertainty.

One of the important aspects of daily family life is attending to caregiving (diapering, bathing, feeding). Basic to survival, these activities often are underrated in terms of the impact they can have on the child and parent's development. Movement and communication development, in particular, can be stimulated in the caregiving context. Communication and movement promotion, facilitated through natural parent-child interactions involved in caregiving activities, is a developmental goldmine for enhancing the health and physical well-being of young children with Down syndrome.

But before looking at enhancement possibilities, let us look briefly at what can happen when caregiving (for example, feeding) is not going well because a young son with Down syndrome is not responding to his mother's feeding attempts, possibly lying flaccidly across her legs during her attempts to bottle-feed him, perhaps showing no change in facial expression when she attempts to ignite his interest through her earnest feeding attempts. These impaired movement-related and communication-related behaviors jeopardize caregiving itself at its most fundamental level. After all, few mothering activities are as emotionally significant to a woman as feeding her baby successfully!

Viewed from a different perspective, between the day a child with Down syndrome is born and the age when the child is able to feed himself or herself with a spoon (at an age of 29 months on average, as compared with 14 months for a child without disabilities), a parent will have *at least* 2,610 opportunities to offer food to his or her child in one way or another.*

Other caregiving activities such as diapering and dressing also offer opportunities to promote the child's development. Couple these caregiving opportunities with parents' social interaction while picking up, rocking, and carrying-about activities that accompany caregiving, and the number of hours runs into the multi-thousands before the child is 2 years old. The point is that the quality of caregiving/social interactions has a profound influence on the child's *and* the parent's development.

What can parents do to take advantage of these numerous and important natural learning times? At least four significant things can happen during these times:

1. The child's skill level can be advanced. For example, a child can be helped to learn to use a spoon as an eating instrument rather than as a "paintbrush."

---

* Three feedings per day × 30 days per month × 29 months. This calculation is a conservative one because during infancy the child will nurse or take a bottle much more often than three times in 24 hours.

2. The child can become socialized to the parent, and vice versa, so their interactions become more harmonious, richer, and more respectful.
3. The child's main ways of responding to the parent—*movement* and *communication*—are strengthened. As examples, the child becomes more skilled in using a spoon (movement) as the parent varies the type of food to be spooned; the child smiles as the parent presents the spoonful of pudding with a bright voice (communication).
4. The parent can develop stronger and progressively more rewarding caregiving skills, reflected back to the child, who then responds to the parent more strongly and skillfully, which in turn....

You get the picture. The parent and child enter into the classic, upward spiraling cycle of mutually beneficial, positive, reciprocal interactions. In the midst of this pleasurable and productive caregiving activity, the parent and the child not only are becoming better socialized and more physically adept, but they also are becoming healthier, as physical health and mental health are intertwined. At the same time, the two areas in which the child with Down syndrome generally shows the greatest weakness—movement and communication—are stimulated.

To illustrate how a parent can use caregiving/social interaction to promote movement and communication, we will provide a few examples of how it can be done and direct parents' attention to resources in the appendix that will help round out their repertoire of caregiving techniques.

## POSITIONING THE BABY TO PROMOTE NUTRITIVE SUCKING[8]

Babies with Down syndrome often have less tone in the small muscles needed to suck and in larger body muscles needed to maintain a good body orientation for nursing. A mother can achieve positive control of the baby's head and mouth for feeding by gently holding the back of the baby's head with one hand while using her other hand to stimulate her baby's lip closure for sucking. In doing this, she can support the baby's body as the baby lies in her lap, raising one of her legs slightly to provide a comfortable brace for the child's back, allowing the infant to stay in contact with her breast.

## PROMOTING THE BABY'S ROLLING OVER RESPONSE[9]

In helping the baby with Down syndrome roll over from back to stomach, the parent should take hold gently of one of the baby's legs, bend it slightly at the knee, and bring it forward slowly across the other leg in the direction the child is to roll (with an interesting rattle or toy animal for the baby to see while rolling over). The parent should make certain that the baby's arms are positioned so the baby can bring them forward under his or her chin (maybe with a little bit of gentle assistance if needed) as the roll is completed. The baby's parent might practice this sequence of rolling-over movements himself or herself, getting back in touch with a complex motor skill to which the adult caregiver no longer gives a thought; it has become an automatic response.

## INCREASING AWARENESS OF BODY AND NEARBY OBJECTS

Placing various objects safely over the child's crib, where the child can contact them with hands and feet, provides a simple but important play activity. It can occur in interaction with a caregiver and also can be self-directed if the object is positioned properly for the child's contact. Things that can be pulled, pushed, can make a sound, and have visual interest are available commercially and also can be found in a typical household. Important to this activity is to facilitate *contact* between the child's feet or fingers and simple objects. In contrast, suspending a huge flashing, buzzing thing-a-ma-jig out of the child's reach is likely to have a negative effect because it is out of the child's control and may "drown" the child's senses.

Burns and Gunn[10] have some nice ideas about increasing the young child's body awareness, orientation in space, muscle tone, and enjoyment in caregiver contact through body massage. They recommend gently massaging the baby's entire body, including the face. The caregiver should stroke the length of arms, body, and legs firmly but lightly with the palm of the hands, when the baby is in both the prone and supine position.

As voluntary movement starts to develop, the massage activity can be extended to encourage kicking. With the baby lying on his or her back, the adult grasps the lower leg and foot and moves them alternately in a kicking or bicycling movement. The baby's hands can be clapped together gently, too, providing movement experience in the midline and—equally if not more important—sharing the enjoyment. And the baby's feet can be clapped together and brought up to his or her mouth to help the child see and feel movement of the legs.

## FOSTERING MANIPULATIVE PLAY

When EDGE individuals were babies, their parents tried out a number of objects and toys, using language-enriched play to promote their child's receptive vocabulary. One of the things we wanted to find out was which toys or objects the parents liked especially well because their young children responded positively to them. The number-one favorite was a toy called Kitten in a Keg, a set of small plastic nesting kegs that, if taken apart properly, revealed the presence of a small plastic kitten inside the smallest keg. Using Kitten in a Keg, parents promoted their child's understanding of the words "big, biggest," "small, smallest," and phrases such as "find the kitten." At the same time, the skillful motions the young child needed to take apart and put together graduated-sized kegs sequentially were stimulated.

As can be seen from these examples, movement and communication abilities in the young child can be promoted in concert with caregiving. This is one of the reasons why early stimulation can be so effective: The young child's development shows an openness to interactive developmental building by the parent, an openness that will diminish later. The immaturity of a young human—dependent on a caregiver for food, warmth, removing the discomfort of diaper wetness—offers the caregiver a golden opportunity to influence his or her child's development precisely because of this dependency.

Gradually the child's dependence is replaced by striving for independence and, if all goes well, eventual partial independence. But the unique openness of the first 6 months of life, with its astonishingly large variety of learning opportunities, never will be duplicated in the life span of that parent-child relationship.

# OTES*

1. R. L. Spicer, *Pediatric Clinics of North America* 31(6), December 1984.
2. D. Smith, *Recognizable Patterns of Human Malformations*, 3d edition (Philadelphia: Saunders, 1982).
3. C. L. Marcus, T. G. Keens, et al., *Pediatrics* 88(1), July 1991.
4. S. M. Peuschel and J. C. Pezzullo, *American Journal of Diseases of Children* 139, June 1985.
5. C. E. Cronk et al., *Pediatrics* 81(1) (1988).
6. G. Anneren et al., *Archives of Disease in Childhood* 61(1) (1986).
7. S. M. Peuschel, *Pediatrics* 81(6), 1988.
8. Y. Burns and P. Gunn, *Down Syndrome: Moving Through Life* (New York: Chapman & Hall, 1993).
9. V. Dmitriev, *Time to Begin: Early Education for Children with Down Syndrome* (Milton, WA: Caring Inc., 1982).
10. Burns and Gunn.

---

\* Referencing in this chapter (and also Chapter 10) has been done in traditional medical journal style, where the title of an article is not included.

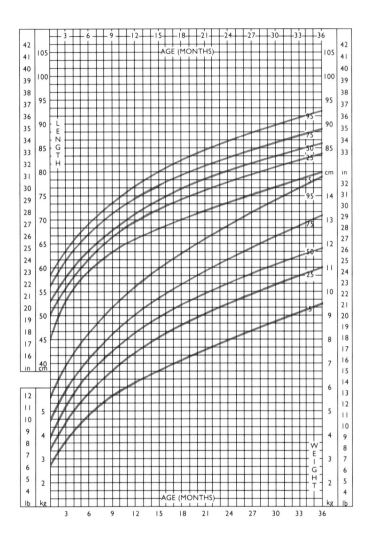

## 𝒻IGURE 2

Percentiles for stature and weight of boys with Down syndrome, ages 1 to 36 months

From an article by C. Cronk, *Pediatrics* 81(1) January 1988. Growth charts reproduced with the permission of *Pediatrics*.

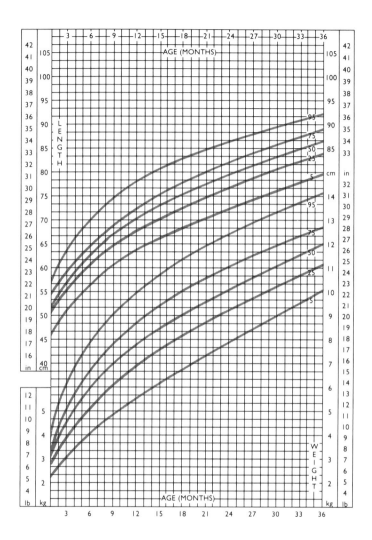

## FIGURE 3

Percentiles for stature and weight of girls with Down syndrome, ages 1 to 36 months

From an article by C. Cronk, *Pediatrics* 81(1) January 1988. Growth charts reproduced with the permission of *Pediatrics*.

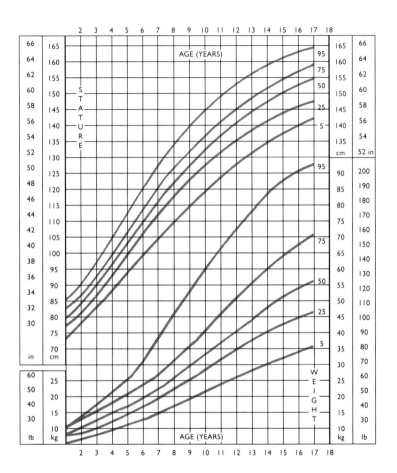

## ℱIGURE 4

Percentiles for stature and weight of boys with Down syndrome, ages 2 to 18

From an article by C. Cronk, *Pediatrics* 81(1) January 1988. Growth charts reproduced with the permission of *Pediatrics*.

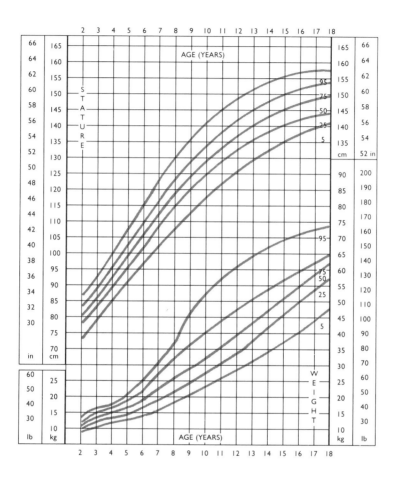

**IGURE 5**

Percentiles for stature and weight of girls with Down syndrome, ages 2 to 18

From an article by C. Cronk, *Pediatrics* 81(1) January 1988. Growth charts reproduced with the permission of *Pediatrics*.

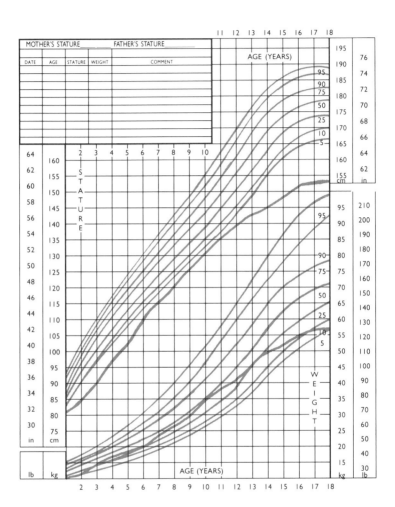

IGURE 6

## NCHS physical growth percentiles

Adapted from "Physical Growth: National Center for Health Statistics Percentiles," by P. V. V. Hamill, T. A. Drizd, C. L. Johnson, R. B. Reed, A. F. Roche, and W. M. Moore, in *American Journal of Clinical Nutrition* 32 (1979): 607–629. Data from NCHS, Hyattsville, MD. © 1982 Ross Laboratories.

# FLEMING FAMILY

Dad: Wayne
Mom: Judy
Sister: Kim
Sister: Kristy
Sister: Kerri
Brother: Scott
Brother with Down syndrome: Rick

Begin each day with a smile.

Age 16: Bodybuilding competition. (This should help break down the stereotype about all kids with Down syndrome being couch potatoes.)

Hot checker game. (Look at that concentration.)

## $\mathcal{F}$LEMING FAMILY (continued)

Buddies always!

C'mon, let's go.

On the way to Special Olympics.

High school graduation.

~*5*~

TIMULATION
OF THE
YOUNG CHILD'S
DEVELOPMENT

John Rynders

"What can I do to get my young child with Down syndrome as ready as possible for kindergarten?" is a question parents often voice. In responding, we begin by letting them know that we know of no miraculous school readiness intervention programs, but that parents can do some practical, nondisruptive things to benefit their child as well as them as parents. Next, we inform them that their child's development will generally parallel the developmental pattern of nondisabled children. Does this mean that children with Down syndrome, given enough time, will catch up with normal children's accomplishments? In some areas the answer is "yes"; in other areas, such as those requiring manipulation of complex numerical symbols, the answer is "no."

From a physiological perspective, the extra dose of genetic material on the 21st chromosome in each cell of the child's body produces the external physical traits that characterize the condition, such as almond shaping of the eyes, flattened nasal bridge, and so on. Physiological differences—including the chromosomal abnormality—do not, however, obliterate or overwhelm normal child growth and development. An individual with this chromosomal condition is first *a child* and second *a child with Down syndrome*. That is why we insist (and you should, too) that people talking about a youngster with this syndrome use the words "child *with* Down syndrome" rather than "Down syndrome child." Putting the child first also reduces the possibility that someone will think of him or her as somehow "less than human" (see the portion of Chapter 2 again, where this problem is illustrated).

Delays and differences in the development of children with Down syndrome, while important to appreciate, tell us little in terms of what to do about the delays and differences. Suppose a psychologist seated beside a 4-year-old girl with Down syndrome shows her how to draw a vertical line with a crayon, hands her the crayon, and asks her to make a line just like the one he drew (pointing to an open area of the paper next to his line). Suppose the child responds by making a few scribbling motions and then lays down the crayon. The psychologist repeats the line-drawing demonstration (many assessment instruments for young children provide two trials on each item), and this time the child makes one quick stab at the paper with her crayon and lays down the crayon again. How does the psychologist score this test item and interpret the child's performance? First, both of the child's drawings would receive low scores because they do not fare well in comparison with a norming group, usually composed of nondisabled children of the child's age. In comparison with nondisabled 4-year-olds, the girl has demonstrated a relatively immature drawing response. But, why?

In interpreting the child's response, the psychologist might conclude that the young girl didn't do well because of relatively poor tone in the muscles needed to move the arm, hand, and fingers in a coordinated way (common in young children with Down syndrome). Or perhaps the psychologist might interpret the girl's relatively immature drawing performance as a function of not yet having a good understanding of some of the words the psychologist used in giving verbal directions (also fairly common in young children with Down syndrome). Or the psychologist could conclude that the child has not done well because of retarded intellectual development (also relatively common in children with Down syndrome).

All three of these conclusions are plausible. The psychologist, however, could look at the girl's performance as reflecting not only what abilities are or are not in her repertoire but, rather, what supports might not be in her environment. For instance, the psychologist might ask himself: In providing the girl with crayons and paper, do the girl's parents also provide her with sufficient opportunities to use them? Do they talk with her about what she is drawing so object-word matching and shape discrimination occur? Have her parents socialized her for learning—rewarded her for trying tasks that are challenging and taught her to think about where to begin a task rather than jumping quickly into it, making mistakes that are easier to prevent than to correct? Educational psychologists who are worth their salt are concerned not only with the child's ability to draw shapes with a crayon but also with the quality and quantity of environment supports available for bringing about proficient performance in drawing with crayons.

In the last thirty years or so educational psychologists have looked to early intervention programs as a special kind of environment support, one that might give young children with Down syndrome an early (and, it is hoped, lasting) boost to their development. Let us turn briefly to the results of these studies to see if they were effective.

# &#x214C;NTERVENTION RESEARCH _____

A few years ago we conducted a computerized search of the early intervention* research literature involving young children with Down syndrome. Approximately fifty studies showed up in the computer printout. In selecting from among these studies, we used a "quality-control" checklist to judge each study's strengths and weaknesses, ultimately leading us to report on only those that withstood scrutiny of their experimental procedures (eight of the fifty studies).

In the first of these eight studies,[1] mothers of young children (ages 12 to 33 months) with Down syndrome learned to use behavior modification techniques (for example, systematically rewarding children for language accomplishments with words of praise and smiles) to promote communication, self-care, and movement abilities. A second group of mothers of children with Down syndrome received only general health care counseling. After six months, children in the group receiving behavior modification from their mothers showed significant improvement in their language development (but not in the other areas) as compared with the counseling-only group.

A second group of researchers[2] taught early two-word verbalizations, known as pivot-open type phrases (for example, "allgone dinner," in which *allgone* is the pivot word and *dinner* is the open word) to two preschool children with Down syndrome who were vocalizing at the one-word stage of language development. Instruction took the form of play, in which a teacher, having taught the children several nouns and verbs, dropped objects such as a toy car into a box and brought them back when the child voiced the correct two words. Not only did both children learn to produce two-word pivot-open verbalizations, but they also generated several of these verbalizations without training later on.

In another study[3] twenty-one preschoolers with Down syndrome, all under the age of 27 months, were enrolled in a program featuring biweekly, 1-hour stimulation sessions focused on speech and movement development. Parents were given specific directions in how to promote these types of accomplishments at home. Results showed no significant improvements in language or movement abilities in the twenty-one children who received the program as compared with sixteen children who did not receive it.

A fourth group of researchers[4] prepared parents of six preschoolers with Down syndrome to be language stimulators. The goal of the program was to make children's verbalizations longer and more complex. Parents used

_____

* Early intervention studies that were medically oriented in terms of the intervention emphasized were not included in our review.

play, imitation activities, and conversations as stimulation vehicles. Significant improvements occurred in children's verbalization length and complexity.

A fifth group of researchers[5] provided a language program to preschool children with Down syndrome that began with verbal requests (for example, "Bounce the ball on the floor"), progressing to a demonstration of the activity paired with a verbal cue, and ending with verbal directions for actions alone. Results showed significant improvement in the expressive language of children in the program group when compared with the language of children who were not in the program, who also had Down syndrome.

We experimented with a program to promote language development through specially prepared play activities.[6] Called Project EDGE (Expanding Developmental Growth through Education), the program served thirty-five home-reared children with Down syndrome (seventeen in a treatment group and eighteen in a nontreatment group), from the time they were newborns up to age 5. Parents in the treatment group provided structured play lessons that consisted of interactive play with simple objects and toys (such as a brush-comb-mirror-doll set; paper and crayons), a step-by-step activity sequence for each object or toy along with a suggested vocabulary list, and photographs of items to promote reading readiness.

At the end of five years of the EDGE program, significant differences favored the treatment group in terms of intellectual and motor development. The two groups, however, were highly similar in language development, the project's main curricular emphasis. Hence, results of the study were interpreted as providing general support for the early stimulation of young children with Down syndrome but not for the EDGE curriculum per se. Therefore, the curriculum never has been published.

In a seventh study[7] experimenters emphasized a broad spectrum of stimulation activities for sixteen preschool children with Down syndrome living in a small nursing home in Sweden. In this study special attention was given to social and movement stimulation. After eighteen months the sixteen children in the treatment group showed significant improvement over a comparable nontreatment group. One year later the effects of the stimulation had disappeared in the treatment children as a group, but differences among individuals continued to favor children who had received treatment in terms of both speech and movement stimulation.

The eighth early stimulation study[8] focused on techniques from physical therapy. Ten children with Down syndrome received stimulation based on objectives written for each child (such as, "Will maintain prone on elbows, with head at 45° for 12 seconds"). Sessions took place at home, each lasting about forty minutes, and were carried out three times per week for nine months. At the end of that time, significant differences favored the children who had undergone treatment, but not in all respects. They did well on individual therapy objectives but not on general measures of cognitive and movement performance.

Summing up, in these eight fairly well done (but not perfect) studies involving young children with Down syndrome, the outcomes are generally encouraging. *First*, seven of the eight studies showed significant improvements in children who received the support of early intervention as contrasted with those who did not, although the differences were not always in areas the experimenters had targeted as their main concerns. *Second*, in most of the successful interventions, the wise use of behavior modification techniques shows up, as does application of these techniques within a verbal learning context—for example, parent-child interactive play with language used for stimulation and reward. *Third*, the proportionately large number of positive findings in these relatively strong studies gives reason for optimism because, taken together, they show that the development of children with Down syndrome can be improved substantially through a variety, and possibly a combination, of approaches. This leads nicely into the next topic, the importance of whole-child stimulation.

## A SPECIFIC OR A GENERAL APPROACH?

Often, parents who have a young child with Down syndrome have trouble deciding if their child's development delays or impairments are important enough to warrant special attention. And, if the child's delays are deemed to require special attention, parents sometimes are unsure about whether stimulation should take the form of specific stimulation or general stimulation.

In parallel fashion, when we as adults look in the mirror and notice a bulge around our waist, it presents a quandary: Is the bulge a normal part of entering middle age (and perhaps related to a propensity for overweight, as seen in relatives)? Is it a result of our lagging interest in regular exercise (or is it due to both of these factors in some combination)? If we decide the bulge is caused, in part, by lack of exercise, and assuming we wish to take action, we have to decide if exercise is to be specific or general in terms of its target and form and its accommodation in our schedule.

If we decide to target the bulge specifically, we may enroll in a health club and go five times a week to work out on an exercise machine and participate in an accompanying regimen designed specifically to reduce the abdomen, administered under the direction of an exercise therapist. Or we may decide that the bulge reflects an overall neglect of body exercise and choose to work on general fitness by walking regularly and briskly during each noon hour.

The choice of one (or both) of these strategies is largely a matter of personal preference. Both, if done conscientiously, will have a positive effect.

In a similar way, observing that a young child with Down syndrome has a delay or impairment in one or more developmental areas—communication, movement, socialization, or cognition—a decision has to be made about whether to do anything about it and, if so, what. In deciding if it warrants action, parents can consult a growth and development chart (such as the ones in Chapter 4) or seek out a specialist in the area of concern—speech therapist, physical therapist, psychologist, or pediatrician. If the parents decide to take action, it will be helpful to make that decision in consultation with a professional—since focusing on the problem in concert is reassuring. After that, if action is warranted, the parents' decision on how to fit the action into their preferences, schedule, and lifestyle is just as important as the decision on what the action is to be.

For example, two sets of parents may decide to deal with a nearly identical language delay in their preschool children, using two different, but beneficial, approaches. One set of parents may decide to take the child to a speech and language therapist three times a week for practice in labeling objects. The other set of parents may decide to work labeling stimulation into parts of the day when they and the child are together naturally, such as mealtime, bedtime, playtime. Either of the two strategies (if they are enjoyable for the child) can be effective because they fit with the parents' priorities as well as the child's needs.

Is the decision as to how to approach a significant deficit or delay, then, a toss-up? We lean toward finding ways to work on a problem in the context of the parent's natural, daily schedule—possibly with a modest expansion of that schedule to accommodate to a child's area of specific need—rather than relying heavily on a specialist to take over the problem altogether, as long as the parent doesn't take on too much responsibility. We tilt toward this in-family context approach because it usually is less disruptive to the family routine. And, because it involves parents (and perhaps a sibling or two as well), it can build chains of successes across the whole family routine. The importance of weaving together developmental emphases, across activity areas, within a family context is emphasized in the next sections.

## $\mathscr{S}$TIMULATING MULTIPLE DEVELOPMENTAL AREAS ___

Our research findings,[9] as well as the research review by Cicchetti and Beeghly,[10] support the proposition that children with Down syndrome have particular difficulty with tasks centering on verbal learning operations, such as a preschooler needing to understand and then remember a series of vocal directions in order to find a toy that has been hidden. For the school-age child with Down syndrome, mathematics problems involving verbal-to-visual or some other type of symbol manipulation (such as "story problems") present a special challenge, as do tasks requiring internal language manipulation, such as reading comprehension tasks.

This being the case, why not give the child with Down syndrome lots of early practice in specific verbal learning tasks? That should prevent this problem. Right? Not quite. Young children, with and without Down syndrome, are "whole body" learners. Therefore, verbal learning tasks should involve thinking, moving, and socializing, as well as speaking and listening. Research shows that developmental areas are interrelated in young children, suggesting that language, motor, social, and other areas can be improved together and even interactively.

For example, two studies by Cicchetti and his colleagues support the premise that the social and cognitive development of children with Down syndrome are not separate entities; they are interrelated.[11] Cicchetti and his associates studied the interrelation of social behaviors (such as smiling) and intellect in children with Down syndrome. In one of the studies, fourteen infants with Down syndrome received creative types of social stimulation from their parents. The parents were encouraged by suggestions such as, "Using a loud, deep voice, pronounce boom, boom, boom at 1-second intervals"; "Blow gently at the child's hair for 3 seconds; blow from the side across the top of the baby's head"; "Stick out your tongue until your baby touches it (help the infant to touch your tongue with his or her hand, if necessary); and pull your tongue back in as soon as baby touches it."

Infants with Down syndrome in these activities laughed in the same developmental order as nonhandicapped infants did, although their achievement in this behavior was delayed by several months. Infants with Down syndrome, like nonhandicapped infants, laughed first at physically intrusive items and later at items calling for more intellectual sophistication. Intellectual development paralleled and was predicted very well by the level of the child's social development. Furthermore, individual consistency was striking across social, mental, and motor measures, showing the organized, and interrelated, nature of development.

In the second study, Cicchetti and his associate examined the development of mirror self-recognition in young children with Down syndrome, ranging in age from 15 to 48 months. Mothers placed their children in front of a mirror for twenty to thirty seconds, observing and recording their children's behaviors on a checklist. Behaviors on the checklist included gazing at the mother's image, social expressions such as smiling and pouting, communication attempts such as sounds and words, and motor behaviors such as claps and kisses. Of critical experimental concern was the infant's nose-touching response following a hoped-for recognition of a rouge-smeared nose reflected in the mirror. This response was assessed as follows: After children observed their reflections, mothers turned them around and, while pretending to wipe their noses as they would do if the child had a cold, smeared green rouge onto their noses. Then, the children again were shown their images. Mothers were asked to remain quiet and unexpressive throughout the entire session.

As predicted, children with Down syndrome lagged in the development of mirror self-recognition, corresponding to their delayed rate of intellectual development as measured with a popular infant development test. When the typical 22-month-old nonhandicapped infant's image was altered by rouge, he indicated self-recognition by touching his nose while looking in the mirror. In contrast, only a small percentage of children with Down syndrome, those with higher developmental scores, touched their nose by 22 months of age. Thus, when developmental age (not just chronological age) was equated, children with Down syndrome showed socialization development parallel to that of nonhandicapped children.

These two studies show that two crucial aspects of a child's development called "social" and "intellectual" are really not separate entities but instead are interrelated. An ideal medium for promoting this social/intellectual linkage is parent-child play, enriched by language interaction that stimulates and reinforces social and intellectual development—a type of play we might call "edu-play."

# LAY*

Beginning early in the child's life, play can serve a myriad of purposes ranging from enjoying the giggling fun of roughhousing to enhancing the symbolic use of play. The quality of play between parents and their young child can have an important influence on the child's intellectual and social development. For example, three re-

---

\* Some of the activities in this section were developed and field-tested by John Rynders' wife, Barbara, a gifted mother/teacher/grandparent.

searchers[12] found that the frequency of positive verbal interaction, object communication (playing together with toys), and close, nurturing contact between mother and child had a close relation to measures of children's cognitive and language competence at age 2. They concluded that "the mother-infant dyad, not simply the individual infant, may be the most worthwhile focus for change."[13]

Berger addressed the issue of socialization versus quality of interaction involving parents interacting with their infants with Down syndrome.[14] Berger found that difficulties in the social aspects of interacting can lead to problems in joint play between parent and child. Because we cannot explore the topic of play in depth in one chapter (whole sets of books have been written on the topic), we will look at a few activities that lend themselves to providing interesting verbal learning opportunities through play for children with Down syndrome and, equally important, can fit into adult schedules quite naturally and fairly easily.

When we operated the early intervention part of the EDGE program, knowing that children with Down syndrome typically show delays in all areas of development, we knew also that the area of verbal learning tended to be their weakest area. Thus, we made certain that nearly every activity offered throughout the day included a strong verbal learning opportunity. During large-muscle play (for example, jumping in place on both feet), the adult would ask the child to count his or her jumps, or would count with a child to provide a model until the child showed proficiency in counting. Parents who

have a preschool child at home can capitalize on this verbal learning emphasis while embedding language, social, and movement components into a variety of whole-child learning activities. Here are some edu-play ideas:

- *Read books* to your child that educate him or her as well as provide
  enjoyment. Establish a time (each day or evening, if possible) that
  will be your special time for this activity, and allow the child to take
  responsibility for carrying books to and from your reading place (we
  like a rocking chair best). Reading builds verbal learning abilities.
  Handling books with care teaches an important socializing skill. Sitting
  close to a parent while reading gives the child assurance that he or
  she is valuable and valued. Whole-child learning is taking place while
  verbal learning is stimulated.
- *Play "word" games* with your child. Emphasize games that have some
  built-in verbal learning components, such as children's lotto, children's
  bingo, *Chutes and Ladders*, and simplified *Dominoes*. Large-muscle
  games such as children's horseshoes and ten pins, because they have
  simple rules, teach the child verbal learning skills in an enjoyable
  manner and also socialize the child in the importance of playing fairly
  and following directions. And, of course, they have the added benefit of promoting large muscle strength and coordination.
- *Introduce outdoor activities with an educational purpose.* Learning
  to care about the earth is a major concern these days. Caring about it
  often begins with learning to appreciate it. A preschool child with
  Down syndrome can learn things about the environment that will be
  important educationally as well as socially, not only in the early years
  of life but as an adult as well. Outdoor education activities that have
  worked well for us with preschoolers are "gardening" (picking a few
  beans, watering a flower with a sprinkling can), bird feeding (putting seed in a bird feeder, tossing stale bread on the ground for sur-
  face-feeding birds), yard work (raking leaves with a child-size rake
  and then running through them), going on a nature walk in the neighborhood, carrying a plastic bag for "treasures" (a feather, an acorn,
  a pretty stone) that can later be displayed.
- *Share adult chores with the child.* This can be enjoyable for parent
  and child alike. (Besides, parents need to do them anyway). The chores
  have to be adapted so they are reasonably enjoyable for a young child,
  at least in some respects. For example, when shopping at the grocery store, tell the child, who is riding in the grocery cart, what he or
  she is seeing as you pass through sections of the store. Before checking
  out, reward the child with a nutritious treat—an apple or a small box

of raisins—provided he or she did not try to grab things off the shelves (a precondition you set as you began shopping in the store). In this activity, not only is the child's vocabulary increasing, but he or she also is learning to exert self-control and delay gratification for a short while. Another adult chore in which a preschool child can share is food preparation—doing selected operations of cookie making, placing slices of cheese on a plate, and the like.

- *Play dress up.* Trying on dad's hat or mom's shoes can be a lot of fun. Later, when the child matures to the point at which he or she can engage in pretend play, dress-up might be followed by a tea party or a "magic" act.

In all of these activities (except dress-up), parents have assumed a mediating role, guiding the activity, avoiding steps that are too difficult for a young child, enriching an activity with new vocabulary, and so on. Through the parents' role, not only does the child become smarter but better socialized as well. To take advantage of this social-intellectual combination, a parent can use some additional instructional techniques to make the play activities even more enjoyable and productive. These techniques can be used throughout the day, not just during playtime, and will improve a child's task achievement and also the child's *behavior* during the task.

Moreover, these techniques would be of use to the educational psychologist who was assessing the ability of the child with Down syndrome to draw with a crayon, a situation described at the beginning of this chapter. Observing that the child had difficulties imitating a drawn line, the psychologist could recommend that the parents take advantage of the techniques described next to support their child's learning. In doing so, their child will become more skilled in the task and, equally important, easier to discipline. At the same time, parents will be able to advance their own development as childrearing becomes more rewarding. The techniques are grouped under three headings: (a) giving better directions, (b) rewarding task accomplishment and social achievement, and (c) reducing undesirable behaviors.

## GIVING BETTER DIRECTIONS*

The outcome of a child's activity often depends a lot on the directions a parent gives before and during the activity.

- *Parallel talk.* The parent demonstrates how to sweep a floor by talking to the child about every step, what is being used, and what to

---

*Some of these ideas were contributed by an EDGE staff member, Judith Wolf, a speech and language therapist.

look for during sweeping to determine when the floor has been swept thoroughly.

- *Elaboration.* The parent extends the child's language and knowledge. For example, the child says "red." The father says, "Yes, Jim, the crayon is red."
- *Corrective mirroring.* The parent helps the child correct his or her errors or omissions in language (grammatical errors). For example, Susan says, "I goed to the park last night." Mother says, "Oh, Susan, I'll bet you had fun when you *went* to the park last night."
- *Question-answer-question.* When asking questions of a young child, the verbal requirements have to be simple and the parent must obtain an appropriate answer. This sounds trite, but it's surprising how often a question is asked and then left hanging. With a young non-verbal or low-verbal child, the child has to convey his or her answer through a motor behavior (pointing, showing, handling). When no answer is forthcoming, a good teaching technique is to supply the answer and then ask the question again. For example: "John, point to the boy in this picture." (No answer.) "John, the boy is here." (Adult points.) "I'm pointing to the picture of the boy. Okay, John, now can you point to the picture of the boy?"
- *"Show and tell" (modeling with continued verbal directions).* The parent clarifies what the child is to do by showing him or her what to do while telling the child what to do (a form of parallel talk). For instance, showing a child how to use a glue stick correctly, along with parallel talk, usually is far more effective than just telling the child how to use it correctly.
- *Physical guidance (with continued verbal direction).* In this method the parent guides the child's hand or hands toward what the parent wants him or her to do (passive guidance), or takes the child's hand or hands and actually does the complete task with the child (active guidance). Active physical guidance should be used sparingly, as too much help, provided too quickly, can damage the child's self-motivation. A rule of thumb is to use physical guidance only after having tried, and failed, to help the child succeed in the task through show-and-tell instruction.
- *Shaping.* Shaping is defined as a method that rewards a child's successive approximations to the desired final response. The parent helps the child build an adequate response from one that is there at a beginning stage of development. An example is to reward Susan for a scribble that approximates an "S" and to continue to reward Susan for "better scribbles" until she achieves a recognizable "S."

■ *Backward chaining*. This method has been described as "shaping in reverse." Rather than building from successive approximations to a final response, as done with shaping, the parent begins with a final response that lacks just one small element and works backward. Again using the letter "S" as an illustration, that parent presents Susan with a letter "S" that is complete except for the final small tip of the letter. Once Susan draws that final tip, her parent praises her and has Susan draw the final tip plus the final curve. When that is done, the parent has Susan draw the final tip, the final curve, plus the lower curve, and so on, until Susan is producing the complete "S" successfully.

■ *Cuing*. Cuing directs the learner's attention to the task by giving clues to the desired behavior such as:

—*Movement cues*. After the child has circled the incorrect picture, the parent points to the picture the child is supposed to circle.

—*Position cues*. The adult places the correct picture choice closest to the child so he or she is more likely to choose it.

—*Redundancy cues*. The parent places a red dot under one of three pictures he or she wants the child to touch.

—*Match-to-sample cuing*. The parent helps the child select the correct choice from among several choices, all of which are incorrect except one. For example, the child is presented with a picture of a bird and, without removing the picture, is shown a page containing pictures of a bird, a dog, a tree, and a ball.

■ *Fading*. The parent reduces the amount of help given, or gradually eliminates cues, such as gradually reducing the size or darkness of a letter provided to the child as a model, until the model disappears and the child is producing the letter without cues. Using the letter "S" again as an example, Susan's mother draws a heavy, dark "S" on a sheet of paper and asks Susan to trace it. After Susan has done that correctly a few times, her mother draws an "S" lightly and asks her daughter to trace over it. Finally, the mother makes the shape of an "S" with her pencil's eraser only and asks Susan to draw one on the paper. (If Susan also makes the letter with the eraser end, the mother should praise her and ask her to make one more that her mother can see.)

## REWARDING ACCOMPLISHMENT AND ACHIEVEMENT

A technique to get a child to repeat a behavior is to reward the child immediately after he or she achieves the desired behavior. There are many types of

rewards and many ways to use them successfully. Here are a few ideas we have found to be helpful.

- *Social rewards*. Kind words, a pat on the shoulder, are commonly used (or should be) in day-to-day interactions. One should not underrate their importance when delivered judiciously. Rewarding desirable behavior increases the probability of its occurring again.
- *Token rewards*. Pieces of money are token rewards (except in the hands of a miser), because they have value only when traded for something. Money is not used often as a token reward for preschoolers. Instead, plastic chips or some other tokens are used as rewards the child accumulates for increasing some desired behavior. For instance, a plastic chip might be awarded each morning the child hangs his or her pajamas on the end of the bed. When the child collects enough chips (stacking them up as high as a mark on a plastic tube holding them), he or she may trade them for a nutritious food item the child regards as a special treat.
- *Direct rewards*. Sometimes small bits of food (square of whole wheat toast, slice of apple, raisin) can be effective rewards in and of themselves, particularly if the child is a little hungry and you have checked to see that he or she enjoys eating whatever food you have planned as a reward for the desired outcome. Stickers can be effective rewards or can be used as tokens that can lead to a larger reward, such

as a sticker-holding book the child may keep after accumulating a predetermined number of stickers.

- *Activity rewards.* Providing the child with an activity he or she enjoys is an excellent reward, possibly in exchange for doing a task the child does not like to do very much. In our example of helping the child hang up his or her pajamas, we could reward the child with five minutes of listening to favorite music in exchange for hanging up the pajamas.

- *Changing the schedule and amount of reward.* In getting a behavior going, the child usually is rewarded every time he or she demonstrates the behavior desired. Once the rate of correct behaving is judged to be adequate for an individual child, one may decide to reward the child on an every-other-correct-response schedule, or may decide to change some other facet of the reward schedule until, ultimately, the child gains satisfaction from doing the task itself—*intrinsic* reward. At that point, external rewards are no longer necessary, or are used only when the child seems to need a nudge to continue doing something consistently or well. (All of us need a word of praise from a supervisor now and then [external reward] even though we gain intrinsic satisfaction from our work much of the time.)

  Changing the amount of reward per unit of effort expended also can be effective. For example, instead of giving the child one "happy face" for coloring one picture, the amount of reward can be changed by giving the child one happy face for coloring two pages. The rule of thumb is that the value or size of a reward should match the difficulty or size of the desired task, adjusted to match the child's temperament and capability.

- *Beat the clock.* This reward strategy (which also can be used as a cuing technique) can be used effectively to stimulate a child who responds well to having someone set time limits on the task or behavior. One needs to be careful, however, not to promote speed ahead of accuracy for some kinds of tasks—for instance, the early stages of academic learning tasks.

## REDUCING UNDESIRABLE BEHAVIOR

- *Household rules.* Rules can help *prevent* problems and, thus, are extremely useful. The rules, however, must be understandable to a young child and should be stated positively so the child perceives that following the rules leads to something desirable. If rules are stated negatively, infractions cannot be ignored and must be punished or the rule becomes meaningless.

- *Extinction.* In extinction, a behavior (which formerly drew attention each time it was exhibited) is ignored, with the goal of causing that behavior to decrease in frequency or magnitude. This often is a relatively slow process because it takes a while for a child to figure out that you no longer pay any attention to a behavior that you previously attended to every time it occurred. Thus, when beginning to use extinction to get rid of an undesirable behavior, the behavior may get worse while the child figures out the new routine. Extinction is not appropriate to use with a destructive behavior because the child or others may be harmed while you're waiting for the behavior to disappear.
- *Punishment.* Destructive and dangerous behaviors may require punishment—presenting an unenjoyable event (verbal reprimand) or removing a positive experience (time-out from a desired activity). Punishment, such as spanking, should be used rarely and judiciously because it can have undesirable side effects in and of itself and seldom leads to permanent elimination of an undesired behavior. If resorting to spanking, one should be careful to avoid injuring the child. Punishment should be administered with as little emotionalism as possible. At the same time, the child should be taught appropriate behaviors to replace the undesirable ones.
- *The "fair pair."* Attempts to extinguish undesirable behavior should be paired with rewards for desirable behavior at the same time. For example, as the parent ignores fidgeting during reading time, hoping the fidgeting will disappear from deliberate lack of attention (extinction), the parent can reward the child for turning the book's pages carefully. By doing these together, the child will be less likely to maintain the undesirable behavior simultaneously with the desired behavior.
- *Response cost.* Removing a reward already in the individual's possession when he or she misbehaves is called response cost. In essence, it is a "fine" for misbehavior. Fines could include removing points, stars, privileges, or access to a favored activity.
- *Overcorrection.* Overcorrection is a mild form of punishment in that the child must either correct the consequences of misbehavior by restoring the situation to a "better-than-normal" state (restorative correction) or practice an exaggerated form of the behavior as a consequence to each episode of misbehavior (positive correction). For example, a child who says a bad word during bathtime has to say a good word replacement ten times before he or she can leave the bathtub.

▪ *Time-out.* Time-out achieves mild punishing effects by the removal of positive reinforcers, usually in the form of attention. In its most basic form the parent simply turns away from a misbehaving child and refuses to interact for a short time (a type of extinction procedure). Sometimes a brief "time-out in place," having the child put his or her head on the table and rest for a minute—can be effective and is far less time-consuming than removing the child from the room. In its more complex form, time-out involves removing the child from a reinforcing situation and placing him or her in a neutral area, where the child remains for a time. Return to the desired area hinges on no further misbehavior. Neutral places can be as simple as a chair facing the wall. When using time-out:

—Match the type of time-out to the child's age and maturity.

—Use a neutral time-out area, one not associated with either positive or negative activities, if possible.

—Refrain from angry words during the time you actually are sending or accompanying the child to a time-out area.

—Use a time-out area as close as possible to where you are but isolated by a chair or some other barrier. Make certain you can see and hear the child. Not only does this dampen influence on potential misbehavior, but it also is an essential safety measure.

—Use relatively short time-out periods, perhaps keeping track of them with a kitchen timer.

—Do *not* return a child to the original situation while he or she is engaging in disruptive behavior; to do so would be rewarding that disruptive behavior.

Giving better directions, rewarding achievement, and reducing undesirable behavior—the techniques outlined in the preceding pages—are *socializing* the child for learning. These methods, sometimes called *mediated learning techniques*, give meaning to a task through words and questions, help to regulate a child's response, focusing it so it is successful, and give the task importance because of the way the parent gives it importance.[15] The child's social and intellectual abilities, interrelated and supportive of one another, can be advanced together by the *way* a parent interacts with the child. Indeed, the *way* the parent interacts is often much more important than the nature of the task itself.

As the child becomes more socialized and capable, parents are able to enjoy the role of mothering and fathering more fully. Furthermore, the child who is becoming more able, both socially and in learning tasks, also is becoming more *independent*. When their child becomes more independent,

parents are able to pursue other interests, advancing their personal development and development as a couple, while also taking greater pleasure in their
child's advancing development.

## PROMOTING SELF-CARE SKILLS*

According to EDGE parents, young children with Down syndrome thrive in
a home environment where a reasonable routine is established—for example,
where toothbrushing comes just before bedtime (and where bedtime itself
follows a period of reading to the child). Routine seems to not only promote
biological regularity for the child but also offers reassuring social comfort.
Not that routines must be adhered to rigidly, but the child will be better off if he
or she can count on reasonable regularity in caretaking and self-care routines.

　　EDGE parents recommend using pictorial sequences to help the child
remember the steps of a self-care task and a wall chart (perhaps a piece of

---

\* Some of the information in this section comes from the original EDGE book and is
based on a book, *You and Your Retarded Child: A Manual for Parents of Retarded
Children*, by S. Kirk, M. Karnes, and W. Kirk (Palo Alto, CA: Pacific Books, 1968),
and from duplicated materials prepared by Sally Goldberg ("Teaching Self-Toileting
Skills to the Retarded Child," "Teaching Self-Feeding Skills to the Retarded Child,"
"Teaching Self-Dressing Skills," Division of Social Services, Department of Public
Welfare, St. Paul, MN, 1971), and from the 1993 interviews of EDGE parents.

graph paper) where the child can mark an "X" in a square each time the task is completed, providing a satisfying way for the child to record accomplishment (and for the parent to reward it). Charting also helps maintain and strengthen the home routine, which makes family life more pleasant for all of the members.

## EATING HABITS

Most children, including children with Down syndrome, are able to suck as soon as they are born. A bit later, when infants are old enough to swish milk around in their mouth, they do that—and find it enjoyable because nature provides newborns with many nerve endings in the mouth. The only place the newborn has more nerve endings is in the cerebral cortex of the brain. This is why babies spend a lot of time swishing liquid and soft food around in the mouth and why children put all sorts of objects into it, including some things that shouldn't be there.

As children grow out of the newborn period, they begin to show signs of being ready to start feeding themselves. Some of these signs are: enough head control to keep the head erect when sitting in an upright position; ability to balance the trunk reasonably well while sitting in a chair (even if they have to be propped with a soft cloth tied comfortably around the stomach and to the back of the chair); and, most important, indications that they wish to self-feed.

The eating environment should be prepared carefully for comfort, ease, and efficiency, and should be pleasant and quiet. The TV should be turned off. All the food should be prepared in advance and be within the parent's (but not the child's) reach. The glass and spoon should be of a size the child can manage easily. The parent should sit beside the child and not hover over her or him. Even with food the child likes very much, independence training should begin with small quantities. Accidents, and spilling, which are bound to happen, should be handled matter-of-factly.

As the child begins to self-feed, soft finger foods should be introduced—bread, a soft cookie, a cooked vegetable. When the child is ready, these foods afford chewing practice and help keep gums healthy. These should be pieces of food the child can grasp easily. (Remember that young children are not able to make the precise thumb-and-finger kind of pinching grasp that older children can.) Above all, a constant, positive, parental presence during feeding, maintaining vigilance to the possibility of choking, and gaining proficiency in the use of the Heimlich maneuver (as applied to a small child) is essential.

**Drinking from a plastic glass.** The skill of learning to use a glass usually is acquired fairly early in life, but with a lot of trial and error before the young child learns just how far to tip a glass to obtain some liquid without getting drenched. In the early stages of learning, a small, plastic, juice glass is suggested. The child should be allowed enough time to swallow and breathe as the parent holds the glass to the child's mouth. When the child is first learning to self-drink, the parent may have to assist by physically guiding the child's hand when he or she is having difficulty. Then, as the child begins to show better control, more of the task can be turned over to him or her. At first, drinking a milkshake or a malt may be easier for a child because the liquid moves more slowly out of the glass. When giving milk or juice or water, commercially available cups with covers that release liquid slowly may be useful. Above all, when holding a glass to the child's lips, the child's head should not be tipped back very much, as the child may choke.

**Using a spoon and fork.** A young child might well regard a spoon as an "instrument of torture." It involves filling, lifting, aiming, emptying, and refilling, all with precise movements and requiring good aim and split-second timing. Spills and dribbles are frustrating. Chopped and blended foods stay on the spoon more easily than some of the others. The parent's hand should be placed gently over the child's hand and, grasping the spoon together, dipped into the food and guided to the child's mouth and then back to the dish. As with using a glass, the child should be encouraged to assume more and more control of the task.

If the child is having difficulty grasping a spoon, the spoon handle can be built up with tape. Or different sizes and shapes of spoons might be tried. Putting a guard on the edge of the tray may be helpful. Another useful aid is a plate with a suction cup on the bottom so it will stick to the highchair top. Or a wet towel can be wrapped around the outside edge of the plate.

Learning to use a fork is similar to learning to use a spoon, but it additionally requires piercing and cutting. And missing the mouth is more painful with a fork than with a spoon. Therefore, forks should be introduced only after the child has good mastery of the spoon, and thereafter with discretion.

## TOILET - TRAINING

All parents look forward to the time when their children will be toilet-trained. Fortunately, almost all children learn eventually to take care of themselves at the toilet. Nevertheless, toilet training often proceeds slowly, sometimes with performance plateaus and even some regressions, because the process of controlling elimination requires coordinated use of muscles.

What are some of the signs indicating that the child may be ready for toilet-training? First—and here is where the importance of communication becomes apparent—does the child understand what is being asked of him or her when talking about using the toilet? Is the child willing to go into the bathroom with you? Does he or she show signs of discomfort when soiled or wet? Is the child sometimes dry for as long as an hour or two at a time? These are all signs that he or she is ready for training. Here are some additional tips:

1. Concentrate on one toilet habit at a time.
2. Keep the child's outside clothing simple. Trousers or slacks with elastic waistbands can be pulled down quickly.
3. Use training pants instead of diapers. These can be removed quickly and help the child feel more grown up.
4. Don't flush the toilet when the child is seated on it. It may frighten the child. Instead, let the child flush it when he or she gets off the seat and after he or she pulls up the pants (maybe with a bit of help from you).
5. If you get a potty chair, keep it in the bathroom. Some parents think a potty chair is unnecessary and want to put the child on the regular toilet. If so, a child-size toilet seat may have to be put on first. If using the adult-size toilet, provide a box or a footstool to support the child's feet, making elimination ("pushing") easier.
6. Do not leave children unattended on the toilet. Go into the bathroom with them, and stay with them. Five or ten minutes usually are sufficient. If the child doesn't eliminate in that time, remove him or her from the toilet without showing emotion.
7. Do not react with anger or punishment to a child's playing with genitals or a bowel movement. This is normal behavior. Rather, respond with a firm but gentle "no" and an appropriate substitute task. (This problem can be avoided by not leaving the child unattended in the bathroom.)
8. Remain calm when accidents happen, and don't give up. Accidents happen during and after toilet training. Sometimes these accidents are associated with illness, a change in family routine, or a feeling

of insecurity. Soon the child will show progress again.

9. Reward the child for progress. The child will respond to praise, a smile, caress, or hand clap. Reward the child immediately after the desired behavior occurs, but don't overdo it.

10. If the child makes grunting sounds or shows other signs that he or she is in the process of a bowel movement, don't rush the child to the bathroom as if the house were burning down. Rushing makes the child tense and may delay elimination or stop it altogether. Instead, lead the child to the bathroom quickly but calmly and gently.

11. Teach boys and girls to wipe their seats from front to back. This is particularly important for girls, to avoid possible urinary infections.

12. Conclude a toileting session with hand washing and drying. Cleanliness is part of toilet training and should be taught along with it.

13. Make a habit of getting the child to the bathroom at times when the bladder is likely to be full. These times might include mornings upon rising, after meals, mid-morning, mid-afternoon, and before bedtime. If the child is having trouble urinating, giving liquids just prior to taking your child to the bathroom may "prime" the response.

14. Most important, establish an individualized schedule for your child and stick to it.

## GROOMING AND HYGIENE

If the child cannot reach the wash bowl comfortably or see into the mirror, a stable footstool or box should be provided. An easy-to-reach shelf can hold combs and other toilet articles.

**Washing the hands.** For the first couple of times children use the sink, the parent should control the water faucet, as children can get carried away with this fascinating object. If a child doesn't wet the hands spontaneously in the water while the parent is running it, the parent should ask the child to wet the hands (while describing what is going on), then put the soap between the child's hands and see if he or she knows what to do. If the child does not, the parent should apply some soap to the palm of one of the child's hands and, gently holding the backs of the hands, rub the two hands together, followed by helping the child rub the soap over the back of the hands and on the wrists. Rinsing comes next, while talking to the child about what is going on and making it as pleasant as possible. Children should be allowed to do as much as they can for themselves and be guided only when they need it. Of course, children shouldn't be left in the lurch when they obviously need help. Standards of cleanliness may have to be lowered a bit when training begins. If a child is trying, he or she should be rewarded for effort.

**Washing the face.** After learning to wash the hands, the next step is learning to wash the face. This is a more complex task because, in contrast to washing the hands, a child cannot see the face constantly while washing it. And everything is backward in a mirror. Furthermore, children may be plagued by a small child's problems, such as getting soap in their eyes, water dripping down their arms and running off their elbows, and missing parts of the face with the washcloth. As the teaching begins, the parent should squeeze out the cloth for the child, then spread it over one of the child's hands. Standing behind the child, the parent helps the child rub the soap over the cloth. (At first this may be a wet washcloth without soap.) Remaining behind the child, the hand with the washcloth is guided gently over the child's face. The cloth is rinsed and the process repeated, relinquishing the task to the child as he or she progresses.

**Bathing.** Bathtime can be highly enjoyable for a young child, especially these days when so many interesting things are available commercially to play with in the bathtub. At first, turning on the bath water and regulating its temperature must be the adult's responsibility. Eventually, however, the child can begin to take over. At that time, a strip of colored masking tape can be fastened temporarily on the inside of the bathtub to show the child the level where the water should be turned off. But children require supervision in the tub. Leaving the child alone is hazardous if the child has seizures or does not have good postural support. A child also might turn on the hot water by mistake and get scalded. Besides, watching water from the bathtub drip down through the ceiling into the living room is very discouraging.

   The general training suggestions for washing the hands and face are the same for bathing. Again, bathing should follow a specific procedure, with a set time for bathing so the child will get accustomed to a sequence of events. The child should be taught to clean out the bathtub after the bath, and learn where to put dirty clothes—both important components of training.

**Combing hair and brushing teeth.** As with face washing, it's a good idea to stand behind the child so both of you can look into the mirror at the same time. A medium-sized comb often is easier for a child to handle than the small pocket combs, because fingers may get in the way when combing. Initially, the parent can help by gently putting his or her hands over the child's and carefully guiding the comb through the child's hair. Parting the hair is a task with which many older nondisabled children have difficulty, so unreasonable standards should not be set for a young child who has Down syndrome.

   When teaching tooth brushing, parents should brush their teeth and have the child observe. The same type of "show and tell" instruction and physical guidance used with other self-care skill training activities is applicable here. Relatedly, preventive dentistry pays big dividends. Frequent checkups and cleanings, along with applications of sealant and fluoride treatments, can often eliminate cavities right up to the preadolescent period.

## GOOD REST AND SLEEP HABITS

Young children grow quickly and use up a great deal of energy in vigorous play. Generally, the younger they are, the more rest they will require. Some children with Down syndrome need more rest than nondisabled children of the same age. Frequency and length of the rest period should be adjusted to the child's requirements. As with any child, however, he or she should not be allowed to nap so long that it interferes with falling asleep at the normal bedtime in the evening.

Rest and sleep periods should be regular. If a rest time regularly follows lunch, for example, the child will accept the routine more readily and also be more willing to go to bed than if the parent waits an hour or so after lunch and then calls the child from play to take a nap. If a child obviously does not need to sleep after lunch, he or she should be given an opportunity to rest for ten to fifteen minutes after lunch. Children who have trouble sleeping should not be forced to lie in bed for long periods. They will associate the bedroom and bed with unpleasantness, an association that should be avoided.

A quiet activity before rest will help. Children have trouble settling down immediately after active play. Quiet activities include reading a story, playing soft music, or giving the child a picture book to look at.

Children should be encouraged to fall asleep and to rest without assistance. If a child is tense, however, the parent may sit by the child, gently rubbing the back, helping the child relax and fall asleep. A parent's presence alone may be enough to calm the child. Gradually, the parent should fade from the picture so the child doesn't become overly dependent on that presence to fall asleep.

Excessive talking or noise making should be discouraged. If possible, the child should sleep in a room where he or she will not be disturbed or distracted by other children or adults. If the child wants to take a toy to bed, that's a good idea, as long as it's a toy that would not injure the child or make a loud noise if rolled upon. An inexpensive child cry pick up and transmission device, which carries distress sounds to the parents' room, can be helpful.

## DRESSING

Dressing and undressing provide rich opportunities for the child and parents to problem-solve together. In the earliest stages of learning to dress, children often are frustrated when faced with complicated zippers or with buttons that somehow refuse to go through buttonholes. As adults, we have developed our own dressing skills to the extent that they are automatic. Thus, when we analyze what we do when we dress ourselves to be able to help our child dress, we have difficulty breaking the task into the required steps. This reminds us of a familiar story. A centipede moving very well across the floor is asked to describe how it moves each of its 100 legs in sequence. When it stops to think about each step, it gets all tangled up in its legs and collapses. Still, the skills of dressing can be broken down into small steps. This kind of planning can be interesting.

One of the most useful training techniques to promote independent dressing is *backward chaining*, a term defined earlier in this chapter. It starts with the final act or product and works backward. We will look at a few dressing activities and see how backward chaining can be used in each one.

**Putting on underpants.** The sequence is as follows:

1. Put on the child's underpants except leave them down around the knees. Then the only thing you have to teach is how to pull the pants up over the hips. At first you may have to guide this behavior physically, but eventually the child should do what's expected with just a verbal invitation.

2. After mastering the hip pull-over, remove one leg from the underpants and teach the child to stand on one leg and put the other leg through the empty leg hole. You may have to provide physical support for a while or let the child practice while seated, because this kind of balance is not easy at first. Each time the child gets the leg of the underpants on properly, have him or her complete the activity by pulling the underpants up over the hips, too.

3. Hand the child the underpants in the proper orientation (with the front facing away from the body), and have him or her put in both legs and pull them up over the hips. Physical support may be necessary.

4. When the child is able to put on the underpants independently and correctly, hand them to him or her in the wrong position (backward), and see if the child can correct the position and put them on properly. The idea is to develop this skill to the point of complete mastery so it becomes automatic and self-correcting (like yours). Eventually the child will have practiced it frequently and will have worked out all the aspects that can go wrong and, hence, will become more and more independent.

**Putting on a t-shirt.**

1. Using the technique of backward chaining, begin by putting the child's shirt on for him or her except for pulling it down in front and back, and ask him or her to do only that final operation.
2. When the child can do that on your command, remove one arm from its hole and teach the child to replace it in the sleeve and pull it down as before.
3. Remove both arms, and have the child proceed one more step by putting first one arm in the sleeve and then the other, pulling the shirt down front and back.
4. Teach the child to put the shirt over his or her head when you give it to him or her. (A clear marking or label on the inside, back of the shirt will provide a helpful cue.) Continue the sequence of the previous steps.

On each try, the child always should be required to go through all the steps already learned. New steps are not introduced until the earlier ones are mastered and can be done at your command.

**Putting on socks.** For a child, putting on a sock may be like trying to put a wet noodle into a key hole.

1. Seat the child comfortably on the floor, with you seated behind, thumbs inside his or her sock.
2. Place the sock over the foot, pulling the top up around the heel, and then have the child pull it up over the ankle upon your command, "Pull up your sock."
3. When the child will do this on command, put the sock partially on the foot (just over the toes), and have the child pull it up all the way.
4. Fold the sock like a tube squashed from the top, and require the child to put the thumbs inside the top, place it over the toes, and pull it all the way up.
5. Teach the child to fold the sock into the palms before putting it over the toes.

**Tying shoelaces.** Parents can provide the child with shoes that have Velcro strips if the child is having great difficulty with laces. In the early stages of teaching tying, some parents find it convenient not to put the shoe on the child's foot at all but instead demonstrate on a table in front of him or her, or use a commercial or homemade shoe-tying board. By using instructional aids, parents place the problem close by and avoid having the child spend a good deal of time in a bent-over position.

**Zipping.** The hardest part of learning to use a zipper is learning how to get the slide started on the track. In the early stages, some parents put a small safety pin near the bottom of the zipper so the child pulls the zipper down only to a point near the bottom (but not disconnecting the slide from the track) and then slips out of the garment as you would do if removing your pullover sweater.

If the child is having great difficulty with zippers, a commercial or homemade zippering board may be helpful, so the child can have the zipper in front of him or her and operate it more easily than when it's under the chin. When the child learns how to hold onto the fabric to produce tension while pulling the slide up and down, parents can teach him or her to start the slide on the track. This is a complex step, however, and probably will require a great deal of time for mastery, plus a lot of patience by parents.

# YNOPSIS

1. Self-care skill development is crucial to a child's eventual overall social development. It is the basis, actually, for independent or semi-independent living at the adult developmental level.

2. Self-care tasks, such as eating properly and dressing appropriately, provide useful learning opportunities through which a child can sharpen language, social, and muscular skills if these are planned properly.

3. Parents are the child's most important "instructional material," serving as a guide or mediator of learning. Specific things a parent can do in this role are:

   ■ Set the stage for learning by eliminating sources of distraction, such as a loudly playing radio, and have all the articles you'll need for the activity close at hand.

   ■ Make yourself and your child comfortable.

   ■ Before you begin a task involving several steps, analyze the task by going through it several times yourself or with another family member so you can teach it step-by-step without confusion and hesitation.

   ■ Decide if the task proceeds best from beginning to end (shaping) or from end to beginning (backward chaining).

   ■ When the child completes a task successfully, reward him or her with your voice and with a smile or possibly a bit of nutritional food, if it suits the task. Stickers can work well too, as can tokens that can be traded in later for something helpful to the child's development and that is enjoyable to him or her.

4. When the child learns a self-care skill, provide him or her with an opportunity to practice what has been learned until he or she can do the task automatically. Then begin to vary the problem slightly. This is important because problems almost never are identical from time to time and place to place, and you don't want a child's learning to be "brittle" and nontransferable. As you vary the problem, you and your child can have fun with it by making a game out of "fooling the teacher" and other variations of affectionate give and take.

5. As you continue to mediate learning, gradually withdraw your verbal, modeling, and physical guidance, substituting cues that are part of the task itself. This is really the end point of self-help training: to promote independence. As a practical matter, you will not always be available to lead your child through every task with your voice and other forms of help, so he or she needs to become as self-reliant as possible.

6. To the greatest extent possible, try to treat your child with Down syndrome as you would a nondisabled child. Do not abandon sound principles of normal child training because your child has intellectual limitations. On the other hand, your child with Down syndrome will have some problems in learning, so more specific instruction of the sort outlined in this chapter will be helpful to him or her and to you as parents from time to time.

Today, early, direct stimulation of infants with Down syndrome is less emphasized than it was formerly, replaced by more of an emphasis on supporting the early parent-child relationship, helping parents "read" and respond to their babies' signals. Indeed, a major goal of early interventionists who work with parents who have an infant with

Down syndrome is to help parents learn to read the sometimes dampened signals of their infant and then to encourage *doing* while avoiding *overdoing* for the infant. Above all, early interventionists support development of what Winnicott[16] calls the "holding environment"—the nurturing, love, and caring that only the infant's family can provide.

# NOTES

1. R. Bidder, G. Bryant, and O. Gray, "Benefits to Down's Syndrome Children Through Training Their Mothers," *Archives of Disease in Childhood* 50 (1975): 383–386.
2. D. Jeffree, K. Wheldall, and P. Mittler, "Facilitating Two-Word Utterances in Two Down's Syndrome Boys. *American Journal of Mental Deficiency* 78 (1973): 117–122.
3. M. Piper and I. Pless, "Early Intervention for Infants with Down Syndrome: A Controlled Trial," *Pediatrics* 65 (1980): 463–468.
4. J. MacDonald, J. Blott, K. Gordon, B. Spiegel, and M. Hartmann, "An Experimental Parent-Assisted Treatment Program for Preschool Language-Delayed Children," *Journal of Speech and Hearing Disorders* 39, 4 (1974): 395–415.
5. P. Pothier, D. Morrison, and F. Gorman, "Effects of Receptive Language Training on Receptive and Expressive Language Development," *Journal of Abnormal Child Psychology* 2 (1974): 153–164.
6. J. Rynders and J. Horrobin, "Educational Provisions for Young Children with Down's Syndrome," in J. Gottlieb, editor, *Educating Mentally Retarded Persons in the Mainstream* (Baltimore: University Park Press, 1980).
7. M. Aronson and K. Fallstrom, "Immediate and Long-Term Effects of Developmental Training in Children with Down's Syndrome," *Developmental (Medicala Medicine) Child Neurology* 19 (1977): 489–494.
8. S. Harris, "Effects of Neurodevelopmental Therapy on Motor Performance of Infants with Down's Syndrome," *Developmental Medicine and Child Neurology* 23 (1981): 477–483.
9. J. Rynders, K. Behlen, and J. Horrobin, "Performance Characteristics of Preschool Down's Syndrome Children Receiving Augmented or Repetitive Verbal Instruction," *American Journal of Mental Deficiency* 84 (1979): 67–73.
10. D. Cicchetti and M. Beeghly, *Children with Down Syndrome: A Developmental Perspective* (New York: Cambridge University Press, 1990).
11. D. Cicchetti and A. Sroufe, "The Relationship Between Affective and Cognitive Development in Down Syndrome Infants," *Child Development* 47, 920–929; L. Mans, D. Cicchetti, and A. Sroufe, "Mirror Reactions of Down's Syndrome Infants and Toddlers: Cognitive Underpinnings of Self-Recognition," *Child Development* 49: 1247–1250.
12. S. Olson, J. Bates, and K. Bales, "Mother-Infant Interaction and the Development of Individual Differences in Children's Cognitive Competence," *Developmental Psychology* 20 (1984): 166–179.

13. Olson, Bates, and Bales, p. 178.
14. J. Berger, "Interactions Between Parents and Their Infants with Down Syndrome" in D. Cicchetti and M. Beeghly, editors, *Children with Down Syndrome: A Developmental Perspective* (New York: Cambridge University Press, 1990), pp. 101–146.
15. R. Feuerstein, Y. Rand, and J. Rynders, *Don't Accept Me As I Am: Helping "Retarded" People to Excel* (New York: Plenum Publishing, 1988). (See section written by Pnina Klein particularly.)
16. C. Winnicott, R. Shepherd, and M. Davis, *Babies and Their Mothers* (Reading, MA: Addison-Wesley, 1987).

# KRIPPNER FAMILY

Dad: Bill
Mom: Joan
Sister: Paula
Sister: Linda (Richardson)
Brother with Down
    syndrome: Wayne

Life is sweet when you're 6.

Swims like a fish.

Fun in the leaves.

Special Olympics torch bearer.

## $\mathscr{K}$RIPPNER FAMILY (continued)

Storytime with niece and nephew.

Graduation from high school.

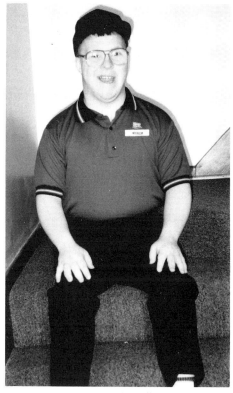

Ready for the world.

It's off to work we go.

# ~*6*~

# AMILY ADJUSTMENT AND ADAPTATION

Brian H. Abery

*J*im and Sally French* were both in their mid-20s in the late 1960s. Sally worked as a teacher, and Jim was employed part-time as an electrical engineer, completing a master's degree with the goal of soon assuming a management level position with his company. During Jim's school years the couple spent a lot of time dreaming about their life in the future. Well-educated individuals dedicated to their chosen professions, they saw themselves buying a house in the suburbs and starting a family. When Sally became pregnant, both parents-to-be were overjoyed and waited for the birth with great expectations. They planned for Sally to take a year off from work and then for her mother to assume child-care responsibilities. The pregnancy itself was without complications and, as the due date approached, extended family members telephoned regularly to see what assistance they might offer the young couple.

On June 26, 1969, Michael was born. At 6 pounds 8 ounces, he appeared to be a healthy little boy. Twelve hours later the attending obstetrician informed Sally and her husband that their son was "severely retarded—a child with Down syndrome." Although Michael had no obvious medical problems, his parents were informed that he would be at high risk for a variety of health complications throughout his life. Professionals suggested on several occasions that the best thing for the family and the child would be to place him in an institution where, according to their physician, "he will get the best care possible." Immediately rejecting this idea, both parents looked to their families for emotional support. Unfortunately, this was not forthcoming, as relatives on both sides of the family seemed to agree that the young couple would not be able to rear a child with a "severe disability" successfully.

---

* Parent names used in this chapter are pseudonyms. The photographs, while representative of families with children with Down syndrome, do not depict the families described. The circumstances described, however, are factual and quotations are taken from transcriptions of interviews with family members.

Michael's birth set into motion a chain of events that, according to Jim and Sally, "drastically changed our lives." Despite a lack of family support, Sally and Jim were adamant that Michael would be reared at home. Twenty-three years later the couple seem sure they made the right decision. Jim describes Michael as "a determined young man who knows what he wants out of life and will probably get it." Sally characterizes her son as someone who sets his goals high and is good at creating the support necessary to reach his objectives. Both parents are quick to point out that rearing Michael (and his two younger siblings) has not been without its struggles, but, as Jim states, "the decisions, accommodations, and changes we have made have been well worth it."

Jean Robinson was 36 when Kathy was born in 1977. At that time she and her husband, Carl, had three other children ranging in age from 2 to 9 years. Jean chose to remain at home with the children, and Carl held both full- and part-time jobs to make ends meet. Living in a densely populated urban area, both parents longed for a better neighborhood in which to rear their children. This would have to wait until Jean returned to work after the last of the children entered school, however, because, as she put it, "both Carl and I agreed that it was important for the children to be raised by their parents rather than a day-care provider." Jean had a number of complications during pregnancy and spent the last weeks before giving birth on "bed-rest." Luckily for the family, a number of close relatives lived nearby and came over to care for the other children, clean house, and help with meal preparation.

After an extended delivery, Kathy was born. Almost immediately her parents were aware that something was wrong. The infant experienced respiratory distress and quickly was given oxygen and moved to an intensive-care unit. Fortunately, Kathy's initial medical problems were not as serious as first thought, and within 12 hours she was back in her mother's arms. During one of these periods, Jean reports, she was "still marveling at her child's birth" when one of the attending nurses asked when Carl would be returning to the hospital. When she questioned why, Jean was informed only that her physician had something she wanted to discuss with her and her husband.

Carl described the meeting he and his wife had with their physician as one of the most "gut-wrenching" experiences he had ever encountered. "Our doctor was direct and to the point, explaining that our daughter had Down syndrome, would likely experience some degree of mental retardation, and need special educational and medical services as she grew up." What made the meeting so difficult, Jean stated, was that she couldn't answer most of their questions at that time—things like how retarded Kathy would be, if she would learn to talk, read, and write, what type of education and medical services she would need. No one at the hospital could (or would) answer these questions for the Robinsons. When they brought Kathy home from the hospital, they knew little about what to expect.

Shortly after completing this past school year, Kathy celebrated her 16th birthday. Despite some of her health difficulties, her mother described her as "just as independent and stubborn as her brothers and sisters when they were that age." During the summer Kathy participates in inclusive recreation programs offered by the local park and is looking forward to returning to school in the fall. Kathy's parents say her persistence and independence has served her well so far in school and in her interactions with peers. Although they indicate that life is going well for Kathy and the family at the present time, they do express concern about what the future holds for their daughter, especially in developing friendships with other young adults.

The Frenches and Robinsons now have had 24 and 16 years of experience, respectively, rearing children with Down syndrome. For both families the process has been one with both its triumphs and disappointments. Over the course of the years, these families have adjusted their expectations and plans for the future, coped with developmental and unexpected sources of stress, and undergone many transitions, each in their own, individual manner. Members of both families also state emphatically that they have grown as individuals and as families as a result of this experience. Even though each family has followed a somewhat different path in achieving what might be called a "psychologically healthy family environment," the process of coping and growth they experienced has many commonalities.

# HE FAMILY SYSTEM

Among the questions parents with children who have Down syndrome ask most often is: How will rearing a child with this disability affect the family? The question can take many more specific forms, including: How will rearing a child with Down syndrome affect the marital relationship, parental relationships with other children, interactions between siblings, affiliations with members of the extended family, friends, and neighbors? How might the family best cope with the stressors that inevitably accompany dealing with educational, health, and social service systems that are something less than "user-friendly?" In what ways can the family support the developing competence of a child with Down syndrome while it provides for the continued physical, cognitive, and emotional needs of the remainder of its members.

These questions have no easy answers. Each individual, with or without a disability, has different capacities and needs, and so does each family. Each family responds to situations such as these in its own unique manner. Some families cope extremely well with rearing a child with Down syndrome. Many do much better than cope; they thrive. Other families, for a variety of reasons, have considerably more difficulty.

The birth of a child with Down syndrome has the *potential* to have many effects upon the family. Conversely, the way in which individual family members and the family as a whole respond to this situation has the capacity to have a profound impact on the child's development. This *bidirectional* process in which the child's behavior affects the family at the same time the family affects the child has begun to be understood only recently. Given that interest in this area has been recent, there is much more we do *not* know about families with children with developmental disabilities than what we do know.[1]

What we know about families with children with disabilities has increased dramatically in the last two decades. Farber was one of the first to note the impact that raising a child with a developmental disability could have on a family, finding a disruption in the "normal family life-cycle."[2] More recent research efforts have found that families of children with developmental disabilities often have added stress,[3] social isolation,[4] more marital discord,[5] more tension among siblings,[6] greater caregiving burdens,[7] and poorer physical and mental health.[8]

Is the situation really this grim? Are most families with children who have developmental disabilities destined to be more dysfunctional than families without children with disabilities? The answer to this question is not simple but might be stated best as a qualified "no." Although past research has furthered our understanding of some aspects of rearing a child with a developmental disability, most of these efforts have focused almost solely upon a search for pathology and dysfunction. Beginning with the notion that "a family with a child who has a disability is a family with a disability,"[9] researchers have used an almost infinite number of methodologies in an attempt to confirm this "maladjustment" hypothesis.

Recent research efforts based upon more complex models of family functioning[10] reveal that positive outcomes may coexist with or be independent of the higher levels of stress reported by many families of children with developmental disabilities. During the decade of the 1980s, research findings appeared suggesting that couples who had children with developmental disabilities more often than not had strong, mutually rewarding marriages,[11] developed innovative ways to cope with higher caregiving demands,[12] adjusted well to adopting children with mental retardation,[13] and had children without disabilities who, based upon a number of family characteristics, were generally well-adjusted.[14] Despite these recent efforts, however, researchers have done a poor job over the years of separating the increased *demands* faced by families with children with developmental disabilities from the *potential stress* and *strain* these demands may create, as well as unquestioningly equating higher levels of demands, stress, and strain with "maladjustment."[15] As a result, despite evidence to the contrary, the notion persists that most families with children with disabilities are not well-adjusted.

## ℛEARING A CHILD WITH DOWN SYNDROME: UNDERSTANDING THE PROCESS_____

An overview of the research literature as well as personal experience suggests that, though some families do have difficulty rearing a child with a developmental disability, many families take it in stride, adjusting over time, adapting to higher demands, and growing as individuals and families along the way. How might one best understand this complicated process of adjustment, adaptation, and coping?

Patterson and her colleagues[16] developed what they refer to as the *Family Adjustment and Adaptation Response (FAAR) Model* (see Figure 7). This model suggests that when an infant with a disability joins a family, a two-phase process of *adjustment* and *adaptation* occurs over time. During the adjustment phase the family and its members make immediate short-term changes to cope effectively with the additional demands of rearing a child with a disability. If a family is to not only survive but also thrive and grow, long-term changes also have to be made over the course of the child's and family's life cycles. These adaptations are in response to the family's attempts to meet the demands it faces from both expected (developmental) and unexpected stressors and strains.

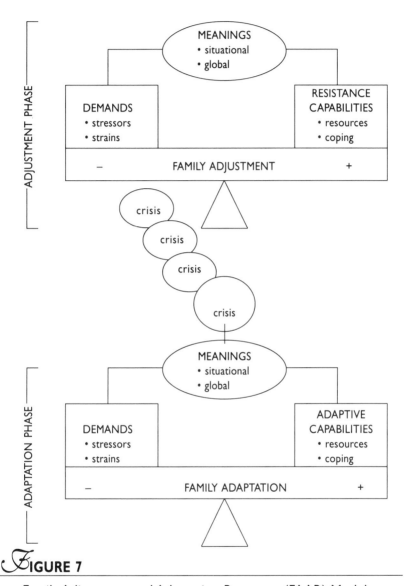

## FIGURE 7

### Family Adjustment and Adaptation Response (FAAR) Model

From "Families Experiencing Stress: The Family Adjustment and Adaptation Response Model," by J. M. Patterson, in *Family Systems Medicine* 5 (1988): 202–237. Used by permission.

## DEMANDS, STRESSORS, AND STRAINS

One of the important distinctions Patterson and her colleagues made is between demands placed on the family, the stressors and strains the family endures, and the experience of stress. It is inconceivable that rearing a child with Down syndrome, or any disability for that matter, will not create additional demands on a family. The external environment acting on the individual often creates a demand, sometimes called a potential stressor. The demands change over time. Some demands result from what are referred to as "normative" sources, the expected transitions and changes over the course of the individual and family life cycle. Expected events that place demands on the family include a child's initial entry into school and the transition from childhood to adolescence. A second set of demands are "non-normative." They are unexpected, as in a divorce or the sudden death of a spouse. For the family of a child with Down syndrome, non-normative demands might include extensive participation in early intervention programming, daily or weekly physical therapy, or the need to meet with professionals (teachers, school psychologists) regularly to ensure that the child is receiving adequate services.

The normative and non-normative demands of a family with a child with Down syndrome potentially can create stressors and strains. A *stressor* is a demand or event that has an impact on the family because it produces changes in the family system.[17] This change may be in any one or more of a number of areas including family boundaries and goals, patterns of family interaction, the quality of relationships, the number or type of roles one must fill, and the values of individuals within the family. Family *stress* is defined as a state that arises from an actual or perceived imbalance between the demands placed on a family and the family's capability to meet these demands. If a family does not have the capacity to respond to additional demands or can do so only by making significant changes, one or more family members may experience stress. *Strain* refers to the actual negative effect on the person or persons as a result of the stress.[18] It is an unpleasant state that most persons seek to avoid or at least minimize. Although all individuals endure some amount of stress and strain, if experienced over a lengthy period, this can lead to both individual and family needs not being met effectively.

Upon the birth of their children with Down syndrome, the French and the Robinson families were faced with a number of demands above and beyond those of most new parents. Both the French and Robinson children, for example, required physical therapy for some time. This requirement placed a demand upon the two families. As pointed out by Glidden, however, the stress caused by the same demand can be different for different families.[19] Because Jim French was working part-time and had some flexibility in his class scheduling, the demand of taking their son for physical therapy could be spread across both parents. Sharing this responsibility, Sally and Jim were able to minimize stress from this demand, and they experienced little strain. The Robinson family, on the other hand, had to deal with the same demand in a different way. Carl was employed full-time and was not able to share the responsibility for taking his daughter to physical therapy with his wife. The stress and subsequent strain this situation created for the family was quite high at first because Jean not only had to take her daughter with Down syndrome to the therapy sessions but also had to bring along her second youngest child. Only when Jean was able to arrange for day-care for Kathy's older siblings was the strain reduced to a manageable level.

To understand a family's response to rearing a child with a Down syndrome, one must consider not only the demands of stressors and strains placed on individuals within the family but also the demands placed on the family unit as a whole. These demands stem from the child as well as the community's response to the child. All of these systems can be viewed as a source of both demands and capabilities. Take, for example, the French family. Upon the birth of Michael, their son with Down syndrome, Sally and Jim French had to respond to caregiving demands that did not exist before his birth. Michael was the French's first child, so they did not have the luxury of previous practice as parents. They had to respond to the demands typical of all infants and also had to attend to the special needs of their child associated with his disability.

The caregiving demands placed on parents of children with Down syndrome obviously are different for each parent and child and are determined by the characteristics of both the parents as well as the child. Some parents who need eight hours of sleep a night often find it difficult to remain alert. Others can get by on five hours of sleep each night. Like their parents, each child with Down syndrome is also a unique *individual*. Some are extremely active, others mellow. Some may quickly develop regular schedules for eating, sleeping, and other biological functions, and others may not.

The birth of a child with Down syndrome also creates a set of demands on the *family,* because mothers, fathers, and siblings often have to redefine their roles within the system. Before the birth of their daughter, Kathy, Jean Robinson undertook most of the child-care responsibilities within the Robinson family. Shorty after Kathy's birth, however, Jean experienced what most family psychologists would term "role overload." As Jean reported, "It became impossible for me to continue to do everything associated with raising the family by myself. It affected not only my relationship with the children but with Carl as well." Carl Robinson, who prior to Kathy's birth worked both full- and part-time jobs to help make ends meet, also felt the strain and observed it in his other children. Over time the Robinsons redefined their roles as parents. Carl quit his part-time job and took over more of the child-care responsibilities, and Jean eventually obtained employment outside of the home.

At a third level, rearing a child with a developmental disability has the potential to create demands (from stressors and strains) at the *community* level. Both the French and the Robinson families have spent considerable time attending meetings related to the education and health care needs of their children. These families estimated that, over the course of their children's lives, they spent an average of 30–50 hours per year participating in meetings to ensure that their children were receiving quality services and necessary supports. Although one might expect the level of community demands to lessen as children mature, families often indicate that these demands decrease only slightly and may even increase as their children move into adulthood.[20]

## SHORT - AND LONG-TERM DEMANDS

Over time a family attempts to balance short- and long-term demands with its capabilities for meeting these demands.[21] The short-term outcome of this balancing effort is termed adjustment, and the long-term outcome is referred to as adaptation. When a family adapts to rearing a child with Down syndrome, it is able to effectively meet the child's needs as an individual as well as its needs as a family.

The demands associated with rearing a family in general and a child with a disability in particular (and the stressors and strains associated with them) change continually. If they are not resolved, demands may pile up, placing the family and child at risk for poor outcomes. This notion of a pileup of demands suggests that families of children with developmental disabilities may be especially vulnerable during periods of major developmental changes.

## FAMILY CAPACITIES

How does a family adjust and adapt to rearing a child with Down syndrome? Why are some families successful while others struggle? Although these may seem like simple questions to answer, we do not yet fully understand all of the complex processes involved in families' adapting and coping. Two decades of research in this area, however, have provided enough information for professionals to begin to understand the process. A number of factors associated with families' success in adapting to rearing a child with Down syndrome or any other disability have been identified. These factors, called family capacities, include:

- The *meanings* the family and its individual members attribute to the demands of the situation and their capability to meet these demands.

- The *resources* the family has available or is able to acquire.
- The *coping behaviors* the family uses in an attempt to achieve a balance between demands and resources.

**Family meanings.** The way family members think about what is happening to them as a group and as individuals has a powerful effect on their success in adjusting and adapting to potentially stressful events of all types,[22] including rearing a child with Down syndrome.[23] This involves the way in which a family defines and perceives the demands associated with the disability as well as its capabilities for coping effectively with these demands. The ability to develop positive, adaptive beliefs and meanings increases the probability of a proactive approach to life, not only for the family but on the part of individual family members as well, including children with disabilities.

Finding meaning in what many may call negative events has been viewed as a way in which families can restore some order and purpose in life, especially during times of great stress and strain.[24] The belief systems that families develop to deal with demands have been found to be global, influencing how a family responds to multiple situations, as well as specific as related to particular situations and demands.[25]

Like other characteristics, the meaning a family attaches to having a child with a disability is subject to change over time. For some families the initial meaning is quite negative but becomes more positive as family members adjust and adapt to the child. If, on the other hand, demands build up to a point where family members no longer have the resources to deal with them, an initially positive or neutral meaning may become more negative. During the first months of their son's life, Sally and Jim French experienced this change in the meaning they attached to having a child with Down syndrome. Jim stated:

> When we first realized that our child had Down syndrome, we were both kind of numb. I don't think either of us saw the situation as anything less than a catastrophe. I had nightmares of my career going up in smoke. Sally quickly realized that she could not go back to teaching after only one year off because finding child care would be impossible. The reactions of our families to the birth of Michael didn't help either. Everyone kept encouraging us to place him for adoption or institutionalize him, even our physician. One strategy they used was to attempt to convince us how difficult...no, how impossible it would be to successfully raise our child. It got to the point where I think we both began to believe that this was a situation we could not possibly endure.

Over time the Frenches were able to meet other families that had children with Down syndrome. As they talked to these parents, they reported that a change seemed to take place. Sally described the change and what it meant to the family:

> We talked to parents who were members of a support group. They all had horror stories to tell about how professionals and family members told them to institutionalize their children. More important, they all had positive things to say about how their families had grown and coped with the difficulties. Most of these people identified some point in their family's life where they as parents came to see their child as a gift...as a person with capabilities and capacities just like any other child. From that point on, it seemed like things got much easier for them. That's not to say that these families didn't make sacrifices along the way. At least at this point, though, they saw the concessions as worth it.

How might the meaning a family and its members attach to having a child with a disability affect the child and the family? Viewing one's child as "less than normal," "sick," or "less capable" may have a number of effects upon interactions between parents and children. This negative meaning has been associated with more dependency on parents, lower levels of competence, and poorer developmental outcomes for the child.[26] Attributing positive or neutral meanings and attitudes to children with disabilities ("Our child is just like other children," "Our child has drawn us together as a family") is a protective factor for families, helping them manage the situation while minimizing stress and strain.[27] The meaning a family and its members attach to a child's disability influences not only the family's ability to adapt but the child's as well. The meaning a child comes to attach to his or her disability, in turn, likely will affect the family's adaptation.

An example may illustrate this point. If a family comes to view the birth of a child with Down syndrome as having meaning or a "good thing," the family is less likely to develop resentment toward the child and more likely to provide the loving, nurturing environment that will facilitate the child's growth and development. This positive family atmosphere increases the likelihood that the child will develop the skills, attitudes, and values that enhance the probability of later independence, autonomy, and a high quality of life. These are all factors that can lessen the demands, stressors, and strains within a family.

The reader may wonder how parents could consider the birth of a child with Down syndrome a "good thing." Certainly most parents do not wish for the birth of a child with a disability. The *frame of reference* within which the family determines the subjective meaning of an event, however, may lead to a view of the birth as a negative and stressful occurrence or something that is neutral or even positive.[28] Consider the meaning of Down syndrome to the following parent, whose frame of reference is children the same age as her son who are average to above average in verbal, academic, and other abilities.

> It was extremely hard for us to not see Thomas's birth as a catastrophe. His sister, who is only a year older, has always been an extremely bright child. She talked at 14 months, learned to read at age 3, and is now in her school district's gifted program. Every time we look at Thomas, we can't help but see that he's falling further and further behind his sister and other children his age, and there is really nothing we can do about it.

It would be extremely hard for this parent to see the child's disability in a positive light. Contrast this situation with that of Jean Robinson, Kathy's mother, who has a distinctly different frame of reference:

> My sister is a nurse in a pediatric intensive care unit. I guess that helped Carl and me a lot because, before Kathy's birth, we had heard all sorts of stories of children born with severe, multiple disabilities, kids with degenerative diseases, children with leukemia and other forms of cancer whose parents knew they would probably never grow to be adults. That kind of helped us put it all into perspective. We know Kathy has a disability. I don't want to minimize that. But when you look at the whole picture, both she and the family were quite blessed. After some early physical problems she's been pretty healthy all these years, was able to take part in an early education program, learned to read, and is now thinking about a career. I guess we were the lucky ones.

Using a different frame of reference, Jean Robinson views her daughter and the family as fortunate. The meaning the Robinson family attached to Kathy's birth and her disability is one of the factors that allowed them to feel empowered and take a decidedly proactive approach to meeting Kathy's education and health-care needs. Viewing Kathy's disability as a challenge rather than a catastrophe, her family was able to take proactive stances and avoid major crises. This has proved especially valuable during major transitions or changes because the family was prepared for these eventualities.

Perceiving the demands associated with rearing a child with a disability as "something we can beat" makes a family (other things being equal) more likely to attempt to find, use, and, when necessary, develop the resources required to rear the child effectively and at the same time meet the needs of other family members. Negative meanings, in contrast, increase the probability that parents and other family members will neglect to seek out resources, such as parent and advocacy organizations, that can provide extensive support and lessen demands. Attaching neutral or positive meanings to the situation also increases the probability that a family will achieve a balance between meeting demands and accepting limits to capabilities through strategies such as lowering expectations to reasonable levels.[29] Jean Robinson related how unattainable expectations at first hindered her family's attempts to cope with Kathy's disability and the positive changes after more realistic expectations were developed.

> Carl and I, like most parents, often got caught up in trying to be the perfect father and mother. Because Kathy has often had physical problems, there were a lot of exercises and activities that her physical therapists wanted us to do with her at home daily. This was fine when the other children were young and weren't involved in a lot of other activities. We could spend the necessary time with Kathy, and the other kids often took part, too. As they got older, though, we began to feel the crunch—school meetings, basketball practice, church functions, choir. The demands on our time as parents quickly built up. We didn't want to deny Kathy's brother and sister the chance to take part in activities their friends were. On the other hand, we felt like "bad parents" when we forgot or didn't have time to work with Kathy.
>
> Things really got out of hand until Carl and I called Kathy's therapist and then had a family meeting with the kids. It turned out that missing a couple of days a week of Kathy's exercises wasn't really going to do any harm. Then we sat down with the kids and informed them that, while we really wanted them to have the chance to do all they wanted, there had to be some limitations. We asked each of them to choose two after-school activities they were really interested in and wanted to pursue. We agreed to support them in those areas—drive them to practice, pick them up after school, and so on. If they wanted to do more, they understood that they needed to figure out ways to do them on their own or with the help of friends.

The meaning a family attaches to rearing a child with Down syndrome also relates to the extent to which specific family meanings are associated with a sense of control and empowerment among family members. A belief that one has some control over life events has been found to be related closely to adjustment and adaptation to stressful events[30] including rearing a child with Down syndrome.[31] Why might this be the case?

Determining the educational and health-care services children with disabilities need is not an exact art. Professionals within education and human services fields often have to guess as to the type and level of services that will facilitate a child's development. As a result, the services provided to these children and their families often do not meet their needs fully. Given the nature of service systems through which children with disabilities receive their education and care, families often have to advocate for additional services they believe are necessary for their children's optimal development. The meaning a family attaches to having a child with Down syndrome is likely to have a profound effect on the extent to which a family experiences a sense of control and empowerment and is able to advocate effectively for their child.

Perceiving themselves as in control of their lives, Sally and Jim French have taken a decidedly proactive stance in advocating for services for their son, Michael. Be it health care, educational, vocational, or other services, the Frenches have, according to Sally, "done whatever was necessary to make sure that Michael gets the services and supports he needs." Provided with these services, Michael has had the opportunity to develop skills and abilities that many children and young adults with developmental disabilities never have the chance to acquire. These capabilities have enabled him to reach levels of independence and self-sufficiency that neither his family nor the professionals with whom they work originally thought possible.

**Family resources.** Family resources consist of the psychological, social, interpersonal, and material characteristics of: (a) individual family members (personal resources), (b) the family unit (informal resources), and (c) the community (formal resources).[32] When available, these can be called upon to reduce stress, solve problems, and facilitate parents' balancing the demands of rearing a child who has a disability with their capacities (see Table 4). Resources at each of these levels are of two general types. The first is *existing resources*, already in place and available to a family and its members before the birth of a baby with Down syndrome and with the potential to minimize the impact of a potential source of stress. Existing resources might include a strong marital relationship, financial stability, and the health of family members.

The second type of resources are *new resources* the family and its members develop in response to new or additional demands associated with rearing a child with a disability. These might include making friends with other families with children with disabilities who can provide a source of support, joining a parent support group, and finding a child-care provider experienced in working with children who have disabilities. Because the demands and strains of rearing a child with Down syndrome (or any child, for that matter) tend to build up over time and vary with the child's stage of development, families must develop new resources continually that will help them meet current and future demands.

The extent to which families have access to and can use specific resources effectively varies depending upon a number of factors. Even so, examining resources that have been helpful to many families that have raised children with disabilities may be instructive.

1. *Personal resources/supports.* Resources at the individual level include, but are not limited to, the individual's physical and psychological health, level of education, intensity of spiritual/religious beliefs, problem-solving skills, and sense of self-esteem and self-confidence.[33] One's *physical* and

# TABLE 4

## Levels and Types of Resources

| Resource Level | Type of Resource | Potential Resource Use |
|---|---|---|
| **Individual** | 1. Physical health | 1. Better physical stamina necessary to meet increased caregiving needs. |
| | 2. Psychological health | 2. Ability to cope with frustration, intense caregiving, etc. |
| | 3. Level of education | 3. More knowledge of disability and service system; financial stability. |
| | 4. Spiritual beliefs | 4. Ability to derive positive meaning from birth of child with disability; sense of empowerment. |
| | 5. Problem-solving skills | 5. Capacity to solve problems/remove barriers necessary to ensure provision of appropriate services; ability to minimize or effectively deal with conflict. |
| | 6. Self-esteem/self-confidence | 6. More persistence; greater likelihood of proactive approach to dealing with child-related issues; enhanced quality of caregiving; higher levels of marital and family satisfaction. |
| **Family** | 1. Family interaction style | 1. Higher levels of family and marital satisfaction; better able to provide intrafamilial support; greater capacity to develop and maintain informal and formal support network; enhanced ability to provide support and nurturance to family members while fostering autonomy; ability to adapt to change. |
| | 2. Marital relationship | 2. High levels of spousal support; agreement on roles, rules, and responsibilities; shared caregiving. |
| | 3. Informal support network | 3. Provision of emotional, informational, instrumental, and companionship support. |
| **Community** | 1. Formal support network | 1. Provision of emotional, informational, and instrumental support; training/education; furnishing of physical support/services; introduction to individuals who may become part of informal support network. |

*psychological health* is essential if a parent is to adjust and adapt to the demands of an infant or child with a disability. Increased demands, such as spending more time in direct caregiving, or attending ongoing meetings with health-care providers and school personnel are potential sources of physical and psychological stress and strain that can lead to anxiety, feelings of incompetence, and depression. As Jean Robinson related:

> It wasn't until Kathy was 5½ years old that she slept through the night without needing some sort of care. Adding up all the sleep I lost over that period of time, it's amazing that I wasn't sick more often. If you add the time demands, frustration, and anxiety Carl and I had from meeting almost weekly with at least one of the many professionals who provided services to Kathy, it's amazing that at least one of us didn't have a breakdown.

The *level of education* of family members also has been found to predict adjustment and adaptation to the stressors associated with rearing a child with a disability. Typically, the higher one's educational level the greater a family's financial resources, the more influence one has with professionals, and the more skills one has in negotiating the service delivery system. Level of education also has been associated with parental understanding of the disability affecting a child, setting appropriate and realistic expectations for the child and others, and participating in support groups. All of these factors have the potential to reduce stress and strain.

The intensity of one's *spiritual and religious beliefs* has been associated with less stress in families who have children with developmental disabilities.[34] At this point, however, we do not know how these beliefs help families adjust and adapt to having a child with a disability. Maybe a spiritual belief system allows one to give meaning to the birth of a child with a developmental disability. Or these beliefs may allow family members to adopt a positive, empowered outlook on life. Religious beliefs also may promote adaptation by providing family members with an additional network of friends who can provide social, informational, and material support. A combination of these factors seems to have aided the Robinson family in developing a set of positive meanings regarding their daughter's Down syndrome. Carl Robinson said:

> Our church has helped us in many way in dealing with Kathy's disability. I think it was at least partially our belief that there is a reason and a meaning to everything that helped us put things into the proper perspective after Kathy was born. It was also through our church that Kathy was able to develop some friendships with children her own age when she was younger. Although many of these friends are no longer around, I know Kathy still remembers them and considers them an important part of her life. And friends

that our family made through its activities with the church have been extremely helpful in helping us care for Kathy when we needed a respite.

Rearing a child with or without a disability, a parent faces many obstacles. The parents of children with developmental disabilities often face more demands as they attempt to navigate a complex social and human services system that includes regular interactions with physicians, nurses, physical therapists, occupational therapists, special and general education teachers, psychologists, and a host of other professionals. Parents' *problem-solving skills and style* may either facilitate or hinder their ability to work with professionals, family members, and others within the community to create an optimal environment in which their child can develop. A preference for and skill in active problem solving rather than self-blame or denial have been associated with psychological health in the general population[35] and with lower levels of distress in parents of children with developmental disabilities.[36]

Both Jim and Sally French have displayed this active style of problem solving throughout their interactions with representatives from the various systems that provide their son with services. For example, after being frustrated with the quality of transition services provided to their son, these parents enlisted the aid of a local parent advocacy organization in an attempt to improve Michael's vocational training. After several meetings with an advocate from this organization, the Frenches met with educational and administrative staff from their son's school. Their level of preparation was so thorough that, according to Sally French, "we obtained the changes in Michael's program that we wanted, and our advocate asked us if we wanted to serve as volunteer advocates for the parent organization."

The *self-confidence* and *self-esteem* of family members, especially parents, are crucial to family adjustment and adaptation.[37] People differ dramatically in their estimates of their ability to deal successfully with new situations. Some individuals believe they can easily handle anything. Others are much more conservative with respect to their levels of self-confidence. Individuals who truly believe they have the skills and experience to adapt to demanding situations will be more proactive and persist in the face of adversity.[38] Past experiences in coping successfully also result in parents' developing positive attitudes about their ability to cope with an infant with a disability. Moderate to high levels of self-confidence, therefore, may help parents avoid crisis situations and take effective action when they inevitably do arise.

Self-esteem in most individuals varies over time. Success tends to build self-esteem, and failure may diminish it. The initial reaction of many parents to the birth of a child with a disability is a sense of failure. If parents have a difficult time caring for the child, their levels of self-esteem may decrease further. This is likely to have a direct, negative impact not only on the quality of care a child receives but on marital satisfaction as well. Establishing realistic expectations, avoiding blame of self or others for difficulties, and utilizing formal and informal supports are strategies that have been found to maintain levels of self-esteem and self-confidence.

2. *Family resources/informal supports.* Informal supports are resources available to the family that are interpersonal and derive from family members' interactions with each other and with individuals they know personally. These resources include the family's predominant style of interaction, the marital relationship, and the family's social support network including relationships with extended family members and affiliations with intimate friends, acquaintances, and neighbors.

Over the past three decades a considerable amount of research has been conducted in an attempt to determine how families adjust and adapt to rearing children with disabilities. In recent years these studies have expanded to include investigations of the extent to which *family interaction* affects the development of children with disabilities. Although much remains to be learned in this area, what we do know is that the style of family interaction has a major impact on the ease and extent of family adjustment and adaptation, parenting competence, and child outcomes. Aspects of family interaction and their relation to rearing a child with a developmental disability that have been studied include family levels of cohesion and adaptability, family structure, sharing of affect, extent of support available, role and task assignments, and many other variables.

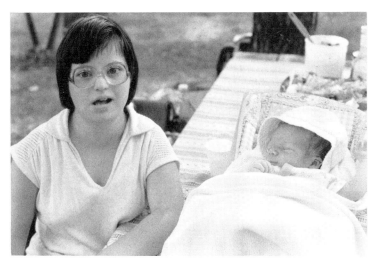

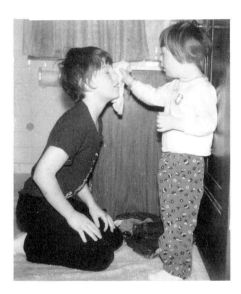

One of the most important findings of this research is that families display a wide variety of styles of interaction. A series of studies of families with children who have varying degrees of mental retardation[39] revealed five distinct styles of family interaction, which the researchers described as:

1. Cohesive–harmonious.
2. Control oriented–somewhat nonharmonious.
3. Low disclosure–nonharmonious.
4. Child oriented–expressive.
5. Disadvantaged–low morale.

Although the severity of a child's disability was found to have an impact on family adjustment, it was not associated with a variety of measures of marital adjustment.

Family interaction research directly relevant to the adjustment and adaptation of families with children who have Down syndrome also has been conducted in recent years. Using the *circumplex model of family interaction*,[40] Abery[41] compared sixty-five families with children with Down syndrome ranging in age from 5 to 18 to a comparison group of families of children without disabilities. This research program considered two basic aspects of family interaction: family cohesion and family adaptability.

*Family cohesion* refers to the extent to which family members are connected emotionally with each other. It ranges on a continuum from enmeshment, or extreme connectedness, characterized by overidentification with the family, to disengagement, or extreme separateness, characterized by extremely low levels of connectedness and the lack of a "sense of family."[42] Continued functioning at either of these extremes is viewed as dysfunctional. Moderate or balanced levels of cohesion (connected or separated) are viewed as more functional as the family strikes a balance between togetherness and separateness, allowing its members to deal more effectively with stressors and developmental change.

*Family adaptability* is defined as the family's ability to change its power structure, role relationships, and relationship rules in response to developmental and situational changes.[43] Families are viewed as being on a continuum of adaptability ranging from rigid (extremely low levels) to chaotic (extremely high levels). Rigid families are characterized by authoritarian leaders, stereotyped roles, and rigid, strictly enforced rules. Chaotic families, at the other extreme, have little to no leadership, dramatic role shifts and reversals, and loosely, arbitrarily enforced rules. Moderate or balanced levels of adaptability (flexible or structured) are more functional to families. Moderate adaptability allows for a sense of stability and at the same time provides room for change. Rules, roles, and the family's power structure are flexible but not constantly changing.

Overall, I found that families of children with Down syndrome displayed moderate levels of both cohesion (connected or separated) and adaptability (structured or flexible) and seemed satisfied with their current styles of interaction. Although no differences were found in the levels of adaptability between families with children with Down syndrome and the comparison group (families with children without disabilities), families of children with Down syndrome were more cohesive than the comparison group. Equally important, families with children with Down syndrome who were moderate in cohesion and adaptability showed more positive communication styles, reported lower levels of stress, were more satisfied with their marital relationships, had lower rates of divorce, and had children whose teachers rated them as having higher levels of social, academic, and behavioral competence than families who displayed extreme levels of cohesion and adaptability.[44] Similar findings have since been reported in a number of studies of families with children with other types of disabilities.[45]

The styles of family interactions of the French and Robinson families provide excellent examples of the way in which different patterns of interaction may facilitate the adaptation of individual families. The French family functioned in a flexibly separated manner (moderate cohesion; moderate adaptability). Given the ages of their children (18, 16, and 14), this style of family functioning allowed enough independence and autonomy for the children and at the same time provided a sense of connectedness that encouraged each

person to feel that, if he or she needed support, it would quickly be provided. Jim French reported:

> Although I think our family is close, we are probably not as close as we
> used to be. I mean, as the children have gotten older, they have spent more
> and more time with their friends. That's something Sally and I think they
> are entitled to and would never dream of telling them that "family comes
> first." What we have been able to do as the kids have grown up, though, is
> set aside a little bit of time each day and week when we do something to-
> gether. During the weekday it's usually nothing more than making sure we
> eat dinner together as a family. It may seem like this is a pretty simple
> thing, but I think it gives us a sense of being connected and an opportunity
> to know what's going on in each others' lives.

The levels of adaptability characteristics of the French family (flexible) allowed Jim, Sally, and their young adult children to strike a balance
with respect to family rules, roles, and leadership so all family members were
able to take part in decision making, had well-defined roles, and understood
the basic rules under which the family functioned. Family leadership, roles,
and rules, however, were open to change and were adapted quite frequently
as the family deemed necessary. Extensive interviews with family members
suggested that this style of interaction was meeting the needs of all members
effectively.

The Robinson family functioned in a structurally connected manner
(moderate adaptability; moderate cohesion). The rules, roles, and power structure of the family clearly were not as flexible as those of the Frenches. Nevertheless, there was a good deal of give and take between Jean and Carl, as
well as between parents and children. Jean said:

> Because of the time-consuming nature of many of Kathy's needs, things in
> our family have to be somewhat structured if we are going to get done what
> needs to be done. But we've always been big on family meetings, and as
> the kids have gotten older, it's been necessary to provide a lot more give
> and take.

The Robinsons also were considerably more cohesive than the French family, and all members reported strong feelings of closeness. Family activities
played a big part in the lives of Jean, Carl, and their children. Both parents
and the children reported engaging in many activities together as a family
each week. Some of these activities revolved around an individual's participation in recreation/leisure activities (for example, the whole family attending one of the children's baseball games and then going out to eat afterward).
Other activities were based on the interests and commitments of the entire
family, such as their participation in church-related events. What is obvious

from interacting with the Robinsons is that parents and children are extremely close and supportive of each other without anyone having to give up his or her individuality.

One of the most important factors in successful adjustment and adaptation to rearing a child with a disability is *marital status and satisfaction.* Single-parent status has been found to be one of the most powerful factors associated with stress and strain in families with children with disabilities.[46] The satisfaction, or lack thereof, that mates derive from their marriage, and reports of marital distress, have been linked to parental stress levels, parental functioning, and feelings of parenting competence.[47]

The importance of a supportive spouse as a resource in parenting a child with a disability should be obvious. Increased parenting demands require that a couple be flexible and reach consensus on the sharing of roles, workloads, and responsibilities. A spouse also is a prime source of a social support. Given the extra demands and difficulties in caring for a child with Down syndrome, the quantity and quality of spousal support not surprisingly is associated with stress and with child outcomes. *Emotional support—* a measure of affection, respect, and satisfaction with the marital relationship—and *cognitive support*—an indication of agreement with respect to child care—are related to mother's and father's parenting competence.[48] Sally French related the importance of this type of support:

> When we brought Michael home from the hospital, we had no idea what to do. I mean, he was our first child. We were new parents. During the early years we were just feeling our way, never really sure if we were handling things correctly. Without the support I got from Jim and he received from me, I think we both would have had a hard time meeting Michael's needs. As I think back to when Michael was young, that was the time we each needed support the most. Neither of us was confident in what we were doing. Jim constantly reminded me that I was a good parent and that things would get better as we learned about Michael's style and needs. It was also important that Jim wanted to be involved in parenting and that we were able to agree on our parenting responsibilities. Without Jim's willingness to be involved, it would have been impossible.

Our *social networks* consist of people with whom we have regular contact and perceive as important.[49] Not only are individuals connected socially and emotionally with each person within their network, but to a greater or lesser extent each person within the network is linked with (has contact with, or knows of) others within the network. Informal social networks include extended family members, intimate friends, neighbors, and acquaintances. Interaction with people within one's social network can promote adjustment and adaptation in families with children with Down syndrome in a variety of ways, the most important being *emotional, instrumental, informational*, and *companionship support* (see Table 5).

The role of social support in helping families cope with the effects of potentially stressful life events and in promoting psychological adjustment is well-established.[50] Some researchers have speculated that it serves as a buffer between the family and upsetting events so the family has fewer adjustments to make.[51] Others believe it aids families in adjusting more quickly to changes brought about by life events.[52] Regardless of the specific processes involved, the research is quite clear: Families with children with developmental disabilities are much better able to adjust and adapt when a significant amount of support is available from their social networks.

What types of support are most effective in enhancing a family's adaptation? The answer to this question depends on the characteristics of the family, its individual members, and its situation. Young parents who have had little experience in rearing children and lack confidence in their abilities may profit most from emotional support. If a family moves to a new community and has little knowledge of the existing service system, informational support may best promote adjustment and adaptation. A child with many health-care and physical needs that require family members to spend a lot of time transporting the child to doctors and therapists might be supported best through instrumental support in the form of transportation. Parents who have spent considerable time advocating for their child with various agencies within the service system may welcome companionship as the most needed and effective form of support.

Although each family must decide for itself the types of support that are most needed, available, and likely to promote adaptation, recent research evidence indicates clearly that support from members of one's informal social network are likely to enhance a wide variety of individual and family capacities. Mothers who have weekly contact with friends, for example, are involved more actively with their infants[53] and have children who are more securely attached.[54] Child-related assistance (instrumental or informational support), which could take the form of a friend providing child care, cooking a meal for a family, or assisting with transportation, is a form of support related to family adaptation and is valued most highly by mothers of children with disabilities, who tend to shoulder the largest share of responsibility for child care.[55] Jean and Carl Robinson related their experience with their informal support network:

> *Jean:* Without the help of aunts, uncles, cousins, friends, neighbors, and people we knew from church, raising Kathy would have been a lot more difficult. We were reluctant at first to maintain contacts with these people immediately after Kathy's birth, but it quickly became clear that we weren't

# TABLE 5
## Types and Functions of Social Support

| Type of Support | Function | Example |
|---|---|---|
| **Emotional** | 1. Reaffirms self-worth.<br>2. Assures individual that her or she is loved and valued. | 1. Reinforces a spouse's competence as a parent.<br>2. Tells a child that he or she is loved. |
| **Instrumental** | 1. Directly provides concrete assistance/ tangible support necessary to solve problems. | 1. Gives financial aid.<br>2. Provides material resources (use of car, etc.).<br>3. Supplies needed services. |
| **Informational** | 1. Gives advice.<br>2. Bestows guidance. | 1. Makes suggestions as to how to deal with a personal problem.<br>2. Refers the person to someone who has resources necessary to help solve a problem. |
| **Companionship** | 1. Serves as supportive person with whom to share activities. | 1. Plays a game with a friend (tennis, cards, etc.).<br>2. Accompanies a friend to a movie or out to dinner. |

going to be able to go this on our own. I think it was our families that first became involved. My sister is a nurse, so she was able to get us a lot of information on Down syndrome that we read and then gave to the extended family. We all learned a lot about the disability and Kathy together. That seemed to calm some of their fears about helping out with Kathy. You know, they quickly found out that she was a lot more like other babies than different from them. Once this happened, things got better. People started calling to ask if they could help out—with the other kids and with Kathy. The support we got was with a lot of different things—having someone to talk to when we were battling the school over Kathy's program, having someone to take care of the kids, including Kathy, when Carl and I needed some time to ourselves, having people available to take the other children places we could not because we were tied up with meetings or therapy sessions.

*Carl:* When Kathy was a baby, Jean's sister and her husband would come over at least a couple of times a week. At first it was usually to do stuff with the other kids, to give us a break. But soon they felt comfortable enough with Kathy so we were able to spend some individual time with the other children. When Kathy got older and started school, Jean decided to go back to work. Well, I don't need to tell you how hard it is to get day-care for a child with a disability. Fortunately, one of our neighbors ran a family day-care. Jean maintained contact with her all through Kathy's infancy, and soon Joyce [the neighbor] got to know Kathy quite well. When Jean returned to work all we had to do was ask, and Kathy had a great day-care situation. That's not to say everything was easy. It was hard work getting people to accept Kathy. Jean and I had to work hard on it with our family, with our friends, and with others. I think it was our belief that if people really took the time to get to know her they would come to love her as much as we did that helped us get through the early part.

How can a family ensure that it will have the adequate support available from its informal support network? One of the most crucial factors is that a family not allow itself to be cut off from others after a child with a disability arrives. Often families of children with developmental disabilities are socially isolated, with smaller friendship networks.[56] The reasons for this isolation vary with the family but have been found to include high levels of emotional and physical exhaustion on the parents' part, parental avoidance of social contacts because of the stigma associated with having a child with a disability, friends' and relatives' avoiding the family because of their uneasiness in handling the situation,[57] and extreme levels of cohesiveness the family adopts as a way to cope with the demands of having a child with special needs.

Although it may be difficult, families can avoid most, if not all, of the scenarios described above. For example, by carefully negotiating role responsibilities within the family, with each spouse providing the other with adequate support, parents can minimize the possibility that one of them will have to shoulder all of the demands and strains associated with rearing a child with a disability. By accepting the disability, learning about it, and educating extended family, friends, and neighbors, families can dispel many of the myths and misconceptions about children with disabilities. This has the side benefit of alleviating the anxiety that many people feel with respect to social interactions with the child or family members.

In attempting to adjust to a child with a disability, one of the most potentially damaging responses a family can make is to develop extreme levels of cohesiveness (closeness) to the point where family members find themselves cut off from the outside world. Even though "standing together as a family" and "taking care of our own problems" may be laudable in some situations, families who are able to adapt to rearing children who have Down syndrome effectively maintain moderate, not extreme, levels of cohesion and adaptability.[58] This allows the family as a whole and its members to maintain and build outside contacts that may serve as valuable sources of support over the long run. Jim French related how difficult, but eventually rewarding, this process can be:

> After Michael's birth Sally and I wanted to crawl into a hole. We were embarrassed to a certain extent to have a child with Down syndrome. It didn't help matters that neither of our families was that supportive and initially encouraged us to place Michael in an institution. I guess it got to the point where it became an "us against the world" thing. We withdrew at first, thinking that the only way to handle this situation was to do it by ourselves. As a result, we found ourselves in danger of losing our connections with family and friends. I think it remained pretty much that way for the first several years of Michael's life. When we decided this wasn't the way to go and we weren't meeting each others' needs or Michael's, it was a long process of rebuilding friendships and connections with family. We've been working on this some time now—hey, Michael's now an adult—and we lost some good friends because of our initial reactions.

Sally French, Michael's mother, also recounted what happened:

> While I'm sort of embarrassed to admit it, I think one of the main reasons why we came out of the shell we had built for ourselves was because of the birth of Michael's brother and sister. It was only then that we started making connections with family and friends again. Our earlier withdrawal made it quite difficult. Talking to one of the friends we had "remade" one day, I was startled to learn that our putting up a wall led them to think that Michael and other children with Down syndrome must be awful because we didn't want our family and friends around to see him. I think our behavior just added to the many misconceptions that people had about Michael and about Down syndrome in general. With no social life or support, we became a "Down syndrome family." Just about everything we did focused on Michael.
>
> Unfortunately, it wasn't until later that we realized this wasn't the best for him. He had us, and we loved him dearly, but he had no one else. His grandparents didn't visit much. Our brothers and sisters, all of whom had their own children, rarely came over, and that meant Michael lost a chance to play with kids his own age. If I had one piece of advice for families, it would be to make sure that in your own coping you're not locking out people who love and care about you. They can be an incredible source of support.

Although developing and using informal social networks for support can greatly enhance a family's ability to cope with a child with a disability, there are several caveats. First, though social networks have the potential to be a source of support, they also may be a source of conflict or criticism.[59] Sally and Jim French found this out shortly after Michael was born, when family members encouraged them, at times quite forcefully, to place their son in an institution. Although this was a common piece of advice to parents of children with Down syndrome in the late 1960s, it created friction between the couple and the extended families. Criticism of parenting styles, disciplinary techniques, the way parents handle the school situation (for example, inclusion versus segregated programming) can all provide fodder for critical remarks by extended family and friends. Relying heavily on one's informal network, with the resulting increase in contact this brings, makes some conflict and criticism inevitable.

Research over the past decade also has shown that some forms of social networks are more beneficial to families than other types of relationships are.

1. Families should strive to develop networks in which they have one or a few intimate friends or relationships with whom they have daily or semi-daily contact. These types of networks seem to be more helpful than those in which an individual has many acquaintances, none of whom is particularly close.[60]
2. It is better if the individuals within one's support network serve multiple needs or are capable of providing a variety of types of support. Each individual's ability to provide many types of support protects the family from losing its sole source of support in a given area if one individual within the network is unavailable for some reason.[61]
3. To maintain a support network over time, one must contribute to the network oneself. Reciprocating with those who have provided support in the past will help ensure that they will continue to do so in the future. Interestingly, it is better if all individuals within the network do not know each other. This eliminates the chance of losing all contributors to the network if problems arise between individual members.[62]

3. *Formal support networks.* The formal support network consists of professionals, community organizations, and agencies the family uses. Even though a network of caring, understanding professionals can be vital to promoting family adjustment and adaptation, no universally available or comprehensive sets of community services exist to promote family and child adaptation and growth throughout the developmental period.[63] In most states, services available to families vary from city to city and county to county.

Some take an approach in which a family deals with one professional for all of its needs. In others a family may find itself working with close to a dozen professionals and organizations. Though the latter approach may provide for specialized services, its potential to create more demands and strain on the family might offset the support it offers. Actually, recent studies have found that many families feel alienated from formal support services[64] and turn to a formal network only when they have been unsuccessful in their attempts to obtain support from family and friends.[65]

Does this mean that trying to build a formal support system will be unproductive? Fortunately, the picture is not quite that dismal. Community services and organizations can be a crucial factor in how well a family adapts to having a child with a disability. In some situations people contacted initially through community organizations and services eventually become part of the family's informal support network. This type of relationship occurs quite frequently in situations in which parents of children with disabilities staff the organization. Within many areas, county ARCs (Associations for Retarded Citizens) provide this type of opportunity.

A number of metropolitan centers have organizations geared toward providing support to parents and families of children with specific disabilities such as Down syndrome. How can participating in such an organization be helpful? While rearing their son Michael, Jim and Sally French relied heavily on this type of support. Sally relayed their experience as follows:

> It was extremely important for us to be able to get to know parents of other children with disabilities, especially Down syndrome. The parent organizations we joined made this possible. As new parents, we had no idea what to expect with Michael. While the professionals we dealt with were competent, and family and friends provided some support, they hadn't been through what we'd been through. They didn't understand why we were asking some of the questions we were asking. It was through joining a number of parent-oriented groups that we were able to connect with people who really understood us, could give us an idea as to what to expect from Michael, what to expect from professionals, and what to expect from ourselves. Sometimes it was important just to have someone available to talk to about your frustrations—someone you knew could empathize because they had probably been through it themselves.

Professionals and the organizations to which they belong also can extend support for families. Though some parents, often with good reason, come to view teachers and the school as their adversary, developing close ties with several individuals within the educational and health-care service systems can help families avoid crises and adapt effectively to having a child with a developmental disability. Think of the differences in the potential sources of support available to the following two families.

When the Johnsons' daughter, Katie, began first grade 3 years ago, her mother waited with her at the bus stop and put her on the bus when it arrived. When she returned home from school at 3 o'clock, her mother was at the bus stop to pick her up. Following the first day of school, Katie's parents met with their daughter's teacher individually during the evening and had periodic contact with this teacher over the course of the school year at parent-teacher conferences.

Contrast this situation to that of Tyler Smith. One week before Tyler began kindergarten, his parents contacted the school and asked for a tour of the facilities. When the school agreed, the Smiths decided they would spend as much time as possible during the tour getting to know *all* of the people with whom their son would be interacting. In addition to meeting Tyler's teacher, they introduced themselves to the school's principal, the school secretary, several paraprofessionals who would be working with their son, cafeteria staff, and the school custodian. Further, they picked up a list of all of the children who would be Tyler's classmates and the names of their parents. The first day of school, Tyler's mother made a point to strike up a conversation with her son's bus driver. When the Smiths attended the school's first-grade orientation, they made it a point of getting to know the parents of his classmates as well. During a relatively short time the Smith family was able to establish connections or links to a relatively large number of people who would be providing services to their son, as well as to other parents. This rich network of connections continued to build over the course of the school year. When things were not going well for Tyler, his parents could rely on a host of people for information and support. If one individual wasn't available, others were.

The situation was quite different for the Johnsons and their daughter. They established only a single source of contact between school and family. When problems arose, the parents had only their daughter's teacher from whom to gain information, ideas, or other forms of support. When Katie's teacher left school in January on a pregnancy leave, the one connection they had established disappeared.

Just as it serves families well to establish a rich, interconnected network of family and friends upon whom they can depend for support, it is also important to develop a similar type of formal support network. In either case the resources available to the family are richer and more varied, and they do not rely upon a single individual who may not always be available or capable of providing the type of support a family needs. Families should note, however, that they could become too dependent upon community organizations or services as providers of support. Some families have been found to rely on community organizations and services so extensively that they jeopardize close relationships with family and friends.[66]

## FAMILY COPING

Family coping refers to the *responses* or *behaviors* that family members use to try to achieve a balance between the demands on the family and the resources it has available. Coping efforts aid in family adjustment and adaptation in a number of ways including:

1. Reducing demands.
2. Increasing resources.
3. Maintaining and allocating resources.
4. Managing unresolved tensions.
5. Altering meanings.

Although resources suggest potential avenues through which a family may enhance adaptation, *coping refers to what the family does*.

**Reducing demands.** The demands on family members differ in a variety of ways. The simplest strategy to reduce demands on any single person is to redistribute them. Family members first might search for individuals within the family who are not overburdened and assign them additional roles. Fathers, for example, who traditionally have not taken as active a role in childrearing or maintaining the family home may be asked to assume more of these responsibilities. Older siblings also may be asked to help out with general household tasks. If all family members are overburdened already, support may be obtained by going outside the family, using the informal support network.

A second strategy to reduce demands involves prioritizing and then eliminating activities and roles that have low-level priority. A family, for instance, might ask its members to prioritize outside activities and limit participation to two activities a week. The Robinson family found this tactic necessary to reduce the demands on parent time as a result of the children's leisure and recreation pursuits.

**Increasing, maintaining, and reallocating resources.** In its coping efforts, the family has to work to ensure that it is utilizing the maximum amount of resources available and is expending them in the areas in which they are most needed. This type of coping is essential for two reasons. *First*, over the course of a child's development, resources will be exhausted if they are not replenished continually. A family, therefore, needs to build continually upon the resources it has available, and be aware of and able to access new forms of support when old forms are exhausted.

*Second*, the demands of having a child with Down syndrome are not constant over time.[67] The skills needed to adapt to an infant with a developmental disability are different from those for an older child. Sally and Jim French first joined a group specifically for parents of children with Down syndrome. While providing them with various types of support over an extended time, members of this group did not have the expertise necessary for helping the Frenches make some dramatic changes in their son's transition program when he was in high school. At that time the French family drew on the support of an organization founded specifically to provide assistance to parents in education advocacy. Without developing this new resource, the French family, in all likelihood, would have had an extremely hard time promoting the educational changes they thought necessary for their son and would have experienced a great deal of additional strain.

**Managing unresolved tensions.** Managing unresolved tensions among family members and between the family and others within the community assures that frustrations, disagreements, and other sources of conflict do not pile up over time to a point at which individuals begin to behave in a dysfunctional manner. Two resources the family can use toward successful conflict resolution are: (a) maintaining a positive, open style of communication so family members have sufficient opportunities to voice their concerns, and (b) fostering a moderate degree of adaptability. The Robinson family developed its own strategy to minimize conflict between family members. Jean Robinson said:

> At least once a week we had a family meeting. Anyone in the family could call one as long as everyone could attend. At first it was usually Carl or myself directing things. As the kids got older, they took more and more of a role. The meetings had two purposes. One was to air our gripes—things we were upset about or didn't like. The other part of these meetings was used to brainstorm, to try to figure out ways to deal with the situations that came up. As I look back, I can't say that everyone always left these meetings with perfect solutions to their problems, because in most cases there was a lot of compromise involved. I think the kids would admit, though, that the family tried its hardest to deal with everyone's complaints as best it could.

**Altering family meanings.** As indicated earlier in this chapter, the meaning a family attaches to having a child with Down syndrome is likely to have a dramatic effect on its ability to adjust and adapt to the child. Just as the demands associated with rearing a child with Down syndrome change over time, so can the meanings attached to this situation. Families who at first think the birth of a child with a developmental disability is catastrophic may come to believe over time that they have some control over the child's development and his or her impact on the family. The belief that one has control over life events has been linked closely to success in coping with potentially stressful situations.[68] A change in the family's belief system or the meaning it attaches to having a child with Down syndrome will be influenced, of course, by many things including the child's characteristics, the family's resources, and the extent to which the family has been successful in coping previously.

This brings us back to the question most families ask: What is the best way to adjust and adapt to a child with a developmental disability such as Down syndrome? This question has no easy answers, for there is no single, best way to cope with having a child with Down syndrome. The coping behaviors that work best for a family depend on a number of factors including the characteristics of the child, the family, and the community.

For some families the most effective way is through extensive use of an informal support system. This has been the primary source of support for the Robinsons. Of course, they were part of what has been called a "kinship-based help-exchange network."[69] As part of a closely knit group of parents, grandparents, more distant relatives, and family friends, the Robinsons had many sources of informal support available to them. To maintain this support, however, the family had to reciprocate with kin. Carl Robinson's profession was in the building trades. He and the family therefore were able to establish reciprocity with kin through Carl's providing significant amounts of free labor when family members decided to remodel or improve their homes. He also was called often to do emergency fix-up work during his free time, such as to install a new water heater when an old one had broken. The Robinson family, while fortunate to have extensive resources upon which it could draw, nevertheless paid a price for the support it received.

Unlike the Robinsons, Jim and Sally French and their family have not made as much use of their kin network in adapting to having a child with Down syndrome. Part of this difference may stem from the fact that, because Jim's family is not from the area of the county in which the Frenches have been living, the family's kin network is limited to Sally's relatives. For this and probably other reasons, the Frenches have relied extensively on a more formal support network. Sally's job as a teacher equipped her well to network with fellow educators and other professionals. Through one of these contacts the French family first became involved in their county ARC and later an organization for parents of children with Down syndrome. Over the years some of the boundaries between the family's informal and formal support network have disappeared. Individuals who once knew the Frenches on a professional or an organizational basis now are considered friends.

# $\mathcal{A}$ LOOK BACK AND AHEAD

Much remains to be learned in the realm of family adjustment and adaptation to the presence of a child with Down syndrome. What is known at this point is that no single, "best" way can be recommended for all families to adapt. Just as each child with Down syndrome is an individual and has unique characteristics that set him or her apart from others, so, too, are the families of children with Down syndrome.

The French and Robinson families were both highly successful in adjusting and adapting to children with Down syndrome. One of the reasons is that each developed a style of adaptation that fit the characteristics of the family and its members. Looking at these two families, they obviously differ in many ways. The Robinsons are an African-American family living in an urban setting. Carl Robinson works in one of the skilled trades, and his wife, Jean, recently has returned to out-of-home work. Kathy, their daughter with Down syndrome, was the last born of their three children, and both parents were in their 30s at the time of her birth. The Robinsons are a reasonably cohesive family that functions in a structured manner. In adapting to rearing Kathy, the family made great use of an informal kin network to obtain necessary supports and relied upon formal sources of support only when informal bases were not available or sufficient.

The French family, on the other hand, is Caucasian and lives in the suburbs. Jim French is an engineer. His wife, Sally, a teacher, went back to work shortly after their youngest child started school. At the time of Michael's birth, both Jim and Sally were in their early to mid-twenties. The Frenches as a family are flexible and considerably less close-knit than the Robinsons. Although family members obviously care about each other, on any given day the parents and children are likely to be independently "doing their own thing." Leadership and the roles family members play are fluid, with parents and children alike assuming a variety of roles and taking turns in positions of leadership based upon the specific issues at hand. In adapting to rearing a child with Down syndrome, the Frenches, for a variety of reasons, made extensive use of their formal support network and relied little, especially during their son's early years, on support from the extended family.

Despite their differences, the ways in which the French and the Robinson families adapted to rearing children with Down syndrome have much in common. The meanings these families attached to having a child with a disability were neutral or positive. They saw it as a challenge rather than as a catastrophe from which they could not recover. Both families worked hard at developing and maintaining the resources necessary to cope effectively with the demands and strains of rearing a child with Down syndrome. They also showed similarities in their communication styles, which were quite positive and open. Despite some differences in their interaction styles, both families adopted styles that allowed for flexibility and resulted in family members' feeling a sense of caring, love, and support while not having to give up their individuality.

Are the French and Robinson families unusual? Although each family is unique, the adaptation of these two families is not unusual. In the only study available to date that specifically studied the adjustment and adaptation abilities of families with children with Down syndrome, the majority were found to be functioning in a healthy manner with moderate degrees of cohesion and adaptability, had low rates of divorce, reported average to higher than average degrees of marital satisfaction, and had developed what they perceived to be adequate sources of support.[70] These results indicate that neither the French nor the Robinson family was unique but, rather, representative of many families of children with Down syndrome who over time are able to cope, adjust, and adapt successfully.

This isn't to minimize the challenges faced by families with children with Down syndrome. All will encounter many difficulties over the course of a child's and family's development. What these results do suggest is that the potential to meet the challenge is there and, with hard work and a willingness to learn and grow, adaptation is within the grasp of most families.

# NOTES

1. L. M. Glidden, "What We Do Not Know About Families of Children Who Have Developmental Disabilities: Questionnaire on Resources and Stress as a Case Study, " *American Journal on Mental Retardation* 97 (1993): 481–495.
2. B. Farber, "Effects of a Severely Mentally Retarded Child on Family Integration," *Monographs of the Society for Research in Child Development* 24 (1959): (Whole No. 71); and "Family Organization and Crisis: Maintenance of Integration in Families with a Severely Mentally Retarded Child," *Monographs of the Society for Research in Child Development* 25 (1960), (No. 1).
3. P. Beckman, "Influence of Selected Characteristics on Stress in Families of Handicapped Infants, " *American Journal of Mental Deficiency* 88 (1983): 150–156; P. J. Beckman-Bell, "Child Related Stress in Families of Handicapped Children," *Topics in Early Childhood Special Education* 1 (1981): 44–54; and S. T. Cummings, "The Impact of the Child's Deficiency on the Father: A Study of Fathers of Mentally Retarded and Chronically Ill Children," *American Journal of Orthopsychiatry* 46 (1976): 246–255.
4. M. Davis and D. MacKay, "Mentally Subnormal Children and Their Families," *Lancet* 23 (1973): 12–16.
5. B. Farber, "Family Adaptations to Severely Mentally Retarded Children," in *The Mentally Retarded and Society: A Social Science Perspective*, edited by M. Begab and S. Richardson (Baltimore: University Park Press, 1975), pp. 247–266; and

A. Gath, "Down Syndrome and the Family: The Early Years" (New York: Academic Press, 1978).

6. Farber, "Effects of a Severely Mentally Retarded Child."

7. M. Erickson and C. C. Upshur, "Caretaking Burden and Social Support: Comparison of Mothers of Infants with and Without Disabilities," *American Journal on Mental Retardation* 94 (1989): 250–258.

8. J. B. Fotheringham, M. Skelton, and B. A. Hoddinott, "The Effects on the Family of the Presence of a Mentally Retarded Child," *Canadian Psychiatric Association Journal* 17 (1972): 283–289.

9. Glidden, p. 482.

10. For example, B. H. Abery, *The Characteristics of Families of Children with Down Syndrome* (paper presented at Annual Meeting of American Association on Mental Retardation, Washington, DC, 1990); K. A. Crnic, W. N. Friedrich, and M. T. Greenberg, "Adaptation of Families with Mentally Retarded Children: A Model of Stress Coping, and Family Ecology," *American Journal of Mental Deficiency* 88 (1983): 125–138; F. J. Floyd and K. A. Phillippe, "Parental Interactions with Children with and Without Mental Retardation: Behavior Management, Coerciveness, and Positive Exchange," *American Journal on Mental Retardation* 97 (1993): 673–684; I. T. Mink and K. Nihira, "Direction of Effects: Family Life-Styles and Behavior of TMR Children," *American Journal of Mental Deficiency* 92 (1987): 57–64; R. R. Orr, S. J. Cameron, L. A. Dobson, and D. M. Day, "Age Related Changes in Stress Experienced by Families with a Child Who Had Developmental Delays," *Mental Retardation* 31 (1993): 171–176; and Z. Stoneman, G. H. Brody, C. H. Davis, and J. M. Crapps, "Childcare Responsibilities, Peer Relations, and Sibling Conflict: Older Siblings of Mentally Retarded Children," *American Journal on Mental Retardation* 93 (1988): 174–183.

11. Abery, *The Characteristics of Families*.

12. K. S. Frey, M. T. Greenberg, and R. R. Fewell, "Stress and Coping Among Parents of Handicapped Children: A Multidimensional Approach," *American Journal on Mental Retardation* 94 (1989): 240–249.

13. L. M. Glidden and J. T. Pursley, "Longitudinal Comparisons of Families Who Have Adopted Children with Mental Retardation," *American Journal on Mental Retardation* 94 (1989): 272–277.

14. B. H. Abery, *Family Interaction and the Psychosocial Competence of Children and Youth with Down Syndrome* (unpublished doctoral dissertation, University of Minnesota, Minneapolis, 1988); Abery, *The Characteristics of Families*.

15. Abery, *Family Interaction*; Glidden.

16. J. M. Patterson, "Families Experiencing Stress: The Family Adjustment and Adaptation Response Model," *Family Systems Medicine* 5 (1988): 202–237.

17. H. McCubbin and J. Patterson, *Family Stress, Resources, and Coping* (St. Paul: University of Minnesota, 1981).

18. R. S. Lazarus and S. Folkman, *Stress, Appraisal, and Coping* (New York: Springer, 1984).

19. For example, Glidden.

20. Abery, *The Characteristics of Families*.

21. Patterson.
22. A. Antonovsky, *Unraveling the Mystery of Health* (San Francisco: Jossey-Bass, 1987); Lazarus and Folkman; S. B. Taylor, "Adjustment to Threatening Events: A Theory of Cognitive Adaptation," *American Psychologist* 38 (1983): 1161–1173.
23. Frey, Greenberg, and Fewell.
24. S. C. Thompson and A. S. Janigian, "Life Schemes: A Framework for Understanding the Search for Meaning," *Journal of Social and Clinical Psychology* 32 (1989): 212–223.
25. D. Reiss, *The Family's Construction of Reality* (Cambridge, MA: Harvard University Press, 1981).
26. J. M. Anderson, "The Social Construction of Illness Experience: Families with a Chronically Ill Child," *Journal of Advanced Nursing* 6 (1981): 427–434; J. D. Campbell, "The Child in the Sick Role: Contributions of Age, Sex, Parental Status, and Parental Values," *Journal of Health and Social Behavior* 19 (1978): 35–51.
27. S. T. Hauser, A. M. Jacobsen, and D. Wertlieb, "Children with Recently Diagnosed Diabetes: Interactions Within Their Families," *Health Psychology* 5 (1986): 273–296; J. Shapiro, "Family Reactions and Coping Strategies in Response to the Physically Ill or Handicapped Child," *Social Science in Medicine* 17 (1983): 913–931; E. Zucman, *Childhood Disability in the Family* (New York: International Exchange of Information in Rehabilitation, World Rehabilitation Fund, 1982).
28. Frey, Greenberg, and Fewell.
29. Patterson.
30. H. M. Lefcourt, *Locus of Control: Current Trends in Theory and Research* (2nd edition) (Hillsdale, NJ: Erlbaum, 1982); L. I. Pearlin and C. Schooler, "The Structure of Coping," *Journal of Health and Social Behavior* 22 (1978): 337–366.
31. Frey, Greenberg, and Fewell.
32. J. McCubbin, C. Joy, A. Cauble, J. Comeau, J. Patterson, and R. Needle, "Family Stress and Coping: A Decade Reviewed," *Journal of Marriage and the Family* 42 (1980): 855–871..
33. W. F. Burr, *Theory Construction and the Sociology of the Family* (New York: Wiley, 1973); McCubbin and Patterson; and L. Wikler, "Family Stress Theory and Research on Families of Children with Mental Retardation," in *Families of Handicapped Children: Research, Programs, and Policy Issues,* edited by J. Gallagher and P. Vietze (Baltimore: Paul H. Brookes, 1986).
34. Farber, "Family Organization and Crisis"; R. Levinson, *Family Crisis and Adaptation: Coping with a Mentally Retarded Child* (doctoral dissertation, University of Wisconsin, Madison, 1975); and G. Saenger, *Factors Influencing the Institutionalization of Mentally Retarded Individuals in New York City* (Albany, NY: Interdepartmental Health Resources Board, 1960).
35. P. P. Vitaliano, R. D. Maiuro, J. Russo, and J. Becker, "Raw Versus Relative Scores in the Assessment of Coping Strategies," *Journal of Behavioral Medicine* 10 (1987): 1–18.
36. Frey, Greenberg, and Fewell.

37. D. Farran, J. Metzger, and J. Sparling, "Immediate and Continuing Adaptations in Parents of Handicapped Children: A Model and an Illustration," in *Families of Handicapped Children: Research, Programs, and Policy Issues,* edited by J. Gallagher and P. Vietze (Baltimore: Paul H. Brookes, 1986).

38. Burr.

39. J. Blacher, K. Nihira, and C. E. Meyers, "Characteristics of the Home Environments of Mentally Retarded Children," *American Journal of Mental Deficiency* 91 (1987): 226–236; I. T. Mink, "Classification of Families with Mentally Retarded Children," in *Families of Handicapped Children: Research, Programs, and Policy Issues*, edited by J. Gallagher and P. Vietze (Baltimore: Paul H. Brookes, 1986); I. T. Mink, K. Nihira, and C. E. Meyers, "Taxonomy of Family Lifestyles I: Homes with TMR Children," *American Journal on Mental Deficiency* 87 (1983) 484–497; K. Nihira, C. E. Meyers, and I. T. Mink, "Reciprocal Relationships Between Home Environment and Development of TMR Adolescents," *American Journal of Mental Deficiency* 88 (1983): 139–149.

40. D. H. Olson, C. Russell, and D. Sprenkle, "Circumplex Model of Marital and Family Systems: VI. Theoretical Update," *Family Process* 22 (1983): 69–83; and D. H. Olson, D. Sprenkle, and C. Russell, "Circumplex Model of Marital and Family Systems I: Cohesion and Adaptability Dimensions, Family Types, and Clinical Applications," *Family Process* 18 (1979): 3–28.

41. Abery, *Family Interaction* and *The Characteristics of Families.*

42. Olson, Sprenkle, and Russell.

43. Olson, Sprenkle, and Russell.

44. Abery, *Family Interaction* and *The Characteristics of Families.*

45. J. W. Gowen, N. Johnson-Martin, B. D. Goldman, and M. Appelbaum, "Feelings of Depression and Parenting Competence of Mothers of Handicapped and Nonhandicapped Infants: A Longitudinal Study," *American Journal on Mental Retardation* 94 (1989): 259–271; M. W. Krauss, "Child-Related and Parenting Stress: Similarities and Differences Between Mothers and Fathers of Children with Disabilities," *American Journal on Mental Retardation* 97 (1993): 393–404; H. McCubbin and S. T. T. Huang, "Family Strengths in the Care of Handicapped Children: Targets for Intervention," *Family Relations* 38 (1989): 436–443; P. M. Minnes, "Family Resources and Stress Associated with Having a Mentally Retarded Child," *American Journal on Mental Retardation* 93 (1988): 184–192; and M. M. Seltzer and M. W. Krauss, "Aging Parents with Adult Mentally Retarded Children: Family Risk Factors and Sources of Support, *American Journal on Mental Retardation* 94 (1989): 303–312.

46. Beckman.

47. W. N. Friedrich, "Predictors of the Coping Behavior of Mothers of Handicapped Children," *Journal of Consulting and Clinical Psychology* 47 (1979): 1140–1141; W. N. Friedrich, L. T. Wilturner, and D. S. Cohen, "Coping Resources and Parenting Mentally Retarded Children," *American Journal of Mental Deficiency* 90 (1985): 130–139; and B. McKinney and R. A. Peterson, "Predictors of Stress in Parents of Developmentally Disabled Children," *Journal of Pediatric Psychology* 12 (1987): 133–149.

48. J. R. Dickie and P. Matheson, *Mother-Father-Infant: Who Needs Support?* (Paper presented at annual meeting of American Psychological Association, Toronto, Ontario, 1984); and Friedrich.

49. L. McCallister and C. S. Fischer, "A Procedure for Surveying Personal Networks," *Sociological Methods and Research* 7 (1974): 131–148.

50. Farran, Metzger, and Sparling; N. Lin, S. C. Light, and M. Woelfel, *The Buffering Effects of Social Support: A Theoretical Framework and an Empirical Investigation* (Paper presented at National Conference on Social Stress Research, University of New Hampshire, Durham, October 1982).

51. McCubbin, Joy, Cauble, Comeau, Patterson, and Needle.

52. Patterson.

53. S. Crockenberg, "Infant Irritability, Mother Responsiveness, and Social Influences on the Security of Infant-Mother Attachment," *Child Development* 52 (1981): 857–865.

54. Crockenberg.

55. Frey, Greenberg, and Fewell.

56. A. E. Kazak and R. S. Marvin, "Differences, Difficulties, and Adaptation: Stress and Social Networks in Families with a Handicapped Child," *Family Relations* 33 (1984): 67–77; A. E. Kazak and B. L. Wilcox, "The Structure and Function of Social Support Networks in Families with Handicapped Children," *American Journal of Community Psychology* 12 (1984): 645–661; and J. McDowell and H. Gabel, *Social Support Among Mothers of Retarded Infants* (unpublished manuscript, George Peabody College, Nashville, TN, 1981).

57. R. Parke, "Fathers, Families, and Support Systems: Their Role in the Development of At-Risk and Retarded Infants and Children," in *Families of Handicapped Children: Research, Programs, and Policy Issues*, edited by J. Gallagher and P. Vietze (Baltimore: Paul H. Brookes, 1986).

58. Abery, *Family Interaction* and *The Characteristics of Children with Down Syndrome*.

59. Frey, Greenberg, and Fewell; Kazak and Marvin.

60. Wikler.

61. J. G. Bruhn and B. U. Philips, "Measuring Social Support: A Synthesis of Current Approaches," *Journal of Behavioral Medicine* 7 (1984): 151–169.

62. Wikler.

63. Farran, Metzger, and Sparling.

64. H. Featherstone, *A Difference in the Family: Living with a Disabled Child* (New York: Basic Books, 1980); A. P. Turnbull and H. R. Turnbull, *Parents Speak Out: Then and Now* (Columbus, OH: Merrill, 1985); and S. Waisbren, "Parents' Reactions to the Birth of a Developmentally Disabled Child," *American Journal of Mental Deficiency* 84 (1980): 345–351.

65. E. Vincent, *Use of Support Networks by Parents of Mentally Handicapped Children* (unpublished report, University of Wisconsin, Madison, 1983).

66. Farran, Metzger, and Sparling.

67. J. Blacher, "A Dynamic Perspective on the Impact of a Severely Handicapped Child on the Family," in *Severely Handicapped Young Children and Their Fami-*

*lies: Research in Review*, edited by J. Blacher, pp. 3–50 (Orlando, FL: Academic Press, 1984); and Farran, Metzger, and Sparling.

68. Lefcourt; Pearlin and Schooler.

69. H. McAdoo, "Societal Stress: The Black Family," in *Stress and the Family: Vol. 1. Coping with Normative Transitions*, edited by H. McCubbin and C. R. Frigley, pp. 178–187 (New York: Brunner/Mazel, 1983).

70. Abery, *Family Interaction*.

*Brian Abery* is the coordinator of school-based services at the University of Minnesota's Institute on Community Integration. Dr. Abery, who has a doctorate in educational psychology from the University of Minnesota, has conducted numerous research and demonstration projects on the impact of family interaction on the psychosocial development of children with Down syndrome and on how the presence of children with this disability affects family functioning. His most recent research has concentrated on developing programs to enhance the social inclusion and self-determination of children with Down syndrome.

# $\mathscr{L}$INDBLAD FAMILY

Dad: Phil
Mom: Barb
Brother: Steve
Sister: Beth
Sister: Molly
Brother with Down
   syndrome: Alex

Mother's Day 1971.

Visiting Santa with big sister.

Ninth birthday: Pizza at Shakey's.

## $\mathscr{L}$INDBLAD FAMILY (continued)

Alex's car won the Pine Wood Derby.

Distinguished!

Father's Day 1985.

Proud parents!

# ~7~

# THE SCHOOL YEARS: BECOMING LITERATE AND SOCIALIZED

John Rynders

*P*arents of a child who has Down syndrome often feel that the school years are—to paraphrase Charles Dickens' famous words—"the best of times, the worst of times." They are the best of times because mothers and fathers can count on having 12–15 years of legally mandated, familiar, continuous, programming for their son or daughter. These same years, however, also can be the worst of times. The secondary schooling years in particular are those during which intellectually demanding tasks and peer pressure magnify the presence of the child's special needs (and perhaps vulnerability).

Excerpts from some of the EDGE parent interviews reveal a few of the challenges of the schooling years, not only for their child but for them as mothers and fathers as well. These interview findings were gathered when sons and daughters of EDGE parents were about 21 years of age.*

> *Father:* I went with Jim to an open house at his junior high. He had a shop class, and I can't even remember what he did in it. I went with Jim to talk to the shop teacher. The teacher said, "It's a good thing there's a volunteer aide who comes in this class. Otherwise Jim wouldn't have done anything."

> *Mother:* I sometimes thought they spent too much time on the vocational skills for Lee and gave up too easily on some of the other skills in his junior and senior year. He had good banking skills. He had good skills with a checkbook and with balancing his checkbook—that kind of thing. Even though he can't read, except for real simple things, I think they could have continued word recognition and sentence recognition training. I think they gave up on academics.

> *Mother:* Teachers seemed to back off academic stuff. Tony was interested in reading and doing math. He actually could do it, and he took pride in that. Tony has a subscription to the newspaper. He looks at the headlines

---

* Names of the children in these quotes have been changed.

every morning. He looks at the sports page. He'll read the television page. He reads parts of stories that have to do with sports. He knows all the box scores.

*Mother:* They stopped any kind of reading in the program. I thought they should have continued that, because even though Bill wasn't the best in the world, you can't get any better if you don't have instruction and practice. That bothered me. Also, they stopped completely with adding and subtracting. They used the calculator and went to the store and just worked on the money skills.

*Father:* Academically, they gave up on Sam. They really did. I can remember saying to one teacher, "Well, what about his reading skills?" She said, "If he hasn't done it by the time he's 16, he's not going to do it." Well, I've got news for them. As soon as he gets out of high school, I'm going to get hold of the Literacy Council,

and I'm going to see if I can get someone to work with him.

*Mother:* When I'd say I want Joe to keep up with his reading and that I'd like him to count the money, they'd say, "Well, have you ever considered that we need to get him out into the community?" Their big thing was to take him to the *woods*! They took him to the zoo. They took him to the apple orchard. It was the same thing every year. *He* didn't even want to go to these places.

*Father:* To this day he doesn't want to go to the zoo—he's been there so many times.

*Mother:* Yes, to the Shrine Circus, too. You know what he says to this day: "If I was still in high school, I'd have to go that darn Shrine Circus." (Laughter)

*Father:* Sally was taken advantage of. And not just the sexual experiences. Some of the boys—classmates—would take advantage of her. They would get her to buy things for them or give them money.

*Mother:* I have mixed feelings about placing students who are mentally handi-capped in high schools with typical peers. The students in special educa-tion have opportunities to meet students in regular ed classes, but they sel-dom are truly included. In a segregated setting students develop the same social strata as typical peers, have many of the same extracurricular and social events, and are included. My son and his friends did attend some of the extracurricular events such as basketball games, the Homecoming game and dance, Prom and the all-night graduation party at the regular high school they attended. They remained in their own group and were not a true part of the larger student body at these events.

Regular ed students may offer a high-five in the hall or say "Hi," but they don't call on the phone, invite special ed students to parties, or call for a date. This isn't a criticism. It's a statement of reality. Did John benefit from attending a regular high school versus a segregated site? It's hard to judge. Is he better prepared for living and working in the real world? He works downtown, rides the city bus to and from work. Did he develop these skills because of his high school experience? We'll never know for sure.

*Mother:* Just putting kids in a room with their chronological peers doesn't mean they're mainstreamed. I've watched carefully when Susan was going through [regular] high school. If she *ever* had made friends, or even an acquaintance, just a normal child to say, "Hi, Susan," it would have been great. I think it was good that she was able to go to that school, that she was with the other kids, but I really don't think Susan got very much out of her classes. Nondisabled kids want to keep up with their peers, and they don't want to be seen with those "strange" people. These are strong words, but still, I haven't seen any effort by the normal kids to be friendly.

We can readily detect two recurring quandaries in EDGE parents' com-ments: Should I argue for a strong and continuing academic emphasis? Should I seek a lot of mainstreaming or a little of it, and should I seek out its most challenging or least challenging forms?

# *M*ORE ACADEMICS OR LESS? _____

This quandary actually stems from an old question: Should a child with Down syndrome ever be in a class labeled "educable" (one that features academ-ics) or only in a "trainable" class (one that features nonacademic subjects such as self-care)? Today, classes labeled either educable or trainable are much fewer than before, but the issue that originally separated one from the other—the presence or absence of an emphasis on academics—is still much in evidence. For instance, many educators doubt that a child with Down syn-drome can *really* learn to read. To them, recognizing signs such as "men" is feasible, but they doubt that children with Down syndrome will ever be able to read with any proficiency. The doubters are in error. How do we know this? Because we have research findings to prove them wrong.[1]

## NEVER EDUCABLE? ALWAYS TRAINABLE?

During the 1970s portrayals of the educational potential of many groups of children with mental retardation were becoming increasingly optimistic. Educational expectations for children with Down syndrome, however, were not keeping pace. In 1975, the same year the Education for All Handicapped Children Act was passed, an article appeared in a popular magazine, *Psychology Today*, that cast serious doubt on the educability of children with Down syndrome. In that article the chief of the Reproductive Genetics Unit in an eastern university hospital was quoted as saying, "You show me just one mongoloid that has an educable IQ.... I've never seen even one [who is educable] in my experience with over 800 mongols."[2] (In 1987, *Psychology Today*, on its own initiative, published an article offering an updated portrayal of the overall achievements of people with Down syndrome.[3])

Up to this point, we have been discussing educability from an academic perspective. But the chief of the Reproductive Genetics Unit who was just quoted is viewing it from an *intelligence test* viewpoint. From an intelligence test perspective, educability generally refers to an intelligence test score (an IQ) falling somewhere between 50 and 75. Because schools often rely heavily on an IQ score as a predictor of academic potential, IQ and academics will be discussed together in the sections that follow.

Responding to the 1975 *Psychology Today* article, we conducted an extensive computerized search of the literature on Down syndrome to determine whether the physician's assertion could be countered with experimental findings. A search through 10 years of research literature yielded nearly 650 references, of which 105 contained data pertinent to the question of educability. Although we were able to demonstrate that several persons with Down syndrome across the 105 studies exhibited educability from an IQ standpoint,[4] our argument for raising educational expectations was far from being strong back in 1978 because long-term evidence of educability was unavailable and academic achievement outcomes that could demonstrate educability from a functional perspective were almost nonexistent at that time. Now, fortunately, at least four early intervention studies have produced findings that bear on these concerns.

## IQ AND ACADEMIC ABILITY IN THE EARLY YEARS OF SCHOOLING

The first of these studies comes from Macquarie University in Australia.[5] Results of this study showed that eight children who had been in an early intervention program with an emphasis on reading through the application of behavior modification techniques and integrated programming were, at around age 8, reading at a level that came close to their chronological age. Moreover, although the IQs of these children were not unusually high (which helps to mitigate the argument that they were reading well only because they were "hand-picked"), five of the eight children had IQs in the educable range.

The second study[6] was directed at the academic abilities of young children with Down syndrome in Great Britain. Buckley and Wood had been teaching a group of fourteen preschool-age children with Down syndrome in a home-based, parent-as-teacher program. Their sample also seemed to be a fairly representative one because it included all of the children with Down syndrome between 2 and 4 years old living at home across two entire health districts. Their findings revealed that several of these young children were developing good beginning reading abilities. Furthermore, twelve of the fourteen had developmental quotients (early indicators of later intelligence quotients) in the educable range.

Nevertheless, parents who have a child with Down syndrome should be alerted to a problem that becomes a trap they sometimes create unwittingly for themselves and then step into. The trap—actually, a trapping misperception—usually is approached through a sequence of two steps:

1. Because young children with Down syndrome who have been in an early education program frequently score in the educable IQ range at the end of that program, parents often stress the importance of IQ in making their educability argument at school entrance. Suppose they are successful in placing their child (who has an IQ in the educable range) in an educable class. So far, so good, but the trap is about to be sprung.

2. Parents, having argued successfully for an educable class placement based on an IQ in the educable range, continue to fight for a succession of educable class placements as their child grows older, continuing to base their advocacy efforts on annual intelligence testing results. They now have all of the "eggs in the IQ basket." The trap is about to catch them because *the IQs of most children with Down syndrome diminish as they grow older, making their parents' argument for an educable placement* more *difficult each year if they rely heavily on intelligence test findings.*

This does *not* mean that children with Down syndrome aren't learning more as they grow older, including lots of things that are more important than what is reflected in an IQ test result—such as how to set an alarm clock accurately, read labels on canned goods correctly, identify the bus that will drop off the child near home, getting on bus 33B rather than 33C.

To offset an overemphasis on IQ as a deciding factor in assigning a child with Down syndrome to a class emphasizing academics or one emphasizing self-help skills, parents should insist that abilities central to the *substance* of educability receive much more attention during the assessment and placement planning process. For example, during a placement conference, parents should talk about their child's interest in books. Relatedly, the child's conceptualization ability, language repertoire, and quality of instructional socialization should be assessed.

Parents will be on firm ground if they insist on a richer and more in-depth assessment of these practical indicators of educability if they look to the results of the Macquarie early education project.[7] After the children in the Macquarie project had been integrated in regular schools, follow-up data were collected. When the children's IQ and reading achievement outcomes were compared, IQ and reading achievement were *poorly* correlated. Hence, if IQ is heavily emphasized, the risk to making a valid educational placement decision should be obvious.

Although these findings might help parents advocate effectively for a trial placement in an educable class for their son or daughter at the time of school entry, these findings are not sufficient to convince skeptical decision makers of children's chances of profiting from academic instruction in their later years.

## IQ AND ACADEMIC ABILITY IN THE MIDDLE YEARS OF SCHOOLING

In one study[8] DuVergeas examined the reading abilities of children with Down syndrome who had been in an early education program in Seattle, Washington, from the time they were 18 months of age. In the University of Washington program, systematic educational stimulation had been offered to fifty children with Down syndrome. Children came from all socioeconomic levels, were from natural as well as foster homes, and were enrolled early in the preschool period—some as newborns. The goal of the Washington program was to promote children's abilities across many curricular areas (cognitive, self-help, motor), with an emphasis on the use of behavior modification. The reading scores and IQs of these children when they were about 14 years old ranged widely, demonstrating grade equivalents that represent substantial academic achievement, although IQs of three of the six children fall currently in the trainable range (IQ below 50).

The second early education study that has investigated long-term academic achievement levels in children with Down syndrome is the EDGE project.[9] We found that across the fifteen children in the experimental group in the Twin Cities, twelve of the children were in educable classes or in regular-educable class combinations at around age 13. (The relatively favorable proportion of educable-to-trainable placements undoubtedly relates to the fact that EDGE personnel helped parents in the Twin Cities area advocate for an educable class if that placement seemed warranted.)

Of central importance for the purpose of addressing the educability issue is that eleven of fifteen EDGE children were *reading with comprehension* at or above the second-grade level as adolescents. To us, one of the "acid tests" for advancing the argument for educability is being able to show evidence of attaining a reasonable level of reading proficiency, particularly reading with comprehension, in children with Down syndrome.

Evidence of educability extracted from the studies reviewed here should not be construed as a rationale for full-time placement of all children with Down syndrome in a class labeled "educable." This might easily happen because we have been advocating here for upgrading educational expectations. Some children with Down syndrome, however, prosper in a *regular* class on a part-time, or even a full-time, basis. To buttress this point, we focus again on the development of eight children with Down syndrome who had gone through the Macquarie early education study and had been placed in regular classes with itinerant specialist support. The investigators in that study reported that children with Down syndrome functioned comparably to the nondisabled students in terms of social and reading abilities (both oral reading and reading comprehension).[10]

In a similar vein, as was pointed out earlier, several of the EDGE Project children were in educable-regular class combinations. By implication, however, a number of children with Down syndrome from the EDGE Project were in trainable classes. Although this should not mitigate our argument for raising educational expectations in general, we do not contend that a trainable placement is never appropriate. To the contrary, some children (but far fewer than once thought) may profit from a trainable class placement, at least part of the time, possibly because of severe cognitive limitations coupled with serious adaptive behavior impairments or absence of the types of support needed to sustain them properly in an educable class.

Based on the corrective influence of updated evidence found in the results of these four studies, parents presumably now should be in an excellent position to argue *convincingly* that children with Down syndrome are *not* always only trainable in terms of their educational functioning. Some profit from a continuous emphasis on academics throughout their schooling, blended in as a part of vocational preparation and community living in general. We do not favor "pushing" academics to the neglect of other school subjects, however, nor do we favor emphasizing formal academic instruction with a youngster who is incapable intellectually or functionally of handling it. We do contend, though, that most children with Down syndrome can become fluent enough in the three Rs to be termed "functionally literate"—for example, able to read essential portions of the newspaper and other documents needed to live relatively independently, capable of handling money in conducting fundamental financial matters such as maintaining a savings account and paying fares on public transportation, and able to print or write notes using correct spelling.

Showing that children with Down syndrome are capable of attaining functional literacy offers little specific information about *how* functional literacy can actually be attained. We turn to this subject next.

# PROMOTING ACADEMICS _____

Students with Down syndrome who have mild intellectual impairments (often referred to as "educable") do not learn to read simply because a teacher chooses the "one best" reading textbook and uses it systematically. First, there doesn't seem to be one best reading textbook series, and furthermore, there is no one best *method* of teaching reading either.[11]

According to Leeper,[12] what is known is that students classified as educable:

—can and do benefit from traditional reading approaches.
—respond to incentive systems—for example, receiving tokens for learning to match words with their corresponding pictures.
—benefit from reading materials that have double-spaced lines of print and uneven righthand margins.
—benefit from a carefully worked out scope and sequence of instruction.*

Several curriculum materials are available for students who are beginning to develop a vocabulary of words based on recognizing their appearance (a "sight vocabulary") and those who are able to sound out some words and parts of words (decoding the sound of words and their parts, also known as "phonics"). For instance, the DISTAR reading program, Sullivan programmed readers, and the Edmark program all have been shown to have good-to-excellent outcomes with students classified as educable.[15]

Another way to help decide which approaches might be effective is to ask experienced teachers of educable-level students what materials or methods they use the most. Their favorites include:

---

* Mainord and Love[13] and Anderson[14] have delineated a helpful scope and sequence for the early stages of reading instruction, presented in the Appendix.

—an instructional approach combining phonic, sight word, and language experience elements.

—assessing student interests and characteristics to determine level and nature of reading instruction.

—teacher probing of students' understanding of content they have read.

—a special reading series or sequence of worksheets.

—small-group or individual techniques to promote reading.[16]

The first item conveys the message that teachers prefer a combined instructional approach, one involving phonics, sight words, and language experience. We've briefly described the phonic and sight word approach, but what is a language experience approach?

Language experience approaches capitalize on the fact that reading is essentially spoken language in printed or written form. Thus, words the child speaks vocally and understands can be used to compose simple sentences that he or she can read as well as speak. An adult or peer tutor can write down these words and give them to the child to read aloud, cementing the understanding of sound-symbol correspondence that is critical to reading. In addition, the child can begin to compose simple stories, possibly using a typewriter or word processor. Typing can be a boon for some students with Down syndrome who have difficulty using a pen or pencil skillfully.

Likewise, it is important for the child to hear words that someone reads at the same time the child sees them in printed form. As conveyed in Chapter

5, the benefits of reading to the child while the child is trying to decode the written words as he or she hears them and looks at pictures supporting the text cannot be emphasized enough. Not only is reading ability advanced in this way, but so is intellect, language, and socialization in the bargain.

Reading for understanding (not speed), comprehension (not just "word calling"), and acquiring not only a sight vocabulary but also learning how to decode words should be emphasized. Above all, it is important to keep in mind that the success of day-to-day living as an adult rests far more on social factors than academic factors. Yes, academic proficiency is nice, and is even linked to some extent to socialization—but the ability to get along with people and work successfully with them will be far more important in the long run.

Many (perhaps most) students who have Down syndrome will find arithmetic to be their most challenging subject. Particularly difficult will be the arithmetic problems called story problems ("If Jane has 8 apples and 3 oranges and gives one orange to...") because they involve remembering and manipulating numerals, words, and symbols in the mind and on paper while moving to a solution. Although children with Down syndrome usually become proficient in using basic arithmetic facts such as adding a column of numbers, many do not do nearly as well with story-type problems.

Because of these difficulties with arithmetic, parents often use "crutches" or alternative devices to help their child over trouble spots or try to help them avoid particularly tough areas altogether if they can. For instance, instead of learning to use a wristwatch with hands, a watch that gives a direct digital readout of the time does the same job just as well. An inexpensive, hand-held calculator can help the person decide how much money to put on the counter to pay for three postage stamps. Or this problem can be "crutched" by teaching the person to reliably identify a one-dollar bill and to feed it into the correct slot of a vending machine in the post office lobby to obtain three stamps, letting the machine make the change.

With respect to writing, students with Down syndrome might be expected to write about as well as they read because of the relation between reading (the meaning of print comes off the page) and writing (the understood print goes back on the page). In contrast to reading, however, writing requires sophisticated arm and finger movements, a fine-motor skill that is difficult for many students with Down syndrome. Because of fine-motor demands in writing legibly, teachers are making more use of the typewriter or word processor with children who can type more easily than they can print or write.

# $\mathscr{S}$CHOOL MAINSTREAMING: WHAT KIND? HOW MUCH? _____

Tom, a student with Down syndrome, and his parents share a dream for his life. The dream is that Tom will become an adult who will be able to live semi-independently in an apartment, hold a job, and participate in a variety of social and recreational activities in his community. If Tom is to succeed in living out this vision, he will need to be able to interact successfully with roommates, bus drivers, store clerks, employers, co-workers, and other people in the community. Thus, each opportunity he has to interact meaningfully with a nondisabled person in school represents valuable preparation for the transition from school life as a student to community life as an adult.

## WHAT IS MAINSTREAMING?

Mainstreaming can be considered a general or a specific term, can be used as a noun or a verb, and can take many forms. Generally, it is used to describe integration or inclusion in a regular school, often in a regular class, for part or all of a student's instructional time. Mainstreaming tends to be an educational term, whereas integration or inclusion refers to broad movements within society in general, including schooling.

Sometimes parents and professionals join in advocating for a given philosophy or policy. A case in point is the push by some to mainstream all school-age children with Down syndrome in regular classes 100% of the time. No exceptions. (This movement is often referred to as "full inclusion.") One has to look beyond the rhetoric of a philosophical statement, however, to see how it squares with the needs of an individual child in a specific setting, matching the support elements in a learning environment to the child. In adopting this perspective, we may decide to enroll a youngster temporarily in a segregated summer camp rather than an integrated camp because the qualities of the integrated camp don't fit the child's needs at that time. In this regard, suppose that a child with Down syndrome tends to behave impulsively (runs away from a group abruptly). Suppose, too, that the integrated camp promotes an open activity arrangement; campers are expected to go from area to area on their own. The segregated camp, on the other hand, offers "follow the child" supervision. For the child's safety, if for no other reason, we would choose the segregated camp because it provides the type of *support* this child needs.

Obviously, an alternative would be to find an integrated camp that provides "follow-along supervision" so as to achieve inclusionary programming. Unless that crucial support element is provided, however, the integrated camp, even though it is in tune with prevailing educational and societal philosophy, is not a good bet for this child. If we push the child into an integrated experience without the supports needed, we risk upsetting his progress because his problem likely will be intensified by the situation, and he (and we) will have to live with its consequences.

A neighbor's daughter, Jean, has Down syndrome. The neighbor insisted on her daughter being in a regular class 100% of the time, even though her regular education classmates never had received any training in how to be a peer companion or to value cognitive diversity. They rejected Jean in dozens of small and large (but all hurtful) ways. Each afternoon when school ended, Jean came home alone, often in tears, withdrawing into the world of TV, eating her way into obesity. The situation worsened as she became heavier and received even more rejection because of it. The regular class teacher, though well-intentioned, was a first-year teacher struggling to survive and had few skills in dealing with large differences in ability.

Jean's self-esteem sank lower and lower, finally reaching the point where she skipped school to wander about aimlessly in the nearby shopping center because school was too painful for her to face. She also developed illnesses (some from environmental causes, some probably psychosomatic), which enabled her to stay home in front of the TV. Encouraging the neighbor to place Jean temporarily in a resource room in the school, where the special education teacher had a flair for building self-esteem, fell on deaf ears. Jean's mother insisted that the *regular* class, and *only* the *regular* class, was appropriate, "even if she's miserable in it every moment" (the mother's words). Sadly, Jean's mother had elevated regular class placement to Holy Grail status, unrealistically so, of course, as most of us have experienced one or more inadequate regular classes.

Fortunately, before Jean developed full-blown depression or ran away from home, the school psychologist referred Jean's case to the school's child study team, which unanimously endorsed special education resource room placement for most of her school day. After several due process hearings, Jean's mother reluctantly agreed to the resource room placement.

After 2 years in the special education resource room, Jean was reintroduced gradually to a regular homeroom class (not the original one), where the teacher had skills in structuring activities for cooperative outcomes, had instructed Jean's regular education classmates in how to be successful peer-companions, and had made the valuing of diversity a central theme of classroom activities. Jean blossomed in that environment, graduating with her regular education classmates and receiving applause from them at the graduation ceremony—applause that was genuine and strong.

The point of this anecdote is obvious: The support elements of an environment, segregated or integrated, or a combination of both, must match the needs of the individual being considered for it. If an integrated environment has the proper support elements, or they can be provided with reasonable dispatch, it is probably a better choice than a segregated environment because of its relatively richer curriculum and the more advanced social and cognitive repertoire of nondisabled peers from which the student with Down syndrome can learn. If, however, a mainstreamed setting is a poor match for the child's needs, it can become a *more restrictive* environment rather than a less restrictive environment, regardless of its philosophical intent.

The environmental supports each child with Down syndrome needs are highly individualistic. Some questions to ask in considering an integrated program are brought up next.

## CONSIDERING AN INTEGRATED PROGRAM

*Does the program aim for mutuality of benefit?* If it is to prosper, integration should provide benefits to students with *and without* disabilities. Fortunately, our research over the last 12 years shows that achieving mutuality of benefit is not difficult if the techniques about to be described are employed properly. Not that the benefits of integration are identical to both groups. They are not. They are equally important though: People with Down syndrome improve their social abilities and activity skills; those without disabilities grow in their self-confidence and regard for people with disabilities and have a better grasp of their own self-worth. (In the old days, that was referred to as "character building"; today it is called "values-based education.")

*Does the program try to include children with Down syndrome in the child's circle of friends?* Well-intentioned, but we believe misguided, insistence that the only legitimate friend for a child with Down syndrome is a nondisabled child effectively excludes relationships with others who have Down syndrome or another type of disability. This in itself is a form of segregation.

Often, insisting on having only nondisabled children interact with a child who has Down syndrome is based on parents' assumption that if their child establishes friendly relationships with nondisabled children, these relationships will become genuine friendships and carry over to adulthood strong and intact. Lasting friendship, however, is based on two people having interests in common, and reciprocally sharing things that enhance the depth of the relationship. This match-up of interests and things to share reciprocally is hard to sustain between people who have highly different levels of ability.

Today, adults with Down syndrome can and do have many nondisabled acquaintances in the community, but few of these can be regarded as close friends as we know them. When we asked EDGE parents to name their young adult sons' or daughters' close friends (buddies, people they like to be with the most), the forty-five individuals named (three each for the fifteen EDGE participants) were, with few exceptions, people with disabilities—many with Down syndrome. Even though most EDGE participants attended regular schools and many attended one or more regular classes throughout their school years and participated in many integrated activities outside of school, their young adult friends are mainly people with disabilities. Actually, it would be surprising if it were otherwise, considering that our own friends are very much like ourselves. Why would we expect this to be different for people with Down syndrome?

Does this finding somehow weaken the social and educational policy that encourages parents to advocate for mainstream placement if they desire it? Emphatically not! It does say, though, that in our earnest attempts to help people with Down syndrome to relate effectively to nondisabled people, we not cut them off from relating to people with Down syndrome and other disabilities.

*Does the program take advantage of choice-making opportunities?* Integration into activities does not automatically guarantee enjoyment for people with Down syndrome. After working many months to achieve schooling integration, parents and teachers may be frustrated because some people with Down syndrome do not want to participate in these integrated activities. Failing to consider personal preferences will undermine even the most noble and enthusiastic integration efforts. Fortunately, individual preferences can be considered by allowing people with Down syndrome to sample various preselected activities and then to choose activities in which they wish to participate from those samples. Research has shown that, when people with disabilities are allowed to choose the activities in which they wish to take part, they are more eager to learn the skills necessary to participate and they generalize in those activities more readily.[17]

*Does the program neglect safety in the name of integration?* A boycott of classes happened at one elementary school when parents kept their nondisabled children at home because of fear for their safety. The concern was evoked by a mainstreamed child with disabilities who was abusive toward other children, being aggressive toward them without warning. Although the school's commitment to including this child in general education classes for the entire school day is admirable, jeopardizing the safety of other students is inappropriate. We should remind ourselves occasionally that our society, while valuing altruism, also has a vigorous litigious element. Emphasizing the safety of all participants as a first concern will reap benefits for everyone in the program. Then, judiciously, inclusion can be done in small doses, moving carefully to larger doses as the student with a disability and his or her peers adapt in a supportive atmosphere.

*Does the program have nondisabled peers assume "adult" teaching roles?* Occasionally a nondisabled peer is asked to assume a role that an adult should assume. Peers without disabilities should not teach "heavy-duty" skills. As examples, a nondisabled peer should not be expected to teach a peer with a disability how to apply deodorant, put on undergarments, or brush teeth. These tasks are best left to adults such as parents and teachers.

## GUIDELINES FOR PROVIDING A GOOD INTEGRATED PROGRAM

The remarkable law, Public Law 94–142, the Education for All Handicapped Children Act of 1975, which mandated that all children, regardless of the type or severity of disability, have a right to a free, appropriate public education in the least restrictive environment, has created unprecedented opportunities for parents seeking to integrate children with Down syndrome into regular schools. To take advantage of these opportunities, we have developed a set of guidelines for parents and teachers.

*Guideline 1: Structure activities to promote cooperative interactions.*[18] Without structuring a mainstream situation for cooperative interactions, nondisabled individuals often view their peers with disabilities in negative ways, feel discomfort and uncertainty in interacting with them, and sometimes even reject them overtly. Unless the setting is structured for cooperative learning experiences, negative competition is likely to emerge and actually socialize children without disabilities to reject peers who have Down syndrome. What does structuring an activity for cooperative interactions mean?

Usually, one of three models of activity structure is applied when instructing a group of people: *competitive, individualistic*, or *cooperative*. Each is legitimate and has strengths in specific situations. Furthermore, these can be combined in an activity at times. We shall define each of them and look briefly at some of their applications.

*Competition* in its traditional application leads to one person in a group winning and all other group members losing. If it is applied to a group in which one or more of the members have disabilities that make success in a particular task difficult, the participants with disabilities likely will come in last in that task. As an example of competitive structuring in camping, imagine five children, some of whom have movement disabilities, lining up at the edge of a lake for a canoe race. Each has a canoe and a paddle to use. The camp director tells them that the person who reaches the other side of the lake first will win a miniature canoe paddle. Children with Down syndrome, who often (though not always) have coordination problems and poor muscle tone, have little chance of winning. Informed program leaders would not use a competitive goal structure in this manner, of course, but would modify the competitive situation or would rely on one or both of the following structures instead.

In an *individualistically* structured situation, each member of a group works to improve his or her own past performance. Potentially, every member of the group, including members with Down syndrome, can win a prize for improvement if the targets for improved performance are not set too high or are not matched inappropriately with a disability condition. Using the canoe example again, suppose the adult leader lines up the group on the lakeshore and says that last week when they paddled across the lake, each person's crossing time was recorded. Then the adult says that every person who improves his or her time will win a miniature canoe paddle, even if the improvement is slight. Now everyone can be a winner. This structure often is used in amateur athletics.

A *cooperative* learning structure, if handled properly, creates a natural interdependence because the group's attainment of an objective, with everyone contributing, is the quality that determines winning. Using the canoe illustration, the adult leader might have the five children climb into a war canoe (a large canoe), give each person a paddle, and tell them they are each to paddle as well as they can and they all will win a miniature canoe paddle if they work together to keep the canoe inside some floating markers (placed in such a way that perfection in paddling isn't required). The adult leader will need to paddle alongside to determine that everyone is paddling and to encourage them to support and assist one another.

To promote positive *social* interactions between participants with and without disabilities, the cooperative structure works better than the other two. In a competitive situation, each child is concentrating on paddling the fastest; he or she doesn't have an incentive for interacting socially. Similarly, in an individualistic structure each child is concentrating on bettering his or her own past performance; again, there is no incentive for interacting socially. In the cooperative structure, however, each person wants to encourage and assist every person in the group to achieve a group goal. This promotes positive interactions such as encouragement, cheering, pats on the back, and informal assistance.

*Guideline 2: Clarify the purpose of a mainstreaming activity.* If the goal is primarily social, structure it for cooperative peer socialization. If the goal is primarily task skill development, structure it for cooperative peer tutoring. Most programs promote both task skill development and socialization, but one objective may be given priority over the other at times. For instance, a 4-H club leader may designate certain periods of the year for project completion, such as the 2 months preceding the county fair. During these times nondisabled participants will be intent on finishing their individual projects. Socializing will be minimal, and nondisabled 4-H members intent on making "the best bookshelf ever entered at the county fair" may even regard it as a distraction.

The leader must be clear about the intent of the activity to avoid creating a situation in which participants are frustrated by trying to fulfill conflicting objectives. When skill development is the focus, the program must be organized so participants with and without disabilities are able to pursue that objective. When socialization is the focus, the program should be organized to facilitate that, and to do it in a way that will create mutuality of enjoyment. When both skill and socialization are to be emphasized, the organization will be different from either skill or socialization alone.

*Guideline 3: Organize the program to suit the focus.* The usual focus of a *cooperative peer tutor* program is to have a peer without a disability teach a skill to a peer with a disability. In a typical example of a cooperative peer tutor program, a 12-year-old child without disabilities works one-to-one on teaching picture sequencing skills to a 6-year-old child with Down syndrome.

The focus of a *cooperative peer socialization* program is to promote positive social interactions between a child with a disability and a child without a disability. A typical application of this arrangement is one in which two young peers of the same age, one with a disability and one without, make a giant puzzle, then paint the pieces together, glue macaroni and yarn on the pieces together, and so on.

In structuring an activity for cooperative peer socialization, the following factors should be considered:

1. *Age of peers.* Nondisabled peers and peers with Down syndrome should be approximately the same age to create an expectation of friendly socialization, turn-taking, sharing, and so forth. If nondisabled peers are a year or two older, that's fine, but to encourage ongoing relationships, nondisabled peers in general should not be younger than their peers with Down syndrome. Our research shows

that when children with disabilities are older than their nondisabled partners, the social interaction often is awkward. Same-age peer interactions can be thought of as "horizontal"—relatively equal and reciprocal.

2. *Activity*. Choose activities that are not overly skill-oriented but, rather, are socialization-oriented. Structure task directions to reward mutual effort, not individual effort. An example is having a peer with Down syndrome and a peer without disabilities put ingredients on a pizza together and share in eating it later.

3. *Preparing of nondisabled peers for socialization.*
   - Show them how to prompt cooperative interaction ("Chris, let's paint this picture together").
   - Show them how to encourage their partner's cooperative participation ("Bill, I'll bet you're good at sanding. Can you help me sand this tray?").
   - Show them how to reinforce their partner for trying ("I like the way we painted the fence together. You're a *good* painter!").

4. *Adult leader's role during peer socialization interactions.*
   - Encourage cooperative activity ("Mary, I'd like to see you and Joan take turns kicking the soccer ball").
   - Reinforce cooperative interactions ("I *like* the way you're setting the table together").
   - Redirect participants back to the cooperative task when one or both become distracted.
   - Step in if a socialization problem arises between participants.

5. *Limitations*. The purpose of cooperative socialization is to promote positive social interactions. It will not further skill development in a specific task in a child with Down syndrome (unless, of course, the targeted skill is social interaction itself). If the teacher's goal is to assist a child with Down syndrome to become a proficient reader, an older nondisabled peer (peer tutor) or an adult will probably have to provide reading instruction and guided reading practice. Cooperative socialization would not meet this task skill development goal very well.

Structuring a situation for cooperative peer tutoring requires consideration of the following factors:

1. *Age of peers*. Nondisabled companions should be considerably older than the partner with Down syndrome (twice as old is a good rule of thumb), as the main purpose of tutoring is to enhance the tutoring recipient's skill in some task. We refer to this relationship as

*vertical* ("I'm the teacher; you're the student"). And, because it's a vertical relationship, the real teacher has to watch over it so the older nondisabled student doesn't become dictatorial or over-mothering.

2. *Activity.* Activities should feature cooperative skill teaching and practice in the skill instead of socialization. An example is found in the older nondisabled student teaching the younger child with Down syndrome to use a hand mixer. After giving the younger child a chance to show what steps he or she can do correctly in using a mixer, the peer tutor teaches the younger child the steps he or she cannot do.

For instance, if the child with Down syndrome doesn't know how to identify the various speeds on the mixer's control dial, the tutor might label each setting verbally while pointing to the corresponding printed words on the dial. The tutor can show how the printed word on the dial translates into mixer speed as the dial is moved from speed to speed. After that, the tutor might print the words on pieces of cardboard and use them like flashcards until the child with Down syndrome can identify them quickly and accurately. After that is accomplished, the tutor directs practice in locating the dial position ("Turn to high"), watching for errors and hesitations. Finally, the speed dial operation is reinserted into the whole task of using a mixer to mix batter for a cake. Food becomes the reward for achieving this cooperative outcome, and both enjoy a piece of cake together for their joint effort, a cooperative outcome.

3. *Preparing nondisabled peers for tutoring.*
   - Show them how to use a variety of instructional techniques such as modeling, reinforcing, prompting, and fading (see list of instructional techniques in Chapter 5).
   - Show them how to adapt tasks to make them more accessible for a child with Down syndrome (see Chapter 8).

4. *Adult leader's role during interactions.*
   - Reward the nondisabled child's tutorial attempts, and reward attempts by the child with Down syndrome to respond to the tutoring.
   - Model good instructional techniques for the two children.
   - Step in to prevent or correct instructional problems.
   - Redirect participants if off-task behavior occurs.

5. *Limitations.*
   - The social dynamics in a tutoring situation can turn autocratic or over-mothering if not watched carefully.
   - The tutor may lose interest in instruction if the partner's progress is slow. The teacher can blunt this possibility by keeping the co-

operative structure in place, tying rewards to something under the tutor's control, such as number of practice trials given, rather than to the recipient's success (though success usually results when the task, or step of the task, is broken down into small, simplified segments). The outcome of the task can be rewarding itself, as in the case of the batter-mixing task, in which the finished cake becomes a reward for both peers.

A third type of structure—one that should become increasingly popular—is the cooperative tutoring/cooperative socialization combination in which, for example, an older nondisabled peer tutors a younger peer with Down syndrome and at the same time a nondisabled peer of the same age as the child with Down syndrome serves as a socializing partner. This structure has some advantages. First, because of the participants' age differences, the older nondisabled peer can assume either a teaching or a socializing role, one that feels comfortable to him or her. Second, if teaching becomes necessary to achieve a task, the older nondisabled peer is available to do it and the younger nondisabled peer can concentrate on socializing. Third, this structure, with its varying participant ages instead of a single age (a structure we've dubbed the "one-room school" model), takes advantage of age and ability differences that are familiar because they occur naturally in families. As an example, a young nondisabled child and a young child with Down syndrome, both of whom are nearly the same age, ride horses together at the local stable (cooperative socialization). At the same time, an older nondisabled peer teaches riding skills to both of the younger children (cooperative tutoring).

*Guideline 4: Recruit nondisabled participants in an appealing way.* A helpful tool for recruiting nondisabled participants, as well as adult volunteers, is a slide presentation showing people with and without disabilities interacting in natural and interesting ways.* This produces a positive image for prospective participants, many of whom may have negative mental pictures of mainstreaming programs because they lack exposure to people with disabilities, or even have a negative stereotype of those with disabilities. Recruitment presentations that depict positive interactions between individuals

---

* If you photograph your own slides, obtain written photo-use permission for each person in your pictures (for minors or others unable to legally sign for themselves, have the parent/guardian sign). Also, inform all parents or guardians of your intent to provide an integrated program and receive consent to have their son or daughter participate. Although this type of permission may not be required, it is important to avoid misunderstanding. By the way, a videotape can serve this purpose and has some advantages to slides. However, playback requires more planning.

with and without disabilities help create the expectation by potential members that they will have a positive experience in an integrated program. That expectation alone can go a long way toward creating a successful program.

*Guideline 5: Strengthen nondisabled participants' understanding of disability.* Meetings involving nondisabled group members and adult leaders should take place frequently, perhaps immediately before or after a mainstream session. During these meetings the discussion can cover a problem in interaction and how to overcome it, new ideas for interacting, task adaptation, and specific techniques that can be used during one-to-one activities. Knowledge of disabilities and their consequences can be broadened and strengthened in these meetings through the Special Friends curriculum.[19]

The following topics often are discussed with nondisabled participants in short, informal group discussions of 15–30 minutes between interaction sessions. Suggested topics include:

- *How do we play together?* Discuss how companions take turns, say nice things to each other, help each other when a task is difficult, stay close to each other when playing, smile at each other, and so forth. Reinforce the interaction techniques they have been taught to apply during integrated activities.
- *How do we communicate?* Discuss communication tips, such as talking slowly, allowing time for a response, trying another way to communicate if a companion doesn't understand, and not giving up. Common, simple manual signs ("hello," "good," "you," "me") can be introduced, too, if applicable.
- *What is a prosthesis?* Discuss the use of tools (ladder, paintbrush, and the like) that people without disabilities need so they can do certain tasks (such as paint a house). Show examples of a prosthesis (for example, an artificial limb or adapted equipment), and explain how it is like a tool that people without disabilities use.
- *How does a person with a disability live in the community?* Invite a person with disabilities to come and talk about how he or she travels from home to work, goes camping, and performs similar activities.
- *What is a best friend?* Discuss the nature of friendship. Ask participants to think about similarities and differences in their relationship with their friend with a disability and their best friend (if they are not the same person).

*Guideline 6: Develop a cooperative social support network.* The first five guidelines mainly provide information about how to promote cooperative interactions directly—for example, how the teacher rewards cooperative tutorial or socialization interactions. A teacher can use other methods, too, growing out of a group counseling tradition, methods that promote cooperative interactions less directly because the people involved bring their *minds* together for a common purpose. Two of these techniques, which have the cooperative planning approach in common but from a slightly differing perspective, are Circle of Friends[20] and the McGill Action Planning (MAP) system.[21] These two often are used together or sequentially.

The Circle of Friends activity often begins using a target-like piece of paper, which the teacher asks the parents or other key informant to fill out in behalf of the student who has Down syndrome (the student with Down syndrome may be capable of filling out a Circle of Friends sheet, too). In the innermost circle, the parent writes the names of individuals who are extremely close friends of the student, indispensable individuals other than relatives. In the circle next to the center one, the parent writes down names of all the people who are good friends but not indispensable friends. Circles three and four further expand the names of people outward until the list of people involved in the student's life in some manner is exhausted. In this way the teacher and parent are able to determine the number of people who are close to and interact with the person with Down syndrome. These people will become part of the MAP system, along with relatives and staff members who together will become a social support network, an *actual* circle of friends for the individual who has Down syndrome.

In the MAP system the teacher assembles people who are important in the child's environment, especially those in the inner one or two circles of the Circle of Friends. Often a parent becomes the most important member of the planning group, although the teacher usually acts as facilitator. Sitting around a table, the child's parent, siblings, one or two classmates, a teacher or two, perhaps a scout leader or other community-based person who is important in the child's life, and other people, including the child who has Down syndrome, "think out loud" about the following points, keeping in mind that successful integration in the community is the primary goal:

1. What is the individual's history?
2. What is your dream for him or her?
3. What is your nightmare?

4. Who is the individual?

5. What are his or her strengths and weaknesses?

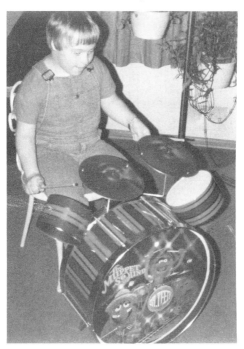

6. What are the individual's needs?

7. What would his or her ideal day look like, and what must be done to achieve the ideal?

These questions are written on large sheets of paper and become a "map" to the individual's future. From the notes generated through this method, short-term and long-term goals are written, followed by a list of steps or tasks that will have to be accomplished to attain the goals. Let's take a look at an example of these two techniques (Circle of Friends, MAP) in action.

Megg is a 10-year-old child with Down syndrome who attends a regular school, where she is mainstreamed into several curricular areas and has a regular class as a homeroom base. Megg is easy to have around—unfortunately, too easy to have around sometimes, because she is very withdrawn socially. Her pencil-drawn Circle of Friends shows no child, older or younger or of the same age, who can be considered as an indispensable ("best") friend. Her mother does show two girls' names in the second circle (the "good friends" circle), though, girls who are in Megg's 4-H club and have shared pizza with her a few times at club meetings.

Working closely with Megg's mother, individuals important to her life, including the two 4-H companions, are brought together to develop a MAP for her. One of the first things brought out is that Megg's mother's nightmare is that Megg will be totally without friends as an adult and that she will be placed in a highly segregated and isolated residential facility when her mother dies, spending her days lonely and depressed.

On the brighter side, Megg's 4-H leader says that Megg has a nice smile (when she displays it, which isn't too often) and good manners. The participants decide to build on these, creating opportunities in which social interaction demands will be moved up a notch but will not be overwhelming for Megg. Her 4-H leader decides that Megg will have a nonspeaking role in the next Share the Fun skit—not a big role but one that perhaps will draw her out a little bit.

Megg's mother and teacher decide that Megg also will be encouraged to train for the Special Olympics volleyball event, joining teammates with and without disabilities through a Unified Sports program that meets at her school twice each week. Megg enjoys volleyball very much and does reasonably well in it. The volleyball coach becomes part of the MAP system, learning more about how to structure cooperative activities for athletes with and without disabilities so they succeed collectively as well as individually. Some of these activities take form in cooperative peer tutoring (nondisabled teammates showing how to serve, pass the ball, rotate, and so forth). Other activities take form in cooperative peer socialization (nondisabled peers encourage Megg during the game, reward her with a word of praise for a good try, and interact with her socially during snack time after a game).

As a result of combining the Circle of Friends, MAP system, and cooperative learning techniques, Megg is beginning to grow in her socialization abilities and volleyball skills. Her day-to-day life shows new vitality, too—new friends, both with and without disabilities; more variety in her socialization sphere; a schedule that gets her out of the house regularly and into worthwhile activities.

OTES

1. J. Rynders and J. Horrobin, "Always Trainable? Never Educable? Updating Educational Expectations Concerning Children with Down Syndrome," *American Journal on Mental Retardation* 95 (1990): 77–83.

2. R. Restak, "Genetic Counseling for Defective Parents: The Danger of Knowing Too Much," *Psychology Today* 9 (1975): 92, pp. 42–46.

3. C. Turkington, "Special Talents," *Psychology Today* 21 (1987).

4. J. Rynders, D. Spiker, and J. Horrobin, "Underestimating the Educability of Down's Syndrome Children: Examination of Methodological Problems in Recent Literature," *American Journal of Mental Deficiency* 82 (1978): 440–448.

5. M. Pieterse and Y. Center, "The Integration of Eight Down's Syndrome Children into Regular Schools," *Australia and New Zealand Journal of Developmental Disabilities* 10 (1984): 10, 11, 20; and D. Lane and B. Stratford, *Current Approaches to Down's Syndrome* (East Sussex, Great Britain: Holt, Rinehart, & Winston, 1987).

6. S. Buckley, "Attaining Basic Educational Skills: Reading, Writing, and Numbers," *Current Approaches to Down's Syndrome,* edited by D. Lane and B. Stratford (East Sussex, Great Britain: Holt, Rinehart, & Winston, 1987), pp. 315–343.

7. Cited in Pieterse and Center.

8. *A Comparative Follow-up Study of Down's Syndrome Children Who Attended the Model Preschool Program* (unpublished doctoral dissertation, University of Washington, Seattle, 1984), cited in V. Dmitriev, "Cognition and the Acceleration and Maintenance of Developmental Gains Among Children with Down Syndrome: Longitudinal Data," *Down's Syndrome, Papers and Abstracts for Professionals,* Jan. 6–11, 1988.

9. Rynders and Horrobin.

10. In Pieterse and Center.

11. J. J. Carney, *What Research Says About Reading for the Mentally Retarded Child* (paper presented at the Annual Meeting of the International Reading Association, 1979).

12. T. Leeper, *Teaching Educable Mentally Handicapped Students to Read: A Review of Research Literature* (special report, Anoka-Hennepin Schools, Minnesota).

13. J. C. Mainord and H. D. Love, *Teaching Educable Mentally Retarded Children: Methods and Materials* (Springfield, IL: Charles C Thomas, 1973).

14. Paul S. Anderson, *Language Skills in Elementary Education* (New York: Macmillan, 1974).

15. This is according to Leeper's review.

16. P. Johnson, *A Study of Selected Aspects of Reading Instruction for the Educable Mentally Retarded: Teacher Opinion, Instructional Procedures, and Materials* (Tampa: University of South Florida, 1976).

17. D. Fletcher, *Ensuring Enjoyment in Integrated Community Recreation and Leisure Activities* (paper delivered at National Conference of American Association

on Mental Retardation, May 1992, Atlanta, GA).

18. D. Johnson and R. Johnson, *Learning Together and Alone* (Boston: Allyn and Bacon, 1994).

19. L. Voeltz, H. J. Hemphill, S. Brown, G. Kishi, R. Klein, R. Fruehling, J. Collie, G. Levy, and C. Kube, *The Special Friends Program: A Trainer's Manual for Integrated School Settings* (revised) (Honolulu: University of Hawaii Department of Special Education, 1983).

20. S. K. Sherwood, "A Circle of Friends in a 1st Grade Classroom," *Educational Leadership* 48(3) (1990): 41.

21. T. Vandercook, J. York, and M. Forest, "The McGill Action Planning System (MAPS): A Strategy for Building the Vision," *Journal of the Association for Persons with Severe Handicaps* 14(3) (1989): 205–215.

# NIGHTENGALE FAMILY

Dad: John
Mom: Wanda
Brother: Matthew
Brother: Stephen
Brother with Down
    syndrome: Andrew

A smile bigger than on the pumpkins.

First
day of
school.

"Dry run": Prelude to water skiing.

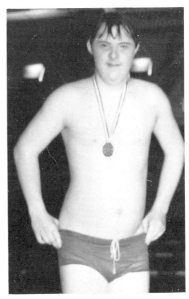

Special Olympics medal winner.

## $\mathcal{N}$IGHTENGALE FAMILY (continued)

Snakes aren't
so bad.

Picnics and smiles go together.

More independence coming.

## ~8~

# ONE FOOT IN SCHOOL, ONE IN A COMMUNITY RECREATION SETTING

John E. Rynders, Stuart J. Schleien,
and Shannon L. Matson

*A*s a student with Down syndrome approaches high school graduation day, the family shifts its attention from school-based concerns to community-based concerns. This "one foot in school, one foot in the community" phase often is referred to as *transitioning*, an event or defined period during which substantial change is occurring (or should occur) in the lives of the individual with Down syndrome and his or her parents and siblings. An example of a transitioning period is the year of halfway house training that precedes the day when a young adult with Down syndrome moves out of the family home into an apartment in a semi-independent living setting. The transitioning event is the day the person actually moves.

The transitioning period leading up to graduation is a major one for the individual and his or her family. As graduation approaches, parents become anxious because of the unpredictability of the post-school period. Adding to parents' general anxiety is their uncertainty about whether the school has prepared their child to hold a job, make good use of free time, invite and maintain friendships, and live as independently as possible outside the parental home. Then, too, they wonder if the school has prepared their child sufficiently in the two areas featured in Chapter 7, socialization and literacy. On top of all this, they worry about their child's health and physical well-being. The latter topics will be covered in this chapter and in the remaining chapters of this book.

## *R*ECREATION AND LEISURE

What is community recreation participation like for young adults with Down syndrome? Is it good, bad, or indifferent? A study of the community recreation/leisure pursuits of young men and women with Down syndrome, as reported by their parents, revealed that the most frequent activities took place in the family home and consisted mainly of watching TV, listening to music, playing alone with toys or games, and spending time with family members.[1] The most common community activities were religious activities, shopping, and going to movies, concerts, or plays. Other researchers and recreation professionals also have noted a "shallowness" in the depth and breadth of the lifestyles of people with developmental disabilities.[2] They found a lack of participation in a variety of community recreation activities, such as outdoor recreation and clubs, that are typical of their nondisabled peers.

Our survey of EDGE parents, whose sons or daughters with Down syndrome averaged 21 years of age, indicated that their children's most popular activity at home was watching TV, followed by listening to the radio or to tape recordings. The third most popular home-based activity was working on hobbies. Outside the home, the most popular activity was participation in sports, followed by shopping (for food, hobby materials, and the like) and visiting friends or relatives (though some of this visiting was in the home).

These results can be misleading because some recreation activities simply do not occur often enough to outstrip, at least in time-per-day, even fairly modest watching of TV, which is accessible 100% of the time, day or night. For instance, bowling in a league once a week for 2 hours could be an individual's favorite pursuit, but watching TV for just 30 minutes a day would show up on the survey as the most popular activity time-wise. Results also may be misjudged in that TV watching undoubtedly would show up as the favorite activity on a time-expended basis for many adults without disabilities as well.

Nevertheless, if we combine the categories of TV watching and listening to the radio and recordings and total the number of hours per week accumulated across the 15 EDGE young adults, participation in these passive activities averages approximately 5 hours per day, 7 days per week, for each individual. Spending this amount of time in a physically inactive pursuit has to be a contributing factor in the obesity that is characteristic of many adults with Down syndrome.

EDGE parents, however, did report that *participation* in sports, not as spectators, is their daughter's or son's third most popular recreation pursuit. Thus, these individuals probably have a substantial capacity for increasing active participation if we can facilitate it somehow. Participation in recreation of an active sort often is dictated as much (sometimes more) by the supports the community provides as by the individual's interests and aptitude. What can be done, therefore, to make community recreation program supports more bountiful and available? And what can be done to cultivate the recreation interests and aptitudes of individuals with Down syndrome and their family members?

# $\mathscr{O\!\!/}$IX STRATEGIES TO PROMOTE PARTICIPATION IN RECREATION _____

In the last 10 years we have identified six strategies that make a significant difference in getting people with disabilities, including those with Down syndrome, out of the house, or at least out of their chairs. Not all of the strategies produce weight loss or significant improvements in physical fitness automatically, but at least they require more expenditure of energy than TV watching or radio and tape listening. More importantly, the recreational activity promoted through these strategies sometimes has been the key to advancing the personal development of young adults with Down syndrome.

In beginning to discuss strategies, parents should not assume personal, long-term, sole responsibility for implementing them. That's too exhausting for anyone! Besides, if parents continue to implement these strategies themselves, community and school personnel may not ever feel a need or responsibility to provide them. When the parent moves away (or becomes exhausted from the effort), the strategy will cease because no one in the community has learned it or is committed to implementing it. This "disappearing act" is all too common. Thus, parents might want to begin to use a strategy to demonstrate its effect, but they then should pass it on to a community professional.

*Strategy #1: Assess the individual's recreation preferences.*

This sounds so "common-sensical" that it doesn't seem worth discussing. Still, it is because it signals to the individual with Down syndrome that his or her preferences are important. The person making the choice is ascribed importance, not a small matter for young adults with Down syndrome. Expressing a preference also has practical importance. Predicting young adults' preferences isn't always easy, as they may change during the transitioning period. Because young adults often are capable of advocating for themselves to some extent—with the attendant motivational benefit—this becomes even more important.

*Strategy #2: Figure out how to get the preferred activity offered in the community in the most convenient way possible by designing a step-by-step working plan.*

Here is where the technical sounding term *task analysis* comes in. Don't be put off by the sound of it. It's not difficult to understand or use, and it can be a powerful tool. It means that a task or activity is broken down into small steps that are observable and teachable. A comprehensive and detailed instructional plan that virtually any adult can use emerges. The parent then is able to suggest to a recreation provider, "I'd like my daughter to play miniature golf at your course" and also say, "Here's a plan that shows how my daughter can learn to play miniature golf at your facility if instruction is offered on an individual, step-by-step basis."

Let's look at a task analysis for Rose, a young adult with Down syndrome, as adapted from one we developed.[3] Rose's recreation preferences were assessed by showing her pictures of young adults participating in various age-appropriate activities such as swimming and playing softball. The pictures were presented in pairs representing all possible combinations. The picture of an adult using a Polaroid™ camera came up as her number-one choice, time after time. Therefore, Rose's father began to develop a task analysis for using a One-Step Polaroid™ camera, a camera that is easy to use and is user-friendly. He made sure that socialization aspects were embedded in the analysis along with the needed camera skills. (After Rose masters this relatively easy photography task, her father will add components to it that also involve adult literacy learning skills—for example, developing a task analysis for Rose's walking to the neighborhood store independently, purchasing film, returning home, and loading the film into the camera. Here is Rose's task analysis for taking a picture of a companion.[4]

1. Ask the companion, "May I take a picture of you?"
2. If the reply is "yes," point to or suggest where person should sit or stand (not more than 12 feet away), with the sun shining on the person's face, but not directly in his or her eyes.
3. Ask the person to smile.
4. Grasp opposite sides of the camera with both hands, the lens facing away from body and toward the person/subject.
5. Raise the camera until you can see through viewfinder.
6. Center the person/subject in viewfinder.

7. Position your index finger directly in front of the shutter release button.
8. Push the shutter release button until it is depressed completely.
9. Wait for the photograph to emerge from the camera.
10. Remove the photograph from the camera.
11. Hold the photograph face up in your palm until it develops fully.
12. Show the photograph to others, then place it in a photo album.

After a task analysis has been completed, it is not only a helpful planning tool, but it also becomes a useful tool for keeping track of (evaluating) progress in the recreation activity and for revealing exactly where instruction is needed. To show how this is so, let's imagine that Rose is not able to perform step 11 of the task analysis (hold photograph until it develops) very well. How does this become evident? Rose's father gave her three chances to take a photo of a companion independently without any instruction, and he put an X in front of each step that Rose didn't do or did inadequately. Thus, he had a written record (three noninstructed attempts to perform the task on her own), which showed that Rose dropped the developing photograph all three times onto the ground after it emerged from the camera. She did not hold onto it and did not wait for it to develop fully.

Having recorded Rose's uninstructed capabilities, her father gave her specific instruction in this step by itself. He demonstrated how the film looks when it's fully developed by taking five photos himself so she could observe how to hold the photograph and wait for it to develop completely. Then, to help her get past this step, he instructed her to count to 60 before touching the front of the photo and then to remove it over a table (Rose can count to 100 easily and accurately).

Each time Rose does this step correctly, he says something pleasant to her such as, "Wow, Rose, look how good that photo looks!" When she does it incorrectly he says something like, "Whoops, you need to count to 60 before you touch the front of the photo, Rose." Then he asks for the camera and he instructs her again. After Rose has mastered this step, it is put back into the context of the whole photography task analysis and she will be given an opportunity to do all of the steps on her own again. If she muffs the step she practiced (or any other step), her father will instruct her in that step until she finally is able to do all the steps correctly and independently, several times in a row.

*Strategy #3: Learn how to adapt a task so that its difficult parts can be avoided or overcome.*[5]

### Material Adaptations

Materials and equipment used in an activity can be barriers to participation because they've been designed by and for individuals without disabilities. These may be adapted, however.

For example, equipment may be modified to permit bowling by individuals with Down syndrome, who often have limitations in fine and gross motor coordination, balance, and muscular strength required to lift and launch a bowling ball down an alley with reasonable skill. In some circumstances the bowling ball may be placed on top of a tubular steel bowling ramp (drawing #1).* The bowler then aims the ramp at the pins and releases the ball. A bowling ball pusher, similar to a shuffleboard stick, also may be used to push the ball down the alley (drawing #2). The pusher may be adjusted to various lengths, allowing ambulatory and nonambulatory, short and tall individuals to bowl. A third adapted bowling device that can be used by a person who is not able to lift and launch a conventional ball is a handle-grip bowling ball. A simple grasp of the handle in the palm of the hand and basic gross-motor arm movements are required to manipulate this adapted device. Once released, the handle snaps back, flush, into the bowling ball, allowing the ball to roll down the alley toward the pins. These three adaptations can permit a greater number of individuals with Down syndrome to enjoy the game of bowling.

Some types of adapted equipment are available commercially and can be purchased from sporting goods and hobby stores, specialty shops, and mail-order houses. Many adapted recreational materials and equipment can be devised by an activity leader (e.g., therapeutic recreation specialist) or a parent. For instance, a tennis racket handle may be enlarged using sponge or foam rubber and then wrapped with masking tape to allow for easier grasping and control of the racket (drawing #3).

A simple adaptation that can make a camera easier to use is to extend the shutter release button by attaching a piece of a crayon or other extension (drawing #4). This makes the button easier to locate and press.

## Procedural and Rule Adaptations

If an individual's physical, intellectual, or social limitation makes a rule difficult to follow, it may result in a potential active participant becoming a passive spectator. Rules may be modified or simplified to make participation possible. They also may be altered when teaching a game, and later rewritten to approximate the rules that nondisabled peers follow. For example, basketball requires a player to bounce or dribble the ball every time a step is taken down the court. A change that permits one dribble for several steps

---

*The drawings in this chapter were created by Jean Larson, certified therapeutic recreation specialist (CTRS) at the University of Minnesota Landscape Arboretum, for the book *Together Successfully* (Rynders and Schleien, 1991).

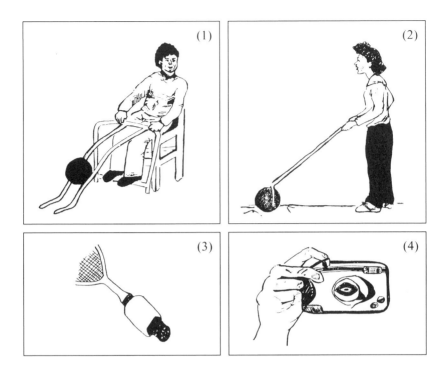

down the court may permit an individual with difficulty in eye-hand-foot coordination to become an active and successful member of the team. Or the individual could learn to bounce and catch the ball instead of using the more difficult, standard dribble. With practice, coordination may improve and the regular rules can be used.

The rules in card games also may be modified. For example, the game "Concentration" requires players to draw two cards consecutively, with the object of drawing the most matched pairs. To make it easier to discriminate between number and picture cards, all picture cards (such as jacks, queens, kings) could be assigned the same value. Another modification of the game would be to use paired photographs of the player and each of his or her friends and family members to create a modified deck of playing cards. This not only simplifies the game but also can make it more motivating and enjoyable.

### Skill Sequence Adaptations

Sometimes a sequence of steps applicable to a nondisabled individual may be too difficult or impractical for a person with Down syndrome. A hobby such as cooking provides a clear illustration of this. When boiling an egg, a nondisabled person might place the egg into a saucepan of boiling water. This could be hazardous (a scalded hand) to an individual with physical or intellectual limitations. To remedy this problem, the sequence of the component steps of the skill could be rearranged. The participant could place the egg into the saucepan, then fill the saucepan with cold water, then place the saucepan onto the stovetop burner and bring the water to a boil. This procedure does not alter the final results (of boiling an egg and making egg salad). It does add several minutes to the cooking time, but it is a safe and practical method of performing this enjoyable task. As another adaptation, a long-handled, slotted spoon could be used to place the egg in and remove it from the boiling water.

A modified skill sequence also is applicable to manipulating a camera. Typically, a photographer first raises the camera to eye level and then places his or her index finger on the shutter release button. An individual lacking fine-motor coordination could be trained to position his or her finger on the shutter release button before lifting the camera to eye level. In this way, he or she merely has to depress the button once the camera is positioned appropriately.

**Facility Adaptations**

The local swimming pool, museum, restaurant, video arcade, library, church or synagogue—all should be accessible to people with Down syndrome. Unfortunately, some individuals have limited access to these places because of narrow doorways, inadequate toileting facilities, and imposing staircases. In addition, transportation to many sites is inadequate. These architectural barriers are being overcome gradually by the installation of wheelchair ramps leading into buildings, enlarged doorknobs, extended handles on drinking fountains, and other adaptations that promote full use by all individuals. Modifications should blend in with standard equipment whenever possible so nobody will stand out as being too different from peers.

For example, the following could make pier fishing accessible to a person with Down syndrome who has physical disabilities requiring the use of a wheelchair:

- An access walk to the pier at least 5 feet wide to allow for turning of a wheelchair (drawing #5).
- A handrail around the entire pier 36 inches high with a sloping top at a 30-degree angle for resting the arm and pole (drawing #6).
- A kick-plate to prevent foot pedals of wheelchair from falling off the pier.
- A smooth, nonslip surface on the access walk and the pier.

## Lead-Up Activity Adaptations

A lead-up activity is a simplified version of a traditional activity or an exercise that allows practice in some component skill. Several lead-up activities may be chained together to teach specific skills necessary to engage in a more complex activity successfully. For example, a player can learn many of the skills involved in volleyball by participating in the game of "Newcomb," which requires participants to catch and throw a ball over a net. The concepts of returning the ball over the net, scoring team points, and rotating players can all be learned during the adapted version. An additional lead-up activity may be necessary to develop the skills needed for tapping the ball over the net. This can be done by having the players form a circle while taking turns tapping the ball to a player in the center of the circle.

By learning a more complex activity in small steps, full participation can be shaped and possibly accomplished eventually. Some individuals with Down syndrome may not be capable of mastering all the skills required to participate in the original activity. In this case, the lead-up activity itself may become a rewarding experience.

These five types of adaptations are the primary ways in which a creative program leader can reduce failure and frustration for all participants. In the Appendix, adaptations are illustrated in the context of four popular areas of recreation and leisure: sewing, woodworking, creative arts, and cooking. In developing adaptations, activity leaders, parents, and the participants themselves must discuss barriers and adaptations. Many of the most creative and effective ideas come from these discussions.

Let's take a moment to see how adaptation strategies are helpful to Sally, a young adult with Down syndrome who doesn't read well or speak clearly. Sally's favorite leisure activity is to go to McDonald's. She usually is able to order what she wants because the task of ordering food has been adapted for her. She uses small cards, each picturing an item from the menu along with the term corresponding to the picture. Sally recognizes the picture but doesn't read the words well; the cashier doesn't need to look at the picture but knows what Sally wants by reading the words on the cards. This adaptation makes this recreation activity accessible to Sally.

*Strategy #4: Put together a focus group along with a circle of friends.*

Similar to the MAP system used with school-age individuals (see Chapter 7), a focus group is composed of people who have a common interest—in this case, an interest in turning the recreational preferences of a young adult with Down syndrome into recreational opportunities. (A focus group also can concentrate on the individual's vocational and independent living preferences while attending to the recreation area because, as we said before, all three areas of community life are interrelated.) The focus group consists of several people who have a stake in the young adult's achieving a goal. The group also may include other adults who are likely to make things happen to reach the goal. To this focus group can be added a small circle of friends, two or three people (with or without Down syndrome or another disability) who volunteer to become cooperative partners, teammates, or tutors during the recreation activity. (See Chapter 5 for information on structuring activities for cooperative learning.)

Together, members of the focus group, with the circle of friends added to it, think aloud (with the young adult with Down syndrome's direct involvement, if possible) about how to fully use a recreation program that is of prime interest to the person with Down syndrome. After making certain that everyone is comfortable and has been introduced to every member of the group, the facilitator focuses the group on the following points:

1. What does the individual with Down syndrome want to do? Where can she or he do it?
2. What barriers exist to her or his achieving the desired goal or goals?
3. How can we, as a focus group, break down these barriers?
4. Who will do what?
5. How can we check for progress?

An important function of a focus group is to identify adults who will either agree to take on facilitation roles themselves or agree to take responsibility for finding others who are willing to take on these roles.

*Strategy #5: Adult facilitation of recreational involvement.*

From the focus group process, at least two adult facilitators should emerge. Of the two, one should take on "coaching" responsibilities—to encourage social interactions and skill development during the recreation activity. This dual emphasis is recommended because recreation activities usually contain both socialization and task skill elements. For example, doing well at a picnic involves using good manners (skill) and engaging in appropriate light conversation (social). Playing bocce (a mix between lawn bowling and horseshoes) involves learning how to toss the ball properly and follow the rules of the game (skill) and to wait patiently to take a turn (social). Riding a public bus requires the ability to recognize the type and number of coins needed for the fare (skill) and, while seated, to not talk loudly or indiscriminately (social).

The coach can develop a task analysis that blends skill and socialization concerns, ensuring that social interactions prosper and task skill inadequacies that are getting in the way of fruitful social interactions are "side-coached." The person may be removed only temporarily from the group for specific task instruction and, as quickly as possible, placed back in the group again to practice what has been learned in the social context (unless the skill of concern happens to be a social skill that is developed best within the group itself).

This coach also should learn to play "What if?" with members of the recreation group and with the individual who has Down syndrome. For example, the coach says to the young adult with Down syndrome, "Suppose you've ordered a hamburger at McDonald's, paid for it, and taken it to your table. When you open the wrapper, you see you've been given a fish sandwich instead (you don't like fish). What would you do? What would you say?" With nondisabled participants the coach says, "You're playing Newcomb (the adapted version of volleyball). The ball is thrown to Larry (who has Down syndrome), but Larry isn't paying attention and the ball hits him in the back and falls to the ground. Larry drops to the ground, beating on the ball with his fists and shouting angrily. What should you do when the person you are with has a childlike tantrum and is a young adult who has Down syndrome?"

The second facilitator that should emerge from the focus group process is an adult who concentrates on making more community recreation personnel, facilities, and programs accessible to young adults with Down syndrome. This facilitator helps connect people, places, and programs into a network of supportive elements. For example, the local YMCA offers an aerobics program that a young adult with Down syndrome who lives 2 miles away would enjoy very much, but arranging public transportation (such as Metro Mobility) for her has become time-consuming and complex. The second adult facilitator (a member of the focus group who is an aerobics teacher at the local YMCA) phones members of the aerobics class until she finds four people who will take turns picking up and returning the person with Down syndrome for the once-per-week class.

*Strategy #6: Promote adult functional literacy as needed.*

It may seem odd to include this topic in a chapter concerning recreation and leisure for young adults, but for some young adults with Down syndrome, reading is an important leisure activity in its own right. Functional literacy enables others to participate in preferred recreation and leisure activities. For example, knowing how to set a timer and turn a dial to a specified temperature allows Jennifer to bake a frozen pizza in her oven (pizza is her favorite recreational food). Knowing how to read the names of two streets and to count the four blocks between their intersection and his place of work enables Paul to catch the bus that stops on the corner of Vermont and Second, which gets him downtown to the movie theater, his favorite recreational site.

These are adult functional literacy skills, built on the academic learning of the earlier school years. Academic learning during schooling, however, may not have taken people with Down syndrome far enough to operate relatively independently in the areas of recreation and leisure (or the vocational and independent living areas either). Adult functional literacy has two interrelated aspects: (a) academic ability, and (b) capability of applying whatever academics have been learned to a practical context. The capability of counting by 5s, 10s, and 25s is an academic ability. Translating that ability into the speedy, accurate counting of nickels, dimes, and quarters to pay a bus fare is the applied capability.

When a person with Down syndrome approaches the final years of schooling, the academic part of functional literacy—such as decoding new words and increasing reading vocabulary from a developmental standpoint— sometimes is abandoned in favor of mastering the sight recognition of whole words and phrases that are important to safety and basic needs—for example, learning to recognize "entrance," "exit," "men," "women," "danger," "do not enter," "bus stop," "wait." For the young adult with Down syndrome who is interested in and capable of further academic growth, however, we believe that abandoning academic training is not a good idea because of its relation to supporting adult functional literacy and community living in general. At the later stages of schooling, teachers and job coaches must concentrate on preparing the individual to function in the adult community where reading signs such as "exit" have to take priority, but to discontinue academics (for example, to stop instruction in phonics or to give up on counting proficiently by 1s, 5s, and 10s) will mean a more restricted adult functional literacy repertoire.

In a way, we have created a dilemma for ourselves. Should we continue academic instruction far into the adult years, hoping that adult functional literacy eventually will improve substantially? Or should we cut off academic instruction, let's say at age 18, substituting only crucial adult functional literacy learning experiences? The answer, in our opinion, relates to the young adult's ability level and motivation.

If at age 18, for example, the young adult is still growing in academics and still interested, why not continue this instruction in parallel with vocational, recreational, and independent living training? If, on the other hand, the individual is not good at academics at age 18 and is not interested in pursuing academics, why not shift to an emphasis on adult functional survival literacy skills such as teaching 150 sight words that are absolutely essential for health, safety, and successful participation in the community?

To argue convincingly that academics should not be abandoned for all young adults with Down syndrome, we must be able to demonstrate that some individuals with Down syndrome have good potential for continuing academic learning in the later years of schooling. Recently an academic achievement test was given to the 15 participants with Down syndrome in the Twin-Cities EDGE group. After testing, academic grade equivalence scores were compared at two points: 11–13 years of age and 20–23 years of age. The results are summarized in Table 6.

As can be seen by comparing the averages from test 1 ($T_1$) to test 2 ($T_2$), the grade equivalence scores of the *group* have increased over the 10-year period, although the magnitude of growth is comparatively small over that time span.

From the perspective of *individual* academic growth, the reading comprehension scores of some individuals were too low to be converted to a grade equivalent when they were about 12 years old, and this difficulty was still present when they were about 21 years old. For them, discontinuing developmental academics (such as learning to decode words through a phonic approach) seems warranted. On the other hand, some EDGE students read quite fluently. Academic instruction has paid off, giving them an important

# TABLE 6

Peabody Individual Achievement Test (PIAT)
Grade equivalents, rank ordered by score value for the 15 EDGE
participants

| Math | | Reading Recognition | | Reading Comprehension | |
|---|---|---|---|---|---|
| $T_1$ | $T_2$ | $T_1$ | $T_2$ | $T_1$ | $T_2$ |
| 0.1 | N.S. | 0.8 | 0.9 | N.S. | N.S. |
| 0.1 | 0.4 | 0.9 | 1.3 | N.S. | N.S. |
| 0.1 | 1.1 | 1.4 | 1.5 | 1.8 | N.S. |
| 0.1 | 1.1 | 1.6 | 1.8 | 1.9 | 2.1 |
| 0.1 | 1.1 | 1.8 | 3.1 | 2.0 | 2.2 |
| 0.3 | 1.5 | 1.8 | 3.1 | 2.0 | 2.2 |
| 0.3 | 1.7 | 3.5 | 4.2 | 2.1 | 2.4 |
| 0.3 | 1.7 | 3.8 | 4.4 | 2.4 | 2.7 |
| 0.4 | 1.8 | 4.0 | 4.4 | 2.4 | 2.9 |
| 0.6 | 1.8 | 4.0 | 4.7 | 2.5 | 3.1 |
| 0.9 | 1.8 | 4.1 | 4.8 | 2.6 | 3.7 |
| 1.3 | 2.1 | 4.1 | 5.8 | 2.9 | 3.9 |
| 1.7 | 2.1 | 4.2 | 7.0 | 3.1 | 6.0 |
| 2.4 | 2.7 | 5.2 | 7.0 | 4.2 | 6.8 |
| 2.7 | 4.9 | 8.9 | 9.6 | 4.9 | 6.8 |
| Average = .8 | Average = 1.7 | Average = 3.3 | Average = 4.2 | Average = 2.2 | Average = 2.9 |

$T_1$ = the first test, given at age 11–13
$T_2$ = the second test, given at age 20–23
N.S. = raw score too low to find a grade equivalent in the PIAT manual

and versatile tool to use, not only functionally in the workplace and living environment, but in community recreation as well. For them, continued developmental/remedial academic instruction, in combination with functional literacy requirements of a work or recreational setting, might be ideal.

# SPECIAL OLYMPICS

We cannot leave this chapter with its emphasis on recreation and leisure without discussing the Special Olympics (S.O.) program in the lives of EDGE children and their families.

For several years now the S.O. program has received "negative press" from some advocates of the full-inclusion movement. Although we would not want a self-contained version of S.O. to be the only outlet through which people with Down syndrome could enjoy competition, neither do we wish to see it eliminated. It has been one of the "mountaintop" experiences for athletes with Down syndrome in the EDGE project. Many of the mini-album pages throughout this book attest to that. Ideally we would like to see a broad array of recreational and sports programs for people who have Down syndrome or other disabilities, ranging from self-contained, such as traditional S.O., to fully integrated programming, such as the adventure programs of Wilderness Inquiry. People with Down syndrome then could have both options available to them and choose to participate in both if they wish. The importance of freedom of choice is illustrated in the findings of a recent study.[6] In the study, 21 young adults with Down syndrome watched a videotape showing nondisabled young adults or young adults with Down syndrome participating in recreational bowling. Of the 21 viewers, 15 said that they would rather bowl with companions who also had Down syndrome.

An example of a young adult who participates in both a self-contained and an integrated recreation program is Rick, an EDGE participant. Rick belongs to a regular community health club that emphasizes body building. He is the only young adult in the club who has Down syndrome. Rick never has taken first place in open competition with nondisabled peers of his age, but he has taken third place in open competition. That's an incredible accomplishment, one that is not only a credit to him and to his family but also should help professionals who have limited expectations of people with Down syndrome raise their sights. Rick also participates in a self-contained S.O. program as a weight lifter, where he has won several medals.

Rick's participation in a regular health club body-building program would appear to challenge the merit of a cooperative learning strategy for those with Down syndrome. Rick, after all, is competing with nondisabled peers, and not in the usual cooperative or individualistic framework. As stated earlier, cooperative, competitive, and individualistic strategies are all legitimate as long as they fit the person's and his or her peers' needs. Rick is one of a relatively few individuals with Down syndrome who has developed his body well enough to compete head-to-head with nondisabled peers. Moreover, his nondisabled peers support his athletic development because the coach has created a cooperative atmosphere within the club, an example of how cooperation can be built into competition.

## $\mathcal{N}$ONTRADITIONAL COMMUNITY RECREATION/LEISURE OUTLETS

When young adults leave school altogether, finding satisfying recreational and leisure outlets in the community often becomes more difficult. The movie theater still exists as it did during the school years, but organized, ongoing activities, many of which are connected in some way with school, tend to diminish rapidly after graduation. Sometimes this void actually becomes the impetus for parents to find a place for the person with Down syndrome to live with other peers who have disabilities. A group home, among other possibilities, represents a built-in group of companions as well as an out-of-home living environment. More will be said about this in the next chapter.

Here again is where a focus group can be extremely helpful in facilitating the participation of a young adult who has Down syndrome in recreation and leisure programs, depending on the individual's interests. Some ideas from EDGE parents and the recreation/leisure literature are as follows:

1. The neighborhood YMCA or Jewish Community Center may have integrated or segregated swimming, aerobics, ballet, or other young adult programs.
2. The local church or synagogue may have a social club, again integrated or segregated, combining socialization opportunities and religious education.
3. Park and recreation programs may offer integrated activities that accommodate young adults with disabilities. We know of an integrated bocce league for young adults that is doing quite well.
4. Of course, finding a young adult who has Down syndrome and interests similar to those of your young adult son or daughter with Down syndrome opens up dozens of opportunities to go for a walk, buy a hamburger at the local fast-food restaurant, attend a movie, go fishing, and do other things that friends enjoy together.

# OTES

1. J. Putnam, S. Pueschel, and J. Gorder-Holman, "Community Participation of Youths and Adults with Down Syndrome" (pp. 77–92), in S. M. Pueschel (ed.), *The Young Person with Down Syndrome: Transition from Adolescence to Adulthood* (Baltimore: Paul H. Brookes, 1988).
2. M. Hayden, K. C. Lakin, B. Hill, R. Bruininks, and J. Copher, "Social and Leisure Integration of People with Mental Retardation in Foster Homes and Small Group Homes," *Education and Training in Mental Retardation* 27 (1992): 187–199; and S. Schleien and J. Werder, "Perceived Responsibilities of Special Recreation Services in Minnesota," *Therapeutic Recreation Journal* 19 (1985): 51–62.
3. J. Rynders and S. Schleien, *Together Successfully: Creating Recreational and Educational Programs That Integrate People With and Without Disabilities* (Arlington, TX: Association for Retarded Citizens of the United States, 1991).
4. Rynders and Schleien.
5. S. Schleien, "Adapting Leisure Skills" (pp. 59–88), in P. Wehman and S. Schleien, *Leisure Programs for Handicapped Persons: Adaptations, Techniques, and Curriculum* (Austin, TX: Pro-Ed, 1981).
6. R. Neumayer, R. Smith, and H. Lundgren, "Leisure Related Peer Preference Choices of Individuals with Down Syndrome," *Mental Retardation* 31 (1993): 396–402.

---

*Shannon Matson* is the coordinator of volunteers for the residence and vocational services programs at Courage Center Rehabilitation facility in Golden Valley, Minnesota. She is also a graduate student in the master's of special education/early intervention program at the University of Minnesota. Shannon was responsible for administering the Peabody Individual Achievement Test (PIAT) to the 15 EDGE young adults, as well as conducting interviews focusing on their wants, needs, and dreams for the future.

---

*Stuart Schleien*, Ph.D., CTRS, is the division head of recreation, park, and leisure studies at the University of Minnesota and is an adjunct professor in the special education program. He designs and implements recreation, sport, and friendship programs for children and adults with disabilities. Dr. Schleien has published extensively on these topics, presented his research in the United States, Canada, Israel, England, Sweden, and Australia, and was recognized for his efforts by the Minnesota Recreation and Park Association and by the Minnesota Association for Retarded Citizens.

# *O*PAT FAMILY

Dad: Harold
Mom: Joan
Brother: Mike
Brother: Vince
Brother: Joe
Sister: Ann
Brother with Down
  syndrome: Tom

One and one-half years old,
surrounded by family.

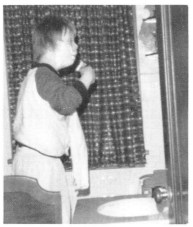

A "little
shaver"—age 5.

In the swim of things.

## ⓟ**PAT FAMILY** (continued)

Rap master!

A terrific weight lifter.

Favorite activity.

Life is great!

# ~9~

# ONE HAND ON THE SCHOOL DOOR, ONE ON THE DOOR TO WORK AND INDEPENDENT LIVING

Alan Fletcher

*N*owadays, nearly all individuals with Down syndrome can be placed successfully within the workforce at least part-time. The range of employment possibilities is as broad as the range of abilities and individual differences across the population of people with Down syndrome. Considering that the period of formal schooling for an individual with mental retardation often ends at around age 22 and that the working years and independent living years may extend to age 60 or more, the 19-plus years of education are relatively brief compared to the 40-plus years of employment. For this reason, opportunities pertaining to preparation for the world of work and independent living must be maximized during the school years.

## ℰDGE PARENT SURVEY

To collectively examine the vocational and independent living preparation of the EDGE participants, a survey was conducted among their parents. Because the EDGE families were distributed throughout a large geographic region, many different school districts were involved in the educational process for the EDGE children. Thus, a variety of approaches were used for vocational preparation. The survey was helpful in identifying training differences, as well as certain recurring themes regarding practices that were the most successful.

The EDGE young adults show a considerable amount of diversity in their patterns of vocational interests as well as responsiveness to various educational strategies dealing with occupational preparation. At the time of this writing, the EDGE young adults were between the ages of 21 and 24. The job titles they held included: clerical worker, stockroom person, warehouse person, bus person, dishwasher, kitchen helper, dining room attendant, assembly worker, packaging person, hotel laundry worker, hotel housekeeper, and janitor. Data from the survey will be incorporated throughout this chapter.

# 𝒯HE LAW ENABLING VOCATIONAL PREPARATION AND COMMUNITY TRANSITION _____

In 1983 the federal government, specifically the U.S. Department of Education, Office of Special and Rehabilitative Services, conducted a campaign to emphasize the importance of transition from school to work as a priority for special education programs throughout the country.

In 1990 the U.S. Congress enacted Public Law 101–476, the Individuals with Disabilities Education Act (IDEA). Because of its significance to this chapter, the following quotes are taken directly from this act:

> *Transition services* means "a coordinated set of activities for a student, designed within an outcome-oriented process, which promotes movement from school to post-school activities including post-secondary education, vocational training, integrated employment (including supported employment), continuing and adult education, adult services, independent living, or community participation."

The *coordinated set of activities* "shall be based upon the individual students' needs, taking into account student preferences and interests, and shall include instruction, community experiences, the development of employment and other post-school adult living objectives, and, when appropriate, acquisition of daily living skills and functional vocational evaluation."

*Individual Education Plans (IEPs)* must now include "a statement of the needed transition services for students beginning no later than age 16 and annually thereafter (and when determined appropriate for the individual beginning at age 14 or younger), including, when appropriate, a statement of the interagency responsibilities or linkages (or both) before the student leaves the school setting."[1]

The law requires that education of students with disabilities be conducted in the least restrictive environment, meaning that: "Removal from the regular classroom occurs only when the nature and severity of the disability is such that education in the regular classroom with the use of supplemental aides and services cannot be achieved satisfactorily."[2] A number of variables, however, must be considered when determining the degree to which a child with Down syndrome should receive vocational preparation services with other disabled students exclusively versus being included in a regular educational/training setting with nondisabled peers.

The benefits of inclusion at the junior high and senior high levels can be substantial relative to social development, such as learning appropriate interaction behaviors, participating in after-school activities with neighbors, and so on. However, limited supportive opportunities and resources, including fiscal resources, within the world of education can limit the capability of a regular education teacher to cater sufficiently to the special educational needs of some students with Down syndrome. This is true particularly during the secondary schooling years.

Removing students with similar levels of disability from the general education class and teaching them in separate classes can sometimes produce a number of important benefits. The special education staff become experts in educating students with similar traits and behavioral needs. Experienced special education teachers and paraprofessionals acquire skills over time that can result in greater successes for some learners, not only from the standpoint of content mastery but also in developing higher self-esteem and happiness with school. Ideally, programming needs to be balanced between an appropriate amount of inclusion time as well as segregated time, provided in accordance with individual student needs and characteristics. A key element in achieving this balance is assessment.

# ASSESSMENT

An ongoing activity throughout the student's educational career, assessment is *the measurement of a child's strengths and weaknesses as well as progress made in specific curricula offered during each successive phase of the child's education.* The term "functional vocational evaluation" in the Individuals with Disabilities Education Act sends a signal that lifetime work activity and occupational direction planning are important in fulfilling the intent of functional vocational evaluation. The comprehensiveness of evaluation is important. Each student with Down syndrome has unique interests, abilities, and undeveloped potential for development in a variety of occupational fields (see the Appendix for a sampling of assessment instruments).

Various paper-and-pencil tests are available for assessing interests and aptitudes. These may be administered by school counselors and special education staff or by qualified vocational evaluators in an evaluation center, following referral by the special education case manager.

A formal evaluation center also may administer *work samples*, mockups of specific tasks associated with various occupations. As part of a comprehensive vocational evaluation, professional evaluators observe and time the performance of the sampled work tasks, write up their findings, and make recommendations. Throughout the process the student's reactions to the type of work being sampled are noted. An extensive amount of interview time is included during and following each of the work samples.

Comprehensive occupational assessment also may include training tryouts, a brief period of participation in a training environment for a specific occupation. This setting provides an opportunity to observe a student's ability to learn the subject matter as well as sample the physical elements of the occupation in the training setting. Of course, assessment also takes place as the student participates in brief career exploration placements in jobs within the community, which includes ongoing dialogue between case managers and work supervisors regarding the student's performance. If it is functional, vocational evaluation should provide direction for the student study team (including the student), which helps to lay out a course of study leading to the student's graduation and placement in an appropriate work setting suited to his or her interests, abilities, and occupation preference.

# *O*CCUPATIONAL SELECTION AND TRAINING _____

Subtle influences affect the path a student follows to eventual occupational placement. For instance, seeds of interest in specific careers may be sown in a child at a young age as he or she observes adults within the family doing various kinds of work. In this regard, a child with Down syndrome is not unlike other children.

During the process of identifying an occupational preference, a child moves through various stages. The preference stated at one age might not be the preference identified at a later age. As the student is exposed to more occupations as an observer and also as a participant through guided introduction by family and school staff, occupational preference most likely will change. Thus, the child is exposed to a multitude of occupational experi-

ences during the school years. We should acknowledge preferences and allow individuals with severe handicaps to make choices "as an expression of personal autonomy and dignity."[3]

When attempting to identify a specific occupational field for more in-depth training and preparation, a variety of criteria should be considered. In the form of questions, these include:

1. What factors are most important for the parents?
2. What factors are most important to the child or young adult with a disability?
3. What factors are most important to the school staff and public agencies that will be assisting the young person with specific education and training as well as support on the job?
4. What specific jobs will be available to the graduate in his or her local community?
5. To what extent are communication skills crucial for success in specific occupations?
6. What level of pleasure does the child or young adult derive while participating within specific occupationally related subject areas?

Because working conditions vary widely among occupations, the individual's personality characteristics and tolerance for various types of job-related tasks and events have to be taken into consideration. The degree to which social interaction with co-workers and with the public is required for success on the job is an important factor for parents and school personnel to consider. The EDGE individuals have a wide range of personality characteristics. Some are gregarious and outspoken, and others are shy and withdrawn. The vocational preparation program and job placement eventually should reflect these personality types.

Earnings potential may or may not be a significant variable depending on other sources of income from the public sector or family. Generally, the public support financial formulas reduce fiscal support in direct proportion to gross earnings of the young adult with Down syndrome. When Amy (my daughter and one of the EDGE participants) was in school and working part-time, her monthly Supplemental Security Income (SSI) payment was $420. After she graduated and began working 30 hours per week at a rate of $4.25 per hour, her monthly SSI payment dropped to $236. This being the case, pursuing a job solely because it has a higher wage scale is not as appropriate as pursuing a job that has characteristics suited to the employee's abilities and interests.

This concept also pertains to the number of hours the individual works per week. At the time of this writing, nearly all of the EDGE participants were out of school, and the average number of hours employed per week was about 25. With regard to wage rate, minimum-wage jobs often are referred to disrespectfully, as though people employed in these jobs are second-class citizens. This, of course, does a disservice to all minimum-wage employees, including individuals with Down syndrome, who often do well in these jobs and derive strong satisfaction from them, which leads to high self-esteem. They take pride in their work and show long-term stability in certain minimum-wage jobs. A successfully functioning society needs good workers in *all* job classifications.

Convenience in getting to a job location ultimately may become a primary factor in determining occupational choice. Obviously, young people with Down syndrome do not have as many job opportunities as nondisabled people. Yet, it is encouraging to see the vast number of job opportunities available today compared to just a few years ago. Many of these are linked to improved public and private transportation services for people with disabilities.

Another occupational attribute that has to be considered carefully pertains to environmental concerns. Does the work environment contain chemicals to which the employee may have allergic reactions or become physically uncomfortable? Is cigarette smoke likely to be a problem? Would other environmental discomforts such as loud noises or wide temperature variations, be incompatible with a specific employee's needs and aptitudes?

Supervisor pressure and tolerance may become significant variables, too, depending upon the employee's responsiveness to various styles of supervision. This information is readily accessible as the child progresses through school and reacts to various teacher styles and personalities.

Endurance and stamina should be taken into consideration. Some jobs require long periods of demanding physical work between breaks. On the other hand, some individuals have enough physical energy to sustain longer periods of work and actually may need more strenuous activity to release tension and stress.

## CAREER AWARENESS AND EXPLORATION

During the career awareness phase of vocational preparation, the student is introduced to the concept of career differences. Career awareness training begins in the elementary years and progresses through junior high school. By late junior high school or early senior high school, the student should be exposed to a variety of career fields more concretely through various kinds of exploratory experiences. These might include assisting the school custo-

dian with basic cleaning tasks, helping in the school office with basic clerical tasks, or assisting in the school's food service area. These types of unpaid work experiences expose the student to various jobs and provide preliminary data for the school staff to use in helping the child make vocational preparation choices.

## CLASSROOM/LABORATORY VOCATIONAL TRAINING

Because of the high cost of secondary vocational education, school districts tend to be limited in the number of vocational training programs they offer. Now school districts frequently cooperate with each other to provide more vocational program choices to their students. Some vocational training also may take place on a smaller scale within special education programs. Although these programs may not have a great variety of training equipment, instruction may cover certain vocational and occupational relations skills. More advanced secondary-level vocational programs have a full array of equipment appropriate for specific occupational fields. This is where hands-on skills training takes place.

To maximize success for students with Down syndrome, the learning environment should have a number of supports in place. Ideally, the curriculum should be individualized and self-paced so the student is not penalized if he or she does not keep up with classmates. When the curriculum is not individualized, regular vocational training programs that accept students with disabilities may accommodate slower learning rates simply by not requiring the same level of mastery for specific tasks or by requiring fewer tasks to be mastered within a given grading period.

Another program adaptation that can make a significant difference in determining success for a youth with Down syndrome in mainstream vocational education is assistance from additional qualified school personnel in the classroom to reduce the teacher-to-student ratio, supporting students with disabilities in specific ways. In some school systems this individual is called a *supplemental resource instructor*, a person licensed in special education as well as vocational education. In other cases the individual might be a paraprofessional with special training to help specific students master vocational skills. This individual can provide behavioral coaching along with needed repetition of instruction or interpretation of specific learning assignments. This model will carry over to a job situation in which a work trainer or job coach will assist the trainee in acquiring specific job skills.

EDGE youth participated in a wide range of vocational training options while in high school. These included food preparation and serving, horticulture, building cleaning and care, woodworking, small engines, metal work, home economics, laundry, and typing.

Another type of related training, which takes place in a laboratory, is called *work adjustment training*. This training generally consists of an assembly line for manufactured product components that an industry or business may subcontract to the school district for assembly work. The purpose of this setting is to provide students with a closely supervised work experience, to observe and possibly modify behaviors, and to provide a productive training environment by strengthening co-worker and supervisor relationships. If the school receives income from a business for the subcontract work, the work adjustment center may pay the students a wage on the basis of the number of pieces assembled.

## WORK EXPERIENCE TRAINING IN THE COMMUNITY

Work experience vocational training often is called *on-the-job training*, or OJT. In this school-sponsored program a certified work experience coordinator works in the community to develop job stations with local employers. Students receive vocational skills training while on the job, under the super-

vision of a regular supervisor who is not employed by the school district. In this situation the student usually is paid, and the employer receives a tax benefit from the federal government in exchange for the employer's willingness to assist with the training. A training agreement is signed by the employer, the school district staff, and the student. Accompanying the on-the-job training is an occupational relations class in the school that teaches appropriate worker behavior such as how to interact with a supervisor and co-workers.

The work experience program contains a parallel program for students with disabilities. In this case, the certified work experience coordinator has had additional coursework pertaining to students with disabilities and labor laws pertaining to sub-minimum wage and other unique laws affecting employment of individuals with disabilities.

A number of the EDGE students participated in community-based work experience programs while in high school. Every EDGE parent indicated that the on-the-job training experience seemed to be more successful than classroom/laboratory vocational skills training.

Although children with Down syndrome usually are developmentally delayed, many are capable of mastering specific job skills necessary for competitive employment. If these skills can be learned while in a school-sponsored, community-based, work experience vocational training program, the transition to post-school employment is more immediate and successful. That continuous vocational training is needed before high school graduation and the follow-through support is necessary while on the actual job is evident in the findings of several studies. Half of the individuals with mild handicaps[4] and more than three-fourths of former students with severe disabilities[5] are unemployed one year after leaving school.

## SUPPORTED EMPLOYMENT

In supported employment a school district employee works with the student in the private sector employment setting. The employee, usually called a "job coach" or "work trainer," works closely with the student with disabilities in a role similar to that of an assistant to the job supervisor. Depending on the need, the job coach might be with the student at all times or only occasionally. Typically the job coach is present more of the time at the beginning of the student's work placement and then tapers off the direct contact as the student learns more job skills. When several students with disabilities are placed at the same job site with one job coach, it is called an *enclave*. In some enclaves individuals work as a team in the same area; in other enclaves individuals work in different locations within the company. Depending upon the young adult's skill level on the job as a result of previous training, experience, cognitive ability, and the like, the level of support from school staff or employer supervisory staff can be reduced to weekly or semiweekly contacts from support staff.

Another form of supported employment involves enhancement of natural supports. *Natural supports* are supervisors and co-workers who modify their normal behavior as appropriate to help employees with disabilities to become more successful on the job. In this situation the job coach from the school district or agency provides information and training to the supervisor and co-workers rather than to the employee with a disability. This model is more successful when the business has characteristics that are receptive to natural supports in addition to a forward-looking policy pertaining to hiring individuals with disabilities.

## SUB-MINIMUM WAGE

Although, the U.S. government establishes a minimum wage for most occupations, it has acknowledged that, for some individuals with disabilities, employment is not possible because of low productivity, unless wages are set lower than the minimum. Thus, the U.S. Department of Labor has established a system to allow qualifying individuals to be paid a sub-minimum wage. The process an employer must follow to qualify for payment of sub-minimum wages to certain employees is quite detailed and involves extensive documentation relative to productivity per unit of time. The person conducting the assessment must identify productivity rates for average workers so the specific rate of production for workers with disabilities can be established in comparison to a norm. Sub-minimum wage assessments and documentation often are done by qualified work experience coordinators from the school system.

This system allows an employer to support community needs with certain sub-minimum wage positions without concern for cost-effectiveness. The worker benefits as a result of having access to a community-based training station that provides an opportunity to work alongside nondisabled peers.

## TRANSITION PLANNING FOR THE POSTSCHOOL PERIOD

Although school system staffs have the primary responsibility for providing educational services to individuals with a disability to age 22, community agency representatives can be helpful by engaging in the post-school planning process beginning as early as age 14. The primary benefit at this stage is that the youth's name can be placed on waiting lists for subsequent services when the young adult exits the school system at age 22 or sooner. During times of limited public fiscal resources, waiting lists are a means by which decisions will be made relative to which individuals of comparable disability level will receive specific services next. Generally, individuals with greater disability receive public fiscal benefits sooner than those with less disability; however, this is relative to a number of variables and varies from county to county and from state to state. The bottom line is that placing the youth's name on community agency waiting lists at around age 14 can make a tremendous difference in the timeliness of services provided during the transition period following secondary schooling 8 years later.

In many cases the community agency with primary responsibility for case management of individuals with disabilities following public schooling (age 22) is the human services department or public social service agency of the county of residence. Following notification by the school district and application by the parents, the county assigns a social worker as case manager to work with the school system and plan for the individual's eventual placement in the community. Although the school system special education case manager may seem to be the primary system person responsible for coordinating the planning for the young person with Down syndrome, the role of the county social worker should not be underestimated. Ideally, the county social worker is just as involved in the long-term planning as the school district case manager is.

Another agency representative typically involved in the planning process pertaining to the student's life after secondary school is the Division of Rehabilitation Services (DRS) counselor. The DRS is a subset of the Federal Department of Labor, and its purpose is to provide assistance in placing individuals with disabilities in long-term employment settings. To this end, the agency provides support services to augment public education while the child is under age 22 and provides tuition and support services to young adults after age 21, as well as support services for employers during the early period of employment. An example is covering the cost of a job coach in an employment setting for up to 18 months to assist with transition and successful employment.

Because of the Individuals with Disabilities Education Act (IDEA), the local education agency (school district) has primary responsibility for overseeing the collaborative effort in providing services to persons with disabilities through age 22. The free public secondary education continues through the school year in which the young adult reaches the age of 22. Following age 22, the responsibility for agency support shifts to the local county for residential and mental health support services and to the Division of Rehabilitation Services for transitional employment services.

After the young adult has made the transition to a permanent employment situation successfully, perhaps taking as long as 18 months with the help of the Division of Rehabilitation Services, DRS direct services are withdrawn. If the individual with disabilities subsequently is discharged from employment and needs more training or support to become reemployable, the Division of Rehabilitation Services enters the picture again, providing support for training and job placement. This pattern of DRS support could continue throughout the individual's adult life.

# INDEPENDENT LIVING

Preparation for independent living begins during the school years through a life-skills curriculum pertaining to topics such as self-advocacy, personal grooming, laundry skills, personal food preparation, money management, social skills, and the like. Also during the school years the county social worker will have placed the youth's name on the desired waiting lists so county, state, or federal fiscal support will be available for a living situation out of the parental home when this placement becomes available during or following completion of the school experience.

Potential living arrangements include foster home placement, group home placement, and semi-independent living situations such as apartment living with a roommate plus agency-person support in the apartment a given number of hours per day or week to facilitate independence. Access to these services often relates to the local county's fiscal condition and funding pattern, augmented with state and federal funds for these purposes. Thus, communities vary widely in the extent to which a young adult with Down syndrome can be placed in an independent living situation outside of the home soon after secondary school graduation. Again, the earlier the agency places the youth's name on desired waiting lists, the better. The following alternative living situations, along with their advantages and disadvantages, are discussed as a stimulus for early planning.

## PARENTAL HOME

The obvious benefit of the young adult with Down syndrome's remaining in the home is that parents can ensure quality of the environment by promoting good eating, sleeping, and personal grooming habits. Parents also can oversee social relationships and daily activities of the young adult quite closely. Therefore, choices that meet family standards can be maintained more easily.

Another benefit of remaining in the home is that it maximizes companionship within the natural family. The parents and young adult may feel very close and derive daily pleasure from satisfying each other's needs through close family ties. Obviously, this is more meaningful in situations where the relationship is strong.

A disadvantage of remaining in the parental home is that the individual may have fewer opportunities for interacting with peers of comparable age and ability level during nonwork hours. Although this may not be viewed as a serious detriment, it is not the societal norm. Normally young adults leave home and spend free time with other individuals of comparable age and ability level during their nonworking hours.

Another disadvantage for the young adult in remaining at home is that, over time, he or she may become less able to adapt to change. Therefore, when the need for placement away from the parents arises as a result of old age, illness, or death, adjustment to the placement could be much more difficult for the individual with Down syndrome.

In the young adult years of the early 20s, the home-living arrangement may be mutually beneficial. Nevertheless, plans for placement outside of the home should be underway to avoid subsequent regret as the inevitable need for placement outside the parental home approaches.

## ADULT FOSTER CARE

In some cases the natural parents need a respite, or other factors within the parental home may make placement in a foster home appropriate. Similar to the parental home, a foster home provides supervision 24 hours a day and the potential for much control over social activities, friendships, and good eating, sleeping, and grooming habits. Even though social activities and friendships can be sought in the community, in-home friendships (in this case, foster home friendships) can facilitate more complete social development because they provide opportunities for conversational and social interaction throughout the week rather than only periodically through community contacts. The foster home also can be viewed as a stepping stone, a bridge from the parental home to a subsequent living arrangement with more independence and autonomy.

A possible disadvantage is that foster home placement may not bring together individuals of a suitable age and ability match. This would negate many of the benefits described.

## INTERMEDIATE CARE FACILITY/MENTAL RETARDATION (ICF/MR)—GROUP HOME

A group home is a licensed residential facility that provides 24-hour care and supervision. The number of residents may be as few as four or as many as six to eight. Benefits of this type of setting include having a peer group of residents of comparable age and ability level. Furthermore, there are planned social activities and an individual program for furthering the development of each resident. Professionally qualified staff interacts with the residents to implement developmental goals. As a licensed facility, outside regulators ensure that facility standards are maintained to established levels of cleanliness, safety, medical care provisions, and the like.

In terms of disadvantages, compromises may be necessary in some situations because of the specific mix of residents. A family might not wish to place the child with Down syndrome in a home with individuals whose disabilities and behaviors seem to be incompatible with their own young adult's needs. The owner/operator of the group home has a challenge in trying to arrange for an ideal mix of residents, because of limitations in funding sources and the variations in disabilities and behavioral characteristics of individuals awaiting placement.

Residents actually can make positive gains by associating with individuals who have various kinds and ranges of disability. Often the individual with Down syndrome has become accustomed to a supportive family that tolerates behaviors that people in other social and residential settings may not tolerate. A group of individuals who are not similar to each other may generate overall development in each other.

## SEMI-INDEPENDENT LIVING

Semi-independent living works best for individuals who do not require 24-hour care or a lot of supervision. Total independence is not expected, because of specific individual needs such as a need to have help to manage money, make appropriate interpersonal safety judgments, plan and prepare nutritionally balanced meals, monitor personal medical needs, and maintain personal hygiene. Semi-independent living situations include apartment living or foster home placement involving a certain number of hours per week of support from agency staff. This support might consist of meal preparation, money management, and other assistance.

A great deal of independence is required in a semi-independent living situation. This may uncover its greatest potential disadvantage—creating vulnerability. For this reason it is not the most popular option for parents of individuals who have Down syndrome.

## OTHER FORMS OF GOVERNMENT SUPPORT FOR PROMOTING INDEPENDENT LIVING

In addition to the agency supports just mentioned, many other types of support programs and services are available from governmental agencies. Supplemental Security Income (SSI) from the Social Security Administration is made available to individuals with disabilities. When the child is below age 18, the monthly dollar amount relates to family income. When the child reaches age 18, he or she is considered an adult and, therefore, the amount is based upon the person's individual earnings rather than family income, even if the child is living at home. As the young adult earns more money in a community job placement, the amount of SSI is reduced. Depending upon several variables associated with the young adult's work history, eventually Supplemental Security Income may be replaced with Social Security Disability Income (SSDI). SSI is considered a public assistance program; SSDI is considered an earned benefit. In Amy's case she began receiving SSDI at age 22 after having worked continuously in part-time jobs as a part of her schooling beginning at age 15. Throughout this time she was making payroll-deducted payments into the Social Security system. The young adult with Down syndrome probably will qualify also for medical assistance, which in turn provides funding for medical expenses related to a wide range of needs for services, including a personal care attendant. The county social worker plays a significant role in assisting the family with accessing needs and arranging for public fiscal supports.

Home- and community-based *waivered services* are another form of federal support (paid through Medical Assistance) for which an individual with Down syndrome generally qualifies. Waivered service, for example, may provide funding for modifying a house to accommodate a specific physical disability. It also provides for necessary home health care, personal care attendant (PCA) services, day programming, and residential programming to teach independent living skills. Day programming following the secondary school experience offers meaningful activities out of the home 5 days a week. It includes things such as independent living skills training, transportation to and from work, social activities, and some kind of work training or habilitation in a work activity center. Day programming encompasses assessment services and employer involvement similar to that provided by the Division of Rehabilitation Services. Again, the fiscal limitations of funding sources result in long waiting lists and not necessarily adequate monies to provide waivered services to all individuals at the time of need.

Another form of financial support in Minnesota, called the Family Subsidy Program, provides assistance to families to enable them to care for their children with disabilities in the home to age 22. The state pays eligible families a monthly allowance for certain home care costs including respite care, transportation, and special diets. Eligibility is based on the family's ability to provide care in the home and is not affected by family income level.

What kind of living arrangement did EDGE parents see for their son or daughter in the future? All believe their young adult child will be ready and able to live outside of the parental home in the future. All of them also believe this move will be good for promoting their child's independence. (Three already have moved out, one into a foster home–like setting and two into a bona fide foster home.)

Without exception, the twelve parents whose children have not yet moved out of the parental home are in no hurry to have them leave. Their statements reflect a loving "separation anxiety." They enjoy their children very much and want to make certain that their adult children move into a place where they will have friends and still have privacy (some believe their child will need to have a room of his or her own; others believe that one or more roommates will be desirable). All believe that some amount of supervision and support from an employee hired for this purpose will be essential, though the amount of help they think will be needed varies a great deal. Parents of daughters are concerned not only about supervision and support but also about their daughters' personal *security.* Safety from rape and other forms of physical harm is an absolute priority.

# AMY'S STORY

At the time of this writing, my daughter Amy is 22 years old, works 30 hours a week (5 hours per day for 6 days) as a dining room attendant at Burger King and is looking forward (with some anxiety) to moving into an adult foster care facility in about 2 months. From most perspectives she is viewed as a success story, having benefited from many educational and supportive opportunities throughout her life.

Amy was fortunate to have enjoyed stability during her lifetime, living with her natural parents the entire 22 years, living in the same home for most of her life, and attending educational programs within the same school district until age 21. Furthermore she had supportive siblings, parents, grandparents, neighbors, fellow church members, and educational and community professional staff. We believe that, because she felt loved and supported throughout the educational years, she developed positive self-esteem and showed a good deal of self-confidence.

Amy was given an opportunity to participate in the EDGE early infant stimulation project between ages 3 months and 5 years. By the time she started public school at age 5, she was focused for learning and functioned well with adult educational providers on a one-to-one basis.

Throughout her public school experience she was in an inclusive environment, although she was the first child with Down syndrome that all of her regular education teachers had in the mainstream. For the most part, she, the teachers, and nondisabled classmates all benefited from this experience. At times, though, educational methodology necessary for her step-by-step success was created daily by the special education professional and paraprofessional staff because her teachers did not have experience dealing with children with Down syndrome. Notwithstanding general success, we believe in retrospect that certain undesirable behaviors were tolerated because of a very strong focus on academic learning. Amy was quite successful at academic learning, yet certain behaviors such as stubbornness and verbal confrontation have persisted and continue to be issues in her present employment setting.

During the elementary years, Amy was accepted socially by nondisabled classmates and neighbors and was invited to birthday parties and overnights along with her sister, Holly, 2 years younger but in the same grade. Most of Amy's playmates at that age did not realize she had disabilities to the extent of being significantly different from other children they associated with. In sixth grade this situation changed abruptly as her peer group realized her differences in the midst of preadolescent anxieties associated with peer acceptance and anticipation of becoming teenagers with more social pressures and competition. From that point on, Amy focused more of her attention on relationships with adults than peers.

During junior high and high school she had a "home base" in the school in the form of a special education resource room within which she received specialized instruction from trained special educators to augment her mainstream classes. She spent about half of the time in regular education classes and the other half in special education classes. Beginning as early as the summer following ninth grade and continuing through age 21, Amy participated in community-based, educationally sponsored, work experience programs. She was a printer's helper, janitor's helper, and attendance slip runner within the educational setting. She spent three years as a dietary assistant, cleaning pots and pans in a large nursing home kitchen. She earned a competitive wage of $5.65 per hour at a time when the minimum wage was $4.00 per hour. During her senior year in high school, she worked 2 hours per day as a dining room attendant at Burger King and 3 hours a day as a dietary assistant at the nursing home in addition to a part-time school program.

With Mom and Dad both leaving for work before she left in the morning, Amy got herself off to school with her backpack, which contained two uniforms and a lunch she made herself. During her 12-hour day away from home, she changed uniforms twice in addition to riding a bus or van eight times during the day, which required several transfers. These details illustrate her stamina and interest in successful employment, as well as a lifelong interest in the educational environment.

As she made the transition to her final year of education at the local intermediate school district, she had the good fortune of participating in a summer apartment living program for 5 weeks. During this time she lived with a group of peers with similar ability levels without daily access to family and neighborhood friends. She visited home only one time (for her birthday party) during the 5-week period. While in the program she worked at the nursing home during the day. The group prepared meals, did laundry, and participated in community social experiences during off hours. This was a valuable experience for Amy and contributed significantly to her understanding of what independent living is all about. As she anticipates moving away from home during the next few months, she remembers the summer apartment living experience that took place 2 years ago.

A major factor contributing to Amy's social development was her participation in competitive athletics. She enjoys competition and always has been physically fit. In elementary school she participated on a mainstream girl's basketball team for 2 years, as well as community soccer and T-ball teams. The reason Amy did not participate in mainstream community athletic competition after elementary school was that the rules assigned athletes to teams on the basis of age. Amy always was short in stature and older than her classmates. She would have enjoyed continuing to play on teams relative to her ability and size, but the rules would not allow this.

During her last 4 years of school, she was a cheerleader for the adaptive athletics sports league for 2 years and an athlete for 2 years, participating in soccer, floor hockey, and softball. During the first year after school, the team invited her back to be an assistant coach. These experiences enhanced her social skills and self-confidence. She was fortunate to have access to these opportunities.

Amy's competitive spirit also flourished during participation in Special Olympics bowling and swimming for a number of years. Although some people within special education circles criticize Special Olympics as inappropriate inasmuch as it is a segregated activity, from Amy's perspective and our perspective as parents, the benefits far outweigh any loss of inclusion.* Most of the EDGE children participated in Special Olympics, and some achieved award-winning status in international competition.

Amy also was fortunate to participate in several social clubs for young people with disabilities from the time she was 14 years old. Although these organized clubs and activities were not readily available 10 years ago, they are much more common today and offer an opportunity for people like Amy to experiment with various behaviors that may or may not be acceptable in a norm-referenced social situation. Observing other people's behaviors in a recreational setting also allows the person to sort out and discuss probable outcomes resulting from certain behaviors. These social occasions also provide the atmosphere in which boy-girl relationships may develop, sometimes leading to dating opportunities. Amy has had attention from several young men over the years (although for the time being she still is hoping to marry a movie star).

One of the most significant curriculum units to which Amy was exposed during her entire school career was a unit called "Body Basics." Although she participated in this curriculum more than 2 years ago, she still refers to it daily while analyzing her own behavior in the context of social situations and the daily stresses of incomplete and misunderstood communication. She can readily recite the five body basics:[7]

---

* Recognizing the need for integrated as well as segregated participation options, the Special Olympics program is developing an increasing number of integrated options called Unified Sports programs.

1. Face the person.
2. Make eye contact.
3. Use the right voice tone.
4. Have the right facial expression.
5. Keep the right body posture.

In addition to the work experience Amy had while in school, she participated in classroom vocational skills training in the areas of industrial arts, printing, typing, and food service preparation. She has retained a number of the skills she learned during these programs, although she is not using them presently in her work setting. She does use a computer daily for correspondence and graphics, which are major pastimes. She communicates emotional responses to people she interacts with by typing her feelings quite effectively.

Amy's transition to independent living began 5 years ago, when her social worker placed her name on the county waiting list for a waiver to provide funding for a residential facility outside of the home. At this point her name has not come to the top of the list, so the present social worker has been working diligently to come up with alternative funding arrangements to facilitate Amy's transition to a living situation that includes other individuals of her age and level of ability. She is fortunate to have a creative social worker with a great deal of experience, resulting in foster home placement with two other female residents who are Amy's age and with whom she has been acquainted in the past.

One of the services Amy presently is receiving is a personal care attendant (PCA) to assist with grooming and other self-care activities. She also receives a semi-independent living skills service (SILS), which provides a counselor to facilitate Amy's participation in community recreational activities such as softball and to assist with Amy's skill development in areas such as money management, appropriate interactions with males, and schedule planning. She receives day-service programming in the form of transportation to and from work and a job coach who interfaces with her work supervisor and conducts biweekly support group meetings. She has been approved for Metro Mobility, which allows her to ride public transportation including taxi service at reduced rates. She is receiving supplemental security income (SSI) and therefore is eligible for medical assistance (MA), which pays for the above-named services. We now have been informed that, because Amy has been an employee for 5 years, she is eligible for Social Security disability benefits, which will replace SSI. The source of this portion of her fiscal support will be the social security system rather than public assistance.

A number of agencies are working together to provide a comprehensive supportive program for Amy. Her county social worker as case manager oversees coordination of the interagency cooperative planning on Amy's behalf. Currently, this coordination encompasses six agencies including the company sponsoring the foster home arrangement. We believe that Amy would be at a disadvantage were it not for the experience of the social worker, who performs her role as case manager effectively. Although each agency has rules and procedures to facilitate consistency and smooth operation, they often have to be flexible as they cooperate with each other on behalf of the unique needs of specific clients. Amy truly has benefited from a cooperative interagency effort.

Because the EDGE children grew up in many different school districts in the greater Twin Cities metropolitan area, the range of experiences and opportunities afforded to them varies widely. Nevertheless, certain recurring themes relative to vocational preparation emerged from the follow-up survey.

*First*, EDGE parents said that, although academic education is valuable and should be pursued to the extent the child with Down syndrome is capable of mastering it, life skills training seems to be the most relevant curriculum during perhaps the final 5 to 7 years of education. When the young adult enters the outside world away from the protective environment of school staff and legally mandated education and support services, individually acquired skills relating to self-regulation, interpersonal skills, self-advocacy, independent living skills, and to some extent vocational skills play a significant role in the individual's ability to function in society more independently.

*Second*, in the opinion of the EDGE parents, work experience training on the job was more valuable than classroom-based vocational education. Vocational classroom/laboratory training is seen to be valuable and appropriate as a prerequisite or simultaneous component of on-the-job training. A variety of experiences seems to be more helpful than a single vocational subject area during the school years. A range of vocationally related programs and settings helps the individual understand the multitude of job classifications available, and this also helps the person understand himself or herself in the context of the work world. Those experiences, however, must be articulated carefully to avoid a "smorgasbord" of training opportunities.

*Third*, EDGE parents take the position that preparation for independent living is as important as specific occupational skills training. The challenges associated with this planning and eventual placement may be equal to or greater than those associated with occupational skills training. During the final 5 years living in the parental home, a young adult with Down syndrome must come to realize that eventually a move to another living situation is appropriate and desirable, although this may take a lot of finesse on the part of the family and school staff.

The prospects for meaningful and appropriate opportunities for individuals with Down syndrome within the workforce are better today than in any point in history. Because of many legislated changes during the past 15 years, societal expectations influencing employers, agencies, educators, and parents now acknowledge that people with Down syndrome have abilities, interests, and personalities that can enhance the workplace and that the workforce should have ample room for them. Because of these enlightened expectations, schools and employers of tomorrow will be able to place individuals with disabilities more effectively in a wide range of employment situations suited to individual differences.

Amy Fletcher is a product of a supportive environment, including a quality educational experience (beginning at 3 months of age with Project EDGE) that was well-integrated with transitional planning and work experience. She has benefited from effective agency interface with the school system and with employers. As she transitioned to a living situation outside of the parental home, she had mixed emotions. She cooperated with the planning process and talked regularly about the pending living arrangement. She admits she was nervous but no longer suggests that she return home. She will do fine. Her parents, however, are still adjusting to an "empty nest."

**OTES** _____

1. D. R. Johnson, L. Price, and B. Mathie, *Community Transition Interagency Committees*, Community Transition Interagency Committee Technical Assistance Project, Institute on Community Integration, University of Minnesota, Minneapolis, 1992, p. 3.

2. Federal Regulations, 34CFR300.550 (6)(2).

3. D. Guess, H. A. Benson, and E. Siegel-Causey, "Concepts and Issues Related to Choice-Making and Autonomy Among Persons with Severe Disabilities," *Journal of the Association for Persons with Severe Handicaps* 10(2): 79–86, 1985.

4. E. M. Szmanski, C. Hanley-Maxwell, and S. Asselin, "Rehabilitation Counseling, Special Education, and Vocational Special Needs Education: Three Transition Disciplines," *Career Development for Exceptional Individuals* 13 (1990): 29, 38; and William T. Grant Foundation Commission on Work, Family, and Citizenship, *The Forgotten Half: Pathways to Success for America's Youth and Young Families* (Washington, DC: Foundation, 1988); cited in A. L. Phelps, C. Chaplin, and A. Kelly, "A Parent's Guide to Vocational Education," *News Digest* 8 (1987): 1–10.

5. M. Wagner, *The Transition Experiences of Youth with Disabilities: A Report from the National Longitudinal Transition Study*, available from SRI International, 333 Ravenswood Ave., Menlo Park, CA 94025.

6. M. S. Moon, K. J. Inge, P. Wehman, V. Brooke, and J. M. Barcus, *Helping Per-*

*sons with Severe Mental Retardation Get and Keep Employment* (Baltimore: Paul H. Brookes, 1990).

7. J. B. Schumaker, J. S. Hazel, and C. S. Pederson, *Social Skills for Daily Living— Body Basics* (Circle Pines, MN: American Guidance Service, 1988).

---

*Alan Fletcher* is the special education director of a large metropolitan intermediate school district, where he is responsible for overseeing the delivery of transition services. He has also worked as a vocational special needs resource teacher and a vocational director at a technical college. In 1993 Alan authored the Minnesota Department of Education plan for support services for students with special needs in mainstream vocational education. He and his wife have a 23-year-old daughter with Down syndrome, Amy, who has successfully moved from school and home living to competitive employment and community living.

## ℱLETCHER FAMILY

Dad: Alan
Mom: Judy
Brother: Paul
Sister: Holly
Sister with Down
  syndrome: Amy

Amy at 4 months and Dad.

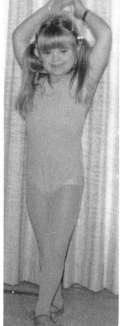

Dance
lessons.

Third birthday: Yum!

Horsing around.

## ℱLETCHER FAMILY (continued)

High school cheerleading.

Amy in her Brownie uniform.

Prom night.

# ~*10*~

# *M*AINTAINING HEALTH INTO ADULTHOOD

Margaret Horrobin

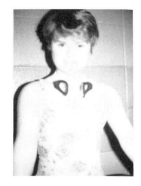

$\mathcal{A}$s children with Down syndrome approach adulthood, some new concerns appear and many of the former concerns of childhood assume less importance. Routine health check-ups continue to be important for early diagnosis of possible problems and also for the opportunity these visits present for counseling and teaching directed toward achieving a healthy way of life.

# $\mathcal{H}$EPATITIS B

Immunizations should be maintained, with consideration to immunization against Hepatitis B, a viral liver infection. Though most people recover uneventfully, it can cause severe, even fatal, liver damage. It also can progress to a chronic, active form in which the patient remains infectious and can pass on the virus to others. In former times, when many people with Down syndrome lived in institutions, many were found to be carriers of the Hepatitis B virus. Because of their immune deficiencies, they seem to have the propensity to become carriers of the disease rather than being able to overcome it. Though institutionalization is largely a thing of the past, a number of adolescents and young people with Down syndrome leave their parents' homes and move into group homes or other communal living arrangements with more contact with individuals other than family members. Therefore, protecting them against this potentially serious disease seems prudent.

# $\mathcal{O}$BESITY

The most common problem in people with Down syndrome is obesity. Almost all adults with Down syndrome are overweight, and this is a complex problem. The simple old equation, "A lot of energy in (food) minus too little energy out (growth and exercise) equals excess weight," is certainly too simple, but it does provide a starting point. The diet should be high in fiber, low in fat, with an emphasis on fruits and vegetables, and should provide a lower calorie intake than would be calculated on the basis of age and weight.

Energy expended depends on many factors, including exercise and metabolism, the latter controlled by the thyroid gland. Thyroid function should be checked by regular thyroid testing. Hypothyroidism, or low thyroid function, generally comes on quite slowly, so people who come into contact with the individual every day may not notice gradual changes. Some studies have suggested that undiagnosed hypothyroidism may be an important contributor to obesity.

Lack of exercise is a major concern. Habits of regular exercise for fitness' sake that are not started until the teenage and young adult years cannot be expected to last. They have to be acquired in earlier childhood and continued. Unfortunately, many young people who formerly were active as children gradually adopt a more sedentary lifestyle, spending a lot of time watching TV and playing video games. Besides being sedentary, these are solitary activities, adding to the social isolation that is one of the most troubling aspects of young adulthood for individuals with Down syndrome. Even physical problems that appear to be minor should be looked for, as these may contribute to lack of activity, particularly orthopedic problems related to the feet. Painful bunions are common, and the long-term effects of positional deformities first seen in childhood may limit activity later on because of pain or awkwardness.

# $\mathcal{H}$EART CONDITIONS

In the teenage and young adult years a condition known as *mitral valve prolapse* is being diagnosed with increasing frequency and may occur in more than 10% of those with Down syndrome.[1] Many cardiologists recommend preventive antibiotic treatment during dental procedures for people with this condition. Medical professionals should listen carefully for its presence during routine health examinations, and if they suspect it, an echocardiogram and a consultation with a cardiologist are appropriate. Other heart conditions, such as rate and rhythm disturbances, may occur, but these are not common.

# $\mathcal{S}$EIZURES

Approximately 8% of people with Down syndrome develop seizures, and about 40% of these start during the 20–30 year age period.[2] These seizures usually are of the tonic-clonic variety with muscular jerking. The indications for seizure medication are the same as for any other person with seizures and many factors have to be taken into account, such as type and frequency of the seizures and their effect on daily activities. The onset of seizures after age 50 or so may indicate Alzheimer's disease (see later discussion on that condition).

# SKIN

Dry, rough skin with calluses seems to be almost the norm and may occur despite the best efforts at lubrication. Chronically chapped lips with fissures are frequent, and the fissures sometimes are hard to heal. Lip problems are always worse if the young person is not able to control his or her tongue.

Chronic fungal infections of the nails giving rise to thickened, deformed nails, particularly on the feet, are a problem for some, and a podiatrist may be helpful in treatment. Medical therapy is tedious and not necessarily effective. Fungal infections of the skin, such as athlete's foot and jock itch, are seen particularly in young men, although we are not sure whether these conditions are truly more common in people with Down syndrome.

# EYE PROBLEMS

Among the eye problems in adults with Down syndrome is a significant incidence of *cataracts*. Approximately half of adults may be expected to develop cataracts, and this obviously will lead to visual deterioration.[3] A condition of the cornea known as *keratoconus* also occurs with Down syndrome and generally is not seen before the teenage years. In this condition the cornea becomes thinner and may change in shape, becoming more bulging. The cause is not certain, but one theory suggests that it may be a late result of chronic eye rubbing. Because of chronic blepharitis, many children with Down syndrome do rub their eyes a lot. Keratoconus generally is diagnosed only by ophthalmologists, which reinforces the importance of regular eye evaluations by an ophthalmologist.

# SEXUALITY AND REPRODUCTION

Changes of puberty in adolescents with Down syndrome occur in the same sequence that they do in other adolescents, though they statistically are somewhat slower. For example, the development of facial hair in young men is somewhat delayed. When development is complete, males with and without Down syndrome do not differ in the size of the mature genitalia. The onset of menstruation is on average 6 months later in young women with Down syndrome than it is for other young women (average age of onset 12½ years contrasted with 12 years).[4]

In dealing with issues of menstruation, developmental age has to be taken into account. A normal girl age 8 who is starting to menstruate is likely to deal with it and comprehend it differently than a girl of 12 or 13, yet the girl with Down syndrome who is starting to menstruate at the chronological age of 13 may be developmentally much more like a girl of 7 or 8. Having said this, however, most young women with Down syndrome are able to handle their menstruation hygiene appropriately and without a lot of help.

The serious question of sex education for young people with Down syndrome has to be addressed. In general, it seems to be woefully lacking. Information is available, and behaviors can be taught. All people with Down syndrome need to learn about normal sexual development. They need to learn social skills and how to avoid sexual abuse. They need to be taught the difference between appropriate private versus public behavior, language, use of body parts, and so on.[5]

## FEMALE FERTILITY

That women with Down syndrome may be fertile is well known.[6] As would be expected, about half of the children resulting from these pregnancies have Down syndrome. When eggs are formed, one chromosome of each pair goes into the egg. Because each cell has three number 21 chromosomes, when this division occurs, 50% of the egg cells receive one number 21 chromosome and 50% receive two, so there is a 50-50 chance that any fertilized egg will develop into a baby with Trisomy 21. Though many pregnancies have been documented in women with Down syndrome, the fertility level is definitely lower. Studies have suggested that about 40% of young women actually do ovulate, 30% possibly ovulate, and 30% do not ovulate.

Understandably enough, families of young women with Down syndrome worry about their daughters and sisters being taken advantage of and becoming pregnant. Thus, parents want to discuss sterilization and contraception. To expect that a young woman with Down syndrome never will be in a situation in which she could be forced or persuaded into sexual intercourse is unrealistic. Families do their best to keep their daughters safe, but as we foster more independent living and encourage job placement and social activities in the community, complete and total supervision is not feasible.

Some choose contraception. The contraceptive pill, though it is an excellent contraceptive, generally is not the first choice because it requires the woman to remember to take it every day, and this may prove difficult. A contraceptive such as DepoProvera, which with one intramuscular injection provides effective contraception for 3 months and also stops menses during this time, is the method of choice for many. It has been subjected to many years of experience overseas and to trials in the United States, though it has been licensed for general use only recently. Side effects are similar to those of oral contraceptives.

Many families request sterilization, and here the issues become more sticky. The specter of sterilizing people with retardation, which in years past was done indiscriminately in some state residential institutions, is an ugly one. In some instances it may have been a thin veil for racist policies. Nevertheless, the notion that no one should be denied the opportunity to become a parent, and that certain outside groups holding strong opinions about the right to procreate know more about and care more about the real needs of their daughters, does not sit well with most families of young women with Down syndrome. Sterilization of minors is a tricky legal issue. Many physicians fear performing sterilizations without a court order. The court order may not be obtained readily, and the legal process may be expensive. A court order, however, often is not legally necessary, and one may find a supportive physician who will perform the procedure after carefully considering the merits of each individual case. Sterilization may be accomplished more easily once a young woman is no longer a minor and it can be ascertained that she agrees with this procedure and is able to give consent for herself with supporting statements from other professionals, if need be, and from her guardian if she has one.

Sterilization is accomplished by *tubal ligation*. A hysterectomy is not indicated for purposes of sterilization. A hysterectomy may be appropriate if the young woman is completely unable to manage her periods with appropriate hygiene or is emotionally overwhelmed by it. These instances are rare, but a hysterectomy curiously may involve less red tape, as the primary purpose of this surgery is to abolish the periods permanently rather than to sterilize the person. Because DepoProvera also abolishes the periods for 3 months with each injection, requests for hysterectomies probably will become increasingly rare.

# ALE FERTILITY

Males with Down syndrome previously were thought to be incapable of fathering children, though this assumption had no scientific grounds. The question was resolved with a 1990 report of a pregnancy proved beyond any scientific doubt to have been caused by a young man with Down syndrome.[7] So the blanket statement must be revised to say that men with Down syndrome rarely father children. This small possibility is enough reason for many parents to ask for a vasectomy for their young adult sons. Interestingly, this procedure is much easier to obtain than female sterilization. Many unanswered questions remain about male sexual function. Erection and ejaculation occur, but information regarding sperm counts and the actual urge for intercourse, for example, does not seem to be available.

In our group of young people from the EDGE project, three of eleven young men have had a vasectomy. One of four young women has had a tubal ligation.

# LASTIC SURGERY

In another area of heated discussion, wide disagreement and great controversy abound regarding plastic surgery for children with Down syndrome. This typically includes tongue reduction and facial reconstruction. Facial reconstruction involves procedures such as building up the bridge of the nose, altering the shape of the eyelids, and building up the cheekbones to give the individual a more normalized appearance. The rationale for tongue reduction has been that it will improve the quality and clarity of speech, as well as reduce the unaesthetic appearance of a thick, fissured tongue that may be hanging out constantly. Many reasons have been given in favor of facial surgery. Some are seemingly straightforward ("The shape of the nose and nasal bridge is such that it is impossible to fit her with the glasses that she needs"). Mostly it comes down to changing some of the physical characteristics of Down syndrome so the stereotypes will not be applied so quickly.

These days, many young people with Down syndrome are doing so much better developmentally and socially than has been the case in the past, and some families believe their children are stigmatized unfairly or stereotyped when their facial appearance gives away their diagnosis. Thus, we can argue that changing the appearance somewhat, making the young person less "Downs-like," may improve a young person's self-esteem and his or her chance of being judged for the inner person rather than the outer person, for abilities and achievements rather than appearance. After all, in the world at large, many people do not hesitate to have plastic surgery to change features they do not find appealing for whatever reason. Should this opportunity be denied to a person with Down syndrome?

Some oppose plastic surgery, saying the parents have failed to come to terms with their child's having Down syndrome and they wish to deny it by changing the young person's appearance. This seems like a simplistic response to a complicated issue. This question has no easy answer, and no blanket approval or disapproval is warranted. Each request should be treated respectfully and sympathetically, and the decision should involve the young person just as much as the family. Surgery is expensive and uncomfortable, and insurance companies usually do not cover it. But, as one father said, "I'm spending a lot of money on my other children sending them to college, so why begrudge this amount of money for my daughter with Down syndrome who's not going to college?" Be that as it may, no hard evidence to date supports the use of facial plastic surgery as a means of improving social acceptance by the public in general.

The effectiveness of tongue reduction is not known. In general, parents seem to respond favorably. Many report an improvement in their adult child's eating habits and better articulation. Unfortunately, speech therapists cannot clearly confirm better articulation. In general, they have not found the post-surgery results to be different from the pre-surgery condition when assessed experimentally. The more involved with the family the people making the judgment are, as family members or regular teachers, the more favorable is the impression of the surgery. The more objective the observers—for example, speech therapists listening to a tape of speech before and after surgery, the less likely they are to be impressed. Perhaps part of the disparity has to do with the fact that, when we are talking to someone, we are not just listening to their words but also are reading their lips and whole face. Maybe this latter aspect is what tongue reduction improves. In any event, as with facial surgery, tongue reduction by no means is generally recommended.[8]

# ALZHEIMER'S DISEASE

Adults with Down syndrome may show signs of premature senility at an earlier age than is seen in the general population. The finding a few years ago of one Alzheimer's gene on the number 21 chromosome may give some theoretical explanation for why Alzheimer's disease is more common in Down syndrome. In addition, postmortem examination of the brain of adults with Down syndrome over age 40 always reveals the typical microscopic findings of Alzheimer's disease. The clinical features of Alzheimer's disease, however, are not seen at this frightening rate, and probably fewer than half of all adults with Down syndrome develop the symptoms of Alzheimer's disease. Though some reports indicate earlier onset, the signs of dementia do not generally occur under age 50 in people with Down syndrome. Even so, this is 10–15 years earlier than in the population at large.

The most frequent early signs are of deterioration of speech, change in gait, and the onset of seizures. The latter in a person of this age with Down syndrome is regarded as evidence of early dementia. Other symptoms of Alzheimer's disease seen in the general population also occur, such as loss of memory or getting lost easily. Neurologic symptoms always must be investigated to rule out other causes before attributing the cause to Alzheimer's disease. When it occurs in an adult with Down syndrome, Alzheimer's disease tends to progress more rapidly, with an average of 5 years from onset of symptoms to death.[9]

To end this chapter by discussing Alzheimer's disease would be to end on a discouraging and depressing note, which is not how most families regard life with their family member who has Down syndrome. Although all the EDGE families try to be realistic about the problems and challenges they face, they are overwhelmingly positive about their past experiences and have much optimism for the future.

This spirit of optimism clearly was in evidence at the close of a recent interview session. EDGE parents had spent about an hour talking about their young adult sons' and daughters' futures. (Much of this material is in Chapter 11.) At the end of the interview, we asked them the open-ended question: "Is there anything else you'd like to say about life with [your son or daughter] that hasn't been covered?" Closing the interview in this way allowed parents to say anything that came to mind. What we hoped for, of course, was that their strongest general impression about living for more than 20 years with their son or daughter with Down syndrome would come to the forefront.

As it turned out, two parents were not asked this question because the interviewer judged that these parents had embodied this content in one or more of their other interview responses (see Chapter 11). A third parent who had been asked the question said she had nothing to add to what she had said already. The other twelve responses follow.*

*Mother:*  Probably the saddest time was when we got the diagnosis, and if I had known then what I know now—what sheer fun life is with him—you know, it wouldn't be so bad.

---

* Statements in some instances have been edited slightly to increase readability, such as removing a statement that essentially is a repetition of a former one, eliminating lengthy "loop-backs" to previous interview answers, and so forth. If our editing attempts distorted parents' answers through inadvertent error, parents had the opportunity to correct the error because they reviewed all of the statements used here, comparing them with the interview transcript.

*Father:* My son is a pleasure to be with, really. He's very, very seldom in the dumps. He's not pessimistic. We wouldn't know what to do without him. He's got a fantastic memory you wouldn't believe. His brother's friends come over and talk about baseball or football and his brother would call him and say, "Jordan's been traded to somebody," and my son would say, "Yeah, he's been traded to Phoenix" or something. He knows. He reads the trades in the newspaper, and he knows what position people play. He must have fifty to seventy-five wrestling dolls. That's one of his hobbies. And he knows every one of them. He knows who they are and, of course, that's one of his big hobbies, along with all the other sports. He watches his wrestling events on TV, he and his buddy from White Bear. They both like the big wrestling events on TV, and they each take turns taping them. And he knows all the wrestlers, the new ones out, and he'll keep up on them.

*Mother:* [referring to wrestlers] The good guys, the bad guys. It depends on what months you're looking at, because the bad guy turns into the good guy!

*Mother:* I think I would have done a couple of things differently. I think I would have done more to make sure he kept regular hours. I think some of those other kinds of opportunities for self-expression are needed. He's not very stubborn. When he gets tired, that's how you know. It's uncharacteristic of him. On the whole, I don't think there are major things I would have done differently. Having him has really pushed my beliefs and values into action. It's been a challenge. It's been extremely complex.

*Mother:* We've talked this over in EDGE groups, about the real surprise at the sexual drive of the boys. It was a real shocker for me, and I know for the others. And how to deal with that has been a big issue. I guess we weren't prepared for the intensity of that, and I think that's something parents of young kids should be aware of. That's been one of the difficult issues.

*Mother:* (Laughs): I don't know. He's just such a love. He really is. They say you shouldn't wrap your life around your kids, and my husband and I...it seems like life, as you get older, means your relationship is...nicer than it was when you were younger. You get all that garbage out of the way. But I have to say that I would like more time with my husband. And maybe we'll work to make that possible. But having my son—I'm not being Pollyanna when I say it—has been a wonderful experience. But it *is* because of the beginning we had. I can't tell you where my attitude would have been if I didn't have all the input we had from Project EDGE. I tell *everybody* that. I always say, "God picked me out because he says, '*This* one really needs help' and puts me right there."

*Mother:* I'm kind of looking to a little bit easier life. She's taken two trips in a year—one trip with us, and then we usually take a grandchild with us. And she loves those trips. She just lives for those trips. She very consciously loves it. And I think with that type of activity, I could see that she could have a happy life. I think I'm feeling much more hopeful and optimistic about her life, and this past year has been very good for her.

*Father:* She's taught us and her brothers and sisters, too, about tolerance.
*Mother:* She's been good for the other children because I think she taught them a lot.
*Father:* And I think she teaches the men and women in the neighborhood, because they see her and they know what beauty she has.

*Father:* I guess I think it has been more pleasure than sorrow. And it's an experience. People who have never had it are missing a real experience in life. Like childbearing is an experience. But this is *really* an experience. You can't just read about it and understand it. You have to *live* it. And it's been a good experience.
*Mother:* I think my feelings are the same as yours. You know, you have to *live* it or experience it yourself. You can't just come up to somebody and say, "Oh, we've been through this, and we've been through that, and they say, "Oh, I *know* what you're going through.'" No, nobody *knows* what you're going through unless they go through it. They don't know. They haven't walked down that road.
*Father:* It's an emotional roller coaster. A lot of highs. Some lows. Always interesting. (laughs)
*Mother:* Never a dull moment. It's been a great experience, really.

*Father:* One of the things he's accomplished a lot more than we ever thought he was going to accomplish is the business about riding the motorcycle, swimming, and the International Special Olympics, even being able to go on an airplane by himself, riding a bicycle, and being in the body building stuff. I guess one of the things we realized was that there seem to be more things where it's normal rather than abnormal.

*Mother:* And more things that are positive rather than negative, really. Add them up. I think probably the one big thing was that body building, and the thing that was the most exciting of all was to see how he would accept it. He was the only person who was handicapped in the competition at all. And to see how he was accepted by the audience and the other body builders was really exciting. It all had to do with the coach and his whole attitude toward our son. It was really a neat experience.

*Father:* Thousands of people gave him a standing ovation.

*Mother:* People always ask me, "Is it really hard [to raise him]?" You know, I don't know. It's a joy to have children. It's hard work. I mean, they are hard work!

*Father:* Yep.

*Mother:* It's been about the same for all three children. It's been hard work, but it's rewarding and joyful.

*Mother:* With a retarded child, there are many, many joys, and there are very hard times. Your life is changed forever with a mentally retarded child. You'll never, never be like other people. But the joys are many. Right?

*Father:* Yeah. He's brought so much into our life. I don't know what it would be like without him. There'd certainly be a really big empty spot. I doubt if either one of my girls would have gone into special education if we didn't have him. So I think he's had a big impact on all of us. I know he has on me. I got into politics and got active in a lot of those things because of him.

*Mother:* And hopefully we can help other people by doing this interview. But it's a hard life. It really is.

*Father:* It's a *different* life. That's certain.

*Mother:* You see things that other people do that aren't possible for us, but that's the biggest part of what he's given to us.

*Father:* Well, when he was born, we thought it was devastating, but the positive things that happened and the positive aspects outweigh the negative by so much. As far as I'm concerned, if this is our greatest cross to bear, well, then, we're not in too bad shape.

*Mother:* He's definitely been a real asset to the family. Our two oldest are living out of state, and they were both home at Christmas, and he took the whole family out to dinner—*treated*, you know. Yeah, it's good. It's not been a big burden, definitely.

*Father:* Then we came home and played the name game. He got into that, too. His brother set up a few names, names he knew our son would recognize.

*Mother:* He just loved that evening. You know, just being with the whole family and then coming home and spending time playing that game. That was ideal. Our family used to go to my sister's cabin for a few days or a week in the summer. All the kids were younger. And he loved that.

# ℕOTES

1. S. Z. Goldhaber et al., *Journal of the American Medical Association* 258 (1987): 1793.
2. S. Pueschel, *Archives of Neurology* 48(3) (1991): 318.
3. A. Hestnes, *Journal of Mental Deficiency Research* 35 (1991): 179.
4. R. Sheridan et al., *Journal of Medical Genetics* 26 (1989): 294.
5. T. E. Elkins et al., *Journal of Reproductive Medicine* 35(7) (1990): 745.
6. S. Pueschel, *The Young Person with Down Syndrome* (Baltimore, MD: Paul Brookes, 1988): 23–24.
7. R. Sheridan et al., *Journal of Medical Genetics* 26 (1989): 294.
8. For a much more complete discussion of this topic, offering differing views, readers may want to read Chapter 10 in *Don't Accept Me As I Am: Helping "Retarded" People to Excel* by R. Feuerstein, Y. Rand, and J. E. Rynders (New York: Plenum Publishing Corporation, 1988).
9. H. M. Evenhuis, *Archives of Neurology* 47 (1990): 263.

## $\mathcal{T}$HOMES FAMILY

Dad: Ray
Mom: Barb
Brothers: Greg, Peter
Sisters: Cathy, Judy, Chris
Brother with Down
   syndrome: Brian

A "beary" good day.

Football isn't as easy as it looks.

Riding with sisters.

# $\mathcal{T}$HOMES FAMILY (continued)

Special Olympics:
First place!

Tired Santa.

Going out.

# $\mathcal{W}$HEELER FAMILY

Dad: Lowell
Mom: Phyllis
Brothers: Greg, Arnie
Sister: Karwyn (Lindahl)
Brother with Down
    syndrome: Eric

I was *born* to be an actor.

Run like the wind.

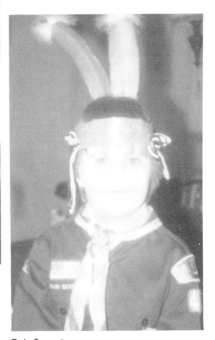

Cub Scouting.

# $\mathcal{W}$HEELER FAMILY (continued)

 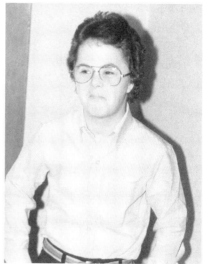

It's okay for guys to have perms.
Before perm.                    After perm.

Billiards with friend Tom.

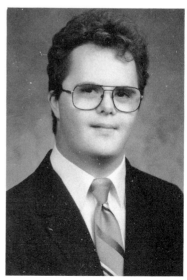

High school graduation.

# ~11~

# $\mathcal{L}$OOKING BACK, LOOKING AHEAD

John Rynders

*W*hat has life been like for parents who have spent approximately 25 years of their lives rearing a son or daughter who has Down syndrome? What would parents do differently if they could somehow repeat those years? To assemble this information, an interviewer asked the fifteen EDGE parents several questions. Excerpts from the responses of each of the parents follow.*

# *P*ARENTS' RESPONSES _____

*"If you could live life over again with [your son or daughter], what things would you change or do differently?"*

*Mother:* I think I would be a stricter disciplinarian. When they're small, they're fun and they're cute and, in my case particularly, indulged, but I would be more strict in certain areas. He's never been a big discipline problem or had any major problems, but I think the things we've struggled with could have been avoided if he had been a little more "scared" of me. The other thing—he has a weight problem. And we're a *family* that hasn't been athletic. I haven't built athletics into my life, and he is much like me. He would much rather watch television or read a book or be quiet than get out and ski. I always tried to encourage him to get out. We've gotten him soccer sets to winter equipment, but nothing has done it because we haven't built it in as a family. I haven't.

*Mother:* Nothing, as far as I'm concerned. Everything went well, don't you think?

*Father:* The early training was really helpful, and going to preschool with

_____
* The responses have been edited only to ensure anonymity.

the other EDGE children was so helpful, too. I wouldn't change anything. We got a lot of support inside this family. I think we're fortunate to have his three brothers and sister, who were always number one to him, and of course his mother. I'm just a fixture around here (laughing). No, we wouldn't change anything.

*Mother:* I think I would have done a couple of things differently. I think I would have done more to make sure that he kept more regular hours. I think more opportunities for self-expression are needed. But on the whole, I don't think there are major things I would have done differently. Having him has really pushed my beliefs and values into action. It's been a challenge. It's been extremely complex.

*Mother:* I probably would do almost everything the same. I think that I wouldn't let him get by with so much, though. He has had problems with authority figures over the years, which may relate to the discipline, or lack of it. His stubborn streak, which is both a Down syndrome and a family trait, has made disciplining more difficult. I also would be more demanding with medical issues. He is partially deaf due to much inner ear infection. More aggressive treatment might have saved not only seven hospitalizations for ear tubes and three mastoid surgeries but more of the hearing. These are all "ifs," though. At the time, we did all we could emotionally, physically, and financially.

*Mother:* Nothing. I can't think of anything I'd do differently. The only thing that comes to my mind as the biggest mistake I've made with him is when his brother died. I didn't allow him to go to the funeral because of the experience I had with a child with Down syndrome in another family trying to climb into her mother's casket. The end result was two years of very bad depression for him [over his brother's death]. So that's the biggest mistake I've made with him.

*Father:* I don't think there's much we could change. Maybe we'd be a little more assertive in getting the community to provide more activities. And we would try to be a bit more active in transporting her to the activities.

*Mother:* Well, when we went into the EDGE program, he was only three months old. I really threw myself into it, as with most things I do. Looking back now, I would have tried to have spent more time with the other two children, who are a little older than he is. I wasn't aware then of the growth and development of children and how important it is to read to them and those things. I did read to them, but I would have done more of that and, in the vernacular of today, spent more "quality time" with the other two children. I don't know of anything I would have done differently with Bruce, because he certainly had an awful lot of attention. He was such an active child. He just demanded a lot of my time and energy. I remember asking Dr. Horrobin, "When is this child ever going to slow down?" and she said, "Oh, maybe when he's twelve." I didn't know if we'd survive that long, but he did slow down. He's a fine young man now, but he really demanded a lot of attention.

*Mother:* I would like to make her more independent. She depends on us for everything. Instead of answering, sometimes she'll look at us to see what we're saying. I think we've made a big mistake there.

*Father:* Yeah, I agree. She could have done more on her own. You don't know it until the years have passed, and with her brothers and sisters being older, they did the same thing. They babied her, took care of her, and did things for her. We thought we were helping her, but we were really hurting her. I think we held her back. I think she could be doing a lot better. It's hard to change now.

*Mother:* Frank being our first child, we really didn't have anyone to compare with, so we just did whatever we thought was best. I guess I'd say we wouldn't do anything different.

*Mother:* I can't say that I would do anything differently. I just feel that we've done the best we could. That's the way I feel.

*Father:* I think if it hadn't been for the EDGE group, we wouldn't have had the support we needed. If I had to do it all over again, I would want to have the EDGE group or something similar to it to help us get through the situation. And I think we'd probably push a little harder in school.

*Mother:* After the EDGE program I didn't keep working with him like I should have, academic-wise. Also, I think I should have stayed more on top of the school situation than I did.

*Father:* I'd say the same thing. I think we should have put more effort into maintaining an academic environment for him somehow. And I'd probably try to have him take part in more social activities. Sometimes he does real well at it, and then he kind of gets away from it and we have to get him back into it. So probably more of a steady social environment would have been better.

*Father:* Well, we [her mother and I] may have different perspectives, so I'll make a general statement. We feel that it's gone very well. I mean, excellent. We're constantly mentioning how lucky we've been. There were problems at the time of the birth, though.

*Mother:* That's right. The doctors weren't very supportive. That was about the only thing.

*Mother:* I think at the time he was born, we did just about everything we could. I wish we had done more. But at the time, we had the EDGE program, which was great. Then he went on to kindergarten, and you couldn't ask for more. Later, though, it was hard. I was always pushing for more academics, and some of the teachers didn't want that. They wanted cutting and pasting. I didn't want that, so it seemed like our name got to be known in the school district, because I feel like we fought for every inch we got, and it wasn't enough.

*Father:* If I had anything to do over, I think I'd fight harder for a better education. I recall the troubles we had just getting him accepted in the schools he was accepted in, and I wish I'd pushed even harder. I don't believe that his potential has been reached or even fully tapped, for that matter.

*Father:* Wow. I don't know. It's been so rewarding, really. However, we're in a situation now where we're thinking about where he's going to be two years from now, or four years from now, and there just don't seem to be a lot of facilities or group homes available. Maybe we could have started sooner working on that. I don't know.

*Mother:* Yeah, when you look back over the years, it's hard to remember the bad parts of it. You tend to remember the good times and the good things. But it's really been good with him. Starting with EDGE, we had groups of wonderful support. He had a good education. St. Louis Park schools have been fantastic! He's been in Special Olympics since he was eight, which has been a really good experience for him and us. But a problem we've had has to do with our third child, who was kind of lost in the shuffle. We had four kids in six years, and Gertrude is the youngest. And Bill and Jim started school shortly after Adam was born. And so Gertrude was kind of the one who was home when I was doing lessons and when I was driving him to the EDGE school. And at the time I thought that gave Gertrude and me some opportunity to spend some time together, but I think she really kind of got lost in our family. She was definitely a middle child.

Reflecting back, perceptions of the first 25 years or so can be summarized as follows. The parents' most frequent comment was that they would do little differently if they could live life over again. The second most frequent comment was that they would push the school, medical profession, or community agencies to do more for their son or daughter. The third most frequent comment had to do with their personal regrets about not doing more for their child with Down syndrome, such as striving harder to make him or her more independent. The fourth most frequent comment had to do with concerns that a child in the family, other than the one with Down syndrome, was "cheated" somehow out of his or her fair share of attention because of the parents' devoting so much time and energy to their child with Down syndrome in the early years.

Nowadays, parents of children who have Down syndrome have support services that EDGE parents did not enjoy. So, with respect to their comments about pushing harder for services, recent laws not only guarantee some of those services, but they contain language guaranteeing parents the right to advocate for services and to ask for a due process hearing if a parent thinks the potential service provider is unreceptive. A good example of a large and comprehensive support service is the Education for All Children with Disabilities Act, which guarantees children with disabilities the right to a free public education in the least restrictive appropriate environment possible.

With regard to several of the EDGE parents wishing they had tried harder to help their son or daughter attain more independence, again far more services and resources are available now to facilitate the development of independence than existed 25 years ago. For example, community-based vocational training, along with job coaching and supported living arrangements, is now common practice (see Chapter 9).

The problem that some EDGE parents encountered (as mentioned in the preceding interviews) in not being able to distribute their time and attention equitably across all the children in their family probably is just as prevalent today, if not more so, because of the number of families in which both parents work outside the home. We do not have a solution to this problem. We do, however, have the statements of several of the brothers and sisters in the EDGE families, which can help us assess the long-term impact of having a sibling with Down syndrome.

# *S*IBLINGS' RESPONSES* _

Around the midpoint in this book's de-velopment, we realized that siblings' thoughts had been neglected. When one of the EDGE parents pointed out this omission, we immediately developed a suggested outline for a short, informal essay and gave copies of the outline to EDGE parents, along with a cover sheet informing siblings of what we were do-ing and inviting their voluntary partici-pation. Parents mailed the invitational outline to their nondisabled sons and daughters, who by that time usually had moved out of the family home, often were married, and in several instances had children of their own.

Because the rate of response was relatively low (eight of fifteen fami-lies), caution must be exercised in forming summary impressions about their experiences as a group. It is conceivable that the other half had experiences (perhaps negative) that they didn't wish to discuss. Nonetheless, here are excerpts from all of the sibling essays we received.

*Sister:* I'm not saying that having a brother with Down syndrome has been easy. I remember the ridicule of those who didn't understand. I remember the stares directed our way. I also remember the frus-tration of the limited level of verbal communication, because he is partially deaf. This was, and still is, played out every day. But, as I grew, it all seemed so slight compared to the relationship I had formed with him. So if someone were to say that I could go back and change things involving his Down syndrome, I would leave it all alone. I wouldn't want to change a thing. The more I learn about him, the more I learn about myself. And that is truly a gift.

*Brother:* Being a close-in-age brother to Philip, my feelings, trials, and tribu-lations were very emotional at times. I remember when I was four years old and Mom and Dad brought him home. He's special, they told me, and they always tried to be positive with and about him. I don't recall their ever showing great disappointment that he has

---

* Pseudonyms have been used throughout this section.

Down syndrome, which I felt was so important in my upbringing—being positive. It truly reflected my opinion of my brother. I felt anger and disappointment when he wrecked my toy train set. I blamed it on the Downs at the time, but after having kids myself—surprise—he was just like any other younger brother or sister. Besides, those were only material possessions.

*Brother:* Growing up with three other brothers and a sister was always a headache. With only one bathroom you can't imagine the fights and arguments that ensued. We all wanted to be first in line—well, all but George. Sharing and patience are his biggest virtues. He's my favorite brother and, next to my wife, he's my best friend, and I love him a ton. That's why he was my best man in my wedding this past November. People say "your family is so good with George." Well, it isn't us. It's George!

*Sister:* Growing up in a family with five children was quite an adventure. Summer days found us in the middle of whiffle ball tournaments in the backyard. We still play today when we're at our parents' house. Recently I became a teacher, and George is a popular topic in my junior high classroom. In fact, I invited him to be a guest speaker so my students could get to know him. During one class the "class bully" tried to challenge his knowledge of sports. Big mistake! George had been introducing the Hoops basketball trading cards to the class when the bully asked him what team Wayne Gretzky played for. George proceeded to inform my student that Gretzky did not play basketball, that he played hockey. He went on to list all of Gretzky's current statistics and when the next game was. Needless to say, my student did not have any more questions for George. Having a brother who has Down syndrome has been a privilege that few people have been given. George has made me realize that most people take life too seriously.

*Another brother:* A clear memory I have of George was formed just two years ago. He was training for a Special Olympics power-lifting event when there was a "regular" meet he competed in as a tune-up. As they announced him as one of the premier Special Olympics lifters in the area, the look on people's faces were of anticipation and doubt. It seemed like people were curious [about] how much he could lift but also wondered why he would compete in a regular meet. Knowing how strong George is, I'll never forget the looks on people's faces and their comments when he went on to win the competition for his weight class. Since I have experienced growing up with a brother who has Down syndrome, I can't even imagine my life any other way. The impact he has made on me and our entire family is unbelievable!

*One more* I don't really ever think of having a brother "with Down syndrome."
*brother:* I think of him and his particular set of circumstances often, but the notion of him as having some kind of justifiable stigma due to Down's was rejected a long, long time ago. Because of him, our family evolved in a way that I doubt ever would have happened otherwise. George has consistently drawn us together in a number of ways: by his innocently haranguing us with reminders to attend various events; by his interest in Special Olympics that pulled us in together to help that organization and recruit our friends to do so as well; by his infectious laugh and the way he can get excited about pro wrestling, basketball, music, or his work; and by his pride of ownership in his contributions to the family. He is a storyteller extraordinaire and has entertained us often with tales of his antics (sometimes too often). Maybe the bottom line for me and the true value of having a brother like George (who happens to have Down syndrome) is his ability to teach. He is a great teacher. His priorities of family, friends, loyalty, honesty, trust, and compassion stand as an example of what should be important for me—an example, I must admit, that I need, and all too often forget, in the haste of my daily life.

*Sister:* My brother was born when I was thirteen years old. I was very excited to have "my own" baby. I had already begun babysitting, and I loved little children. It was really a gift to have a baby as a part of my family.... It has been interesting watching my children, especially my six-year-old son, as he interacts with his Uncle Chris. He told me Uncle Chris's accent is difficult to understand. My four-year-old daughter prides herself on being able to understand him.... They are so young I haven't tried to explain Uncle Chris to them. I enjoy their explanations. Andrew says Chris is better at playing games because he is bigger. Andrew also says he likes playing games with Uncle Chris because Uncle Chris tries very hard, and he is a good loser. Both my four-year-old and my two-year-old like Uncle Chris because he gets excited about everything they show him. He claps and encourages them.

I am a parent now, and for the first time I find there are things I don't like about Chris. He messes with my children's hair, so I have to discipline him. He wants me to give him special attention even though I am trying to keep track of four little ones. He gets jealous when his parents pay attention to their grandchildren. I have surprised myself. I was always cautious not to dislike any behavior in Chris. I always wanted to give him special attention because he is so special to me. But now I see that today I treat him more normally than I ever have in my life. Like every person he has good and bad points. But I love him not for the fact that I feel obligated because he is special, but because he is my brother.

*Another sister:* First I must say that growing up with my brother Chris who has Down syndrome, was and is no different than growing up with my other brother and sister. Each one brought something into the family. Each of them in some way or another has a lasting impression on me. A *big* issue now is "person first." Rather than seeing a disability, you see a person for who he or she really is. I feel that in having Chris in my life, I became aware of this many years ago. He is my brother, who has the same wants and needs as you and I have. He has likes and dislikes, feelings, and a personality of his very own just as you and I have. Imagine that—he's just another person! I really feel that, given the opportunity to go beyond the disability, people may begin to more clearly understand that we are all only human and have many more similarities than differences. If all the world were blind, how would one know if another had a disability or not?

*Sister:* Mark has always been fairly unemotional. I'm not sure if he is afraid to show anger, happiness, and sadness—because I know he is feeling these emotions. I'll never forget, though, when his best friend died. He cried for the first time that I can remember. He was able to show how he felt. I don't think he will ever be quite the same after that devastating experience. I have a very happy, positive outlook about the future in general, and about Mark's future. I feel lucky to have him for my brother, to have been able to grow up with someone with Down syndrome. I've seen what they can accomplish even with the many odds against them. I really believe that I am a better person because of him.

*Sister:* I have never been so proud of my brother as the time he competed in a body building contest. This wasn't a Special Olympics contest, but a contest of all nonhandicapped people and my brother. It was a real big event with Mr. and Mrs. Universe there, as well as many other contestants. Well, my brother had been lifting weights for quite a while and really did have a good, muscular body. We were all very nervous right before the show began, as we weren't sure how he would do up there on stage. It's one thing to be able to remember your whole routine, but to perform in front of hundreds of people is another. Personally, I know I wouldn't be able to do it. Well, to make a long story short, he got up there and did his routine perfectly. (I would guess that some of those people in the back didn't even know he was handicapped.) It still brings tears to my eyes to talk or write about it. He received a standing ovation, and was he ever proud of himself, as we were of him! My brother has had a very lasting impression on me. I went to college and became a special education teacher, and since then have received my master's degree in vocational education for special needs personnel. I truly don't think that I ever would have pursued this career if it wasn't for him. I saw, through him, that he is just an individual like anyone else, only it takes him longer to learn things. There are things that he will never be able to do, but then again, there are things that all of us will never be able to do.

*Sister:*   When I was a young child, growing up with Brad seemed like any other sibling. We were told he was special, but until I was older, I didn't think much of it. Entering into my teenage years was when there was a definite difference. He was still my little brother, but now I was becoming a young adult and image was important! How would my friends accept my brother? He needed to be watched over, and often I was elected. That was how I viewed it at the time. At times it felt unfair, but at that age there could be many other circumstances that could make one feel that way. Still, even during the drastic "teen" years, he was still just my little brother. He is a very excitable and happy person, with a lot of emotion in everything he does. The joy seen in his face when he has done something well is something not soon forgotten. That joy was brilliant when he received his first Holy Communion. It was a day that he was so very proud of. After he received the sacrament, he came back to the pew, threw his arms around my dad, and said, "I did it. I did it." That day was a very special one for him, and one that I will not forget.

*Sister:*   Growing up with my sister was mostly a positive experience. When she was born, the rest of us (siblings) were nine to twelve years older. We were old enough to understand that she was "different," and we were old enough to feel some of the shock and disappointment that my parents felt so deeply. But as she grew, she was just Helen, our little sister. She was sweet and fun and very lovable. I was always the big sister, even before her, so the additional responsibilities seemed natural. My parents never told us we should spend time with her or made us feel like we needed to include her, or work with her. She was who she was. Of course, there were moments—at shopping malls, parks—when someone would stare at her. At first this really hurt me deeply. Over time I came to realize that other people just didn't understand, and I told myself to feel sorry for them because they could never know her as I did. They would never know what a truly pure heart my sister possessed. She grew and developed in ways we were told may not be possible for someone with Down syndrome. With every achievement—and there were many—we all shared in the joy. At her high school graduation I can remember being so proud of her as she walked in the procession with her classmates that I was overcome with emotion. She carried herself with dignity that I pray she never loses.

*Another sister:* Helen has made an impact on all of our lives. At times I felt frustration, though, because there was a lot of attention by my parents that needed to be focused on her with her special needs. Overall I would say that she brought us closer as a family. As a family we worked through one hurdle at a time with her. We have had many special times together over the years. About eight years ago Helen and our sister Diane and I went on a sisters-only camping trip. When we are together, we tell each other how we feel about things. For example, Helen has expressed how she would like to get her driver's license. Growing up with her has taught me many things. Because of her, I feel that I am a more patient, loving parent.

*Sister:* When Donald was born, I was four years old. At the time, we were dealing with my dad being sick, Donald being born with Down syndrome, and then my dad became very sick again. There seemed to be so much change all at once. I remember feeling a loss of my mother to Donald, with all the time she spent with him teaching the daily lessons and the extra time it took to care for him. The feelings I had toward him were mixed. I remember his affection for me and everyone, his kindness and generosity. Sometimes I felt frustration, though, because he needed so much supervision. When he moved to [a special school], I saw a whole different way kids with handicaps lived. I remember walking into the building that had a funny smell, dark halls, and a huge bathroom that everybody shared. The other children were bigger (even adult ages), louder, and rough. I felt bad because I couldn't be there to protect him anymore. This was a dark side to see after being around the EDGE program.

Summarizing these siblings' feelings, their growing-up experience with a brother or sister who has Down syndrome generally was positive, though not always free of rocky times. Not that rocky times are necessarily all bad. They can lead to a higher level of personal development, brought about by having to cope with stresses and with feelings of ambivalence associated with having a brother or sister with Down syndrome. Indeed, this ambivalence is shown clearly in the statement of Sister H, whom we chose to present last. The old adage "there's no free lunch" fits the plight of parents who somehow must struggle to share their attention and affection equitably when forces, both internal and external, to overcommit to the child who has Down syndrome are so strong.

If the looking-back perceptions of siblings are representative of all EDGE siblings, and are not "rose colored" but are reality-based, the feelings of inequity of parental attention in their early years (felt just as keenly by some of the EDGE parents) do not disappear totally over time but seem to be replaced largely by feelings of love and admiration for their brother or sister with Down syndrome and enjoyment in associating with him or her in their grown-up years. That a disproportionately large number of siblings, in comparison to a population of siblings who do not have a family member with a disability, have chosen a vocation in special education seems to validate this impression partially. Not that parents who have young children, one of whom has Down syndrome, can relax in their efforts to distribute their time and attention as equitably as possible, but their earnest struggle to try to be as equitable as they can while giving special attention to a sibling with Down syndrome appears to send an important long-term character-building message to their other children, presenting a model of love and compassion that other children in the family seem to internalize eventually.

# ARRIAGE?

How do parents feel about their son or daughter with Down syndrome's future, not in terms of recreation, vocation, and independent living (these topics are covered in Chapters 8 and 9) but, instead, in terms of a possible long-term relationship with a member of the opposite sex.

The fifteen EDGE parents are unanimous in worrying about their child's

being lonely as an adult, particularly after the parents have died. They voice a consistent concern that their son or daughter with Down syndrome needs to have friends and companions beyond those in their immediate family. When their children have dated, parents support it (that's one of the major reasons for dating occurring in the first place), but they are concerned that their child could be sexually exploited or, at least, be sexually active in circumstances where supervision is not adequate, with the possibility of pregnancy. (None of the parents wants their child to become a parent.)

With regard to marriage as a possibility, EDGE mothers have widely varying views. Three of the fifteen see it as a strong possibility for their son or daughter; three see it as a "maybe, under just the right circumstances"; four see it as a dim possibility but haven't ruled it out entirely; three feel strongly that it is not a possibility; one hasn't given it enough thought to have formed an opinion; and in one family one parent sees it as a possibility and the other does not (both decided to respond).

## CLOSING THOUGHTS

In closing this chapter we think it fitting to see how the fifteen EDGE parents feel about their young adult son or daughter with Down syndrome now that they and their children are approximately 25 years into their family journey. We asked them the following question:

*"What three words would you use to describe [name's] personality?"*

*Mother:* I'd say outgoing and gregarious and happy-go-lucky—stubborn.

*Mother:* Good sense of humor is number one. Sports-minded and usually pretty even-tempered. Never holds a grudge. He's not overly friendly, and he's not obnoxious.

*Father:* What you see is what you get. There are very, very, very few people he really dislikes. I mean, he really gets to know people. It's just amazing. He just grows on people!

*Mother:* He's very curious, and he's almost intuitive...extraordinary sense of a situation, and responds to it very appropriately.

*Mother:* Creative. Strong-willed with a temper. A delightful sense of humor.

*Mother:* He has a wonderful sense of humor. Part of his difficulty has been in not being assertive enough. In the last year he's become more assertive. But he's vulnerable, and I don't know that there's anything you can do to change that. He's a people pleaser...and when he's pushed beyond his limits, he gets very stubborn.

*Mother:* He's the most unconditional loving person. He's the most stubborn person. And he tries 150%.

*Father:* Sometimes she's stubborn, and sometimes she's very cooperative. She seems to be responsible most of the times, but some other times she isn't.

*Mother:* She has a zest for life, she's quite inquisitive, and she's shy.

*Mother:* I guess "loving." He's such a lovable guy, and he just sort of exudes love and sweetness, and he's also very perceptive of others' moods.

*Mother:* She's always happy, she's never sad or unhappy or a problem. She's gentle, easy-going, and loving.

*Mother:* Enthusiastic, personable, polite, and stubborn.
*Father:* We should all do as well (background laughter). Determined, enthusiastic, and gutsy.

*Mother:* Delightful to be with, really, because he does have a good personality. He has a good sense of humor, and he's a person who likes to do things for other people.
*Father:* I guess you would describe him as being outgoing, delightful, easy to talk to.

*Father:* Loves games. He wants to be normal.
*Mother:* Stubborn. He wants to please people, too.

*Father:* Compassionate. She will observe when an adult needs consoling. If any one of us is hurting, she'll notice it. If she's in the middle of a sentence, she'll say, "I love you."
*Mother:* She's very sensitive to others' feelings.

*Father:* Oh, he's outgoing. Overly friendly. Trusting. All those are nice virtues, but they're also a matter of serious concern, too.
*Mother:* Outgoing, friendly, very wonderful.

*Mother:* Reserved. Not really shy. Sense of humor. Friendly.
*Father:* He has a great imagination.

In the EDGE parents' comments about their young adult son's or daughter's personality, two personality traits come through strongly. The first, and *by far the strongest*, is reflected in words indicating that their child with Down syndrome is enjoyable to be with. They use words such as "friendly," "good sense of humor," "happy," "tries very hard," "loving," "sensitive to others." These words dominate the fifteen EDGE parents' summary descriptions of their son's or daughter's personality.

A second trait, one that reflects defensiveness, is found in personality descriptors such as "stubborn" and "digs in his heels." Interestingly, the traits of enjoyability and defensiveness sometimes are used to describe the same child. For instance, an EDGE mother says the three words that come to mind when describing her young adult child's personality are "outgoing, gregarious, and happy-go-lucky-stubborn."

What can be made of this in terms of portraying the journey of EDGE parents at this point in their child's growing up years? Moreover, what do EDGE parents' descriptors of their son's or daughter's personality at around the age of 25 years have to say to parents who have just had a baby with Down syndrome, whose journey as a family is just beginning?

Let's deal with the defensiveness descriptors first. Across the fifteen EDGE families, six of the twenty-three personality summary statements of mothers and fathers contain the word "stubborn." That's a ratio of nearly one in four parents. Stubbornness can be irritating, but it is a relatively benign personality trait as it seems to be expressed in all but one of the EDGE families. But it can be serious, as it is in the one EDGE family where stubbornness occasionally turns into a temper tantrum. (In this case, defensiveness became "offensiveness" and led to curtailment of integrated community living opportunities.)

Stubbornness does not usually indicate a seriously maladapted personality. Each of us uses it as a defense mechanism (though in the most socially appropriate manner we can muster) if pushed beyond our ability to cope successfully in a given situation. But why does this descriptor permeate personality summaries to the tune of nearly a fourth of them? Our hunch is that stubbornness is learned because it is a useful defense mechanism for individuals with Down syndrome, who usually have mental retardation in the mild to moderate range. Having sufficient intelligence to recognize that a given task looks too challenging and

a sufficiently good memory to remember past difficulties with it or similar tasks, the individual may learn to exhibit stubbornness to avoid tasks that portend failure. For instance, "digging in their heels" when faced with an arithmetic task involving story problems can produce an "escape hatch" for the person with Down syndrome who has failed in these types of tasks in the past. Over time, people with Down syndrome (and many persons with mild to moderate levels of mental retardation due to other causes) learn stubbornness as a way to avoid a variety of situations and tasks in which they feel they might fail. Eventually stubbornness becomes a habit and a personality trait they display frequently.

Returning now to the predominant personality descriptors voiced by EDGE parents, pleasantness, sensitivity, and a joy for living characterize their perceptions, revealing that interacting with their son or daughter with Down syndrome as a young adult is enjoyable most of the time. With a lasting painful memory of events surrounding the birth of their child, memories of schooling that often were stressful, and persisting anxiety about what the future holds for their young adult son or daughter with Down syndrome, EDGE parents—and, it seems, most other parents who have a child with Down syndrome—journey through the growing-up years experiencing a rare form of success. This type of success comes only to those who have had to face hardship squarely, earnestly cope with it daily, and ultimately overcome it (but without ever being able to escape it completely).

Parents who have a child with Down syndrome seldom are able to discard all of the negative pieces of baggage that have been laid upon them since 1866, when Dr. Down used the words "mongol" and "degeneracy." Today's parents, though, are transforming the baggage of the past into a new "carry on" form that helps them live with more justifiable pride than ever before in history.

## $\mathscr{L}$OOKING TOWARD THE FUTURE

We began the book with the metaphor of "a journey," which commenced for the participants when EDGE children were born with Down syndrome in the late 1960s and early 1970s. We have traced the diverse paths of their journeys from birth, through the growing-up years, to the present. Although EDGE children are now young adults, the journey continues. Indeed perhaps the longest, and certainly most unmapped paths of the journey—the late adult years—lie before them. In these years some sons and daughters with Down syndrome may very likely walk their paths without a mother or father beside them because of having outlived one or both parents. And all families will encounter paths where the needs for interdependence and independence must be carefully balanced within and across family members in an atmosphere of ever-changing family structures.

EDGE parents had no advance knowledge that their child would be born with Down syndrome. Nonetheless, they all decided to share their family journey with a child with a disability. Does this mean that every parent who has a baby with Down syndrome should do likewise? No EDGE parent can answer this question for other parents, nor should anyone be so presumptuous as to try to do so. What we can say, though, is that all of the EDGE families have a positive, special "personality." Touched by the bittersweet experience of living with a son, daughter, sister, or brother with Down syndrome, family members, almost without exception, express feelings about the advantages of having shared their journey with a family member who has Down syndrome. Somehow, the bittersweet emotions that EDGE parents experienced at the birth of a child who has Down syndrome changed to a sweet-bitter (mostly sweet) feeling about a son or daughter who has made the transition to young adulthood.

This bodes well for new parents who feel inclined toward raising a child with Down syndrome at home. Fortunately, in the 1990s educational and community resources are in place to assist and support families who have children with Down syndrome. People with Down syndrome and other disabilities are included in schools, park programs, employment sites, and other community settings as never before.

The fuller integration of people with Down syndrome in community life also bodes well for society, which can derive immeasurable benefit from the unique contributions, humanizing influence, and renewing perspective on living that people with Down syndrome offer. In Chapter 12 we catch a glimpse of these benefits as revealed through the words of young adults with Down syndrome, speaking for themselves about their lives.

# $\mathcal{W}$OODARD FAMILY

Dad: Richard
Mom: Shirley
Son with Down syndrome: Bob

Bobby's "Hulk Machine."

Age two: What a smile!

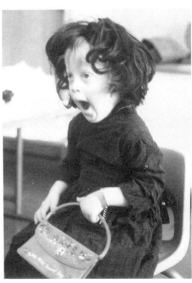

The party is over.

# $\mathcal{W}$OODARD FAMILY (continued)

Clowning around.

Boy and his dog.

Slow dancing.

Grown into a handsome guy.

# ZOLTAI FAMILY

Dad: Tibor
Mom: Olga
Brother: Peter
Sister: Kitty
Sister with Down
    syndrome: Lili

Life is a "ball."

I love books.

A proud moment.

Sister's wedding.

# ZOLTAI FAMILY (continued)

With grandpa.

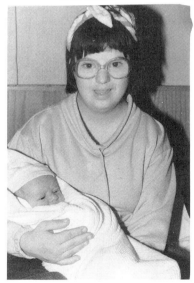

Holding first nephew.

Grown up.

# ~12~

# GIVING VOICE: YOUNG ADULTS' PERSPECTIVES ON THEIR LIVES

I. Karon Sherarts

$\mathscr{I}$n this chapter young adult men and women with Down syndrome speak for themselves about their lives. They share reflections about growing up and their feelings about having Down syndrome, express what gives their life meaning, and discuss their joys and their disappointments. As they talked about their lives, there were moments when each person expressed feelings and ideas with profound eloquence.

Excerpts from interviews with EDGE adults, show the breadth of their interests, and opinions and provide brief glimpses into aspects of their lives. Each of the EDGE adults lives a rich, complex, and multifaceted life. Each also has an imagination and an inner life. All of them have made significant transitions, from childhood to young adulthood, from school to employment. And some have left home to live in group or foster homes, supervised apartments, or independently. Most of them recognize that they will continue to need varying levels of support from their families and society.

Since its "discovery" in 1866, Down syndrome has been an intriguing area for research and scholarship. In each era the results of this work have framed our perceptions of people with this genetic condition and our expectations of their capabilities. Over the past twenty-five years an ever-increasing number of research-based texts and articles about people with Down syndrome have successfully challenged many of the pervasive stereotypes that were considered facts in earlier times. All of this work has important, far-reaching implications for parents, educators, physicians, and society as a whole. We now know that people with Down syndrome have a wide range of abilities, personalities, and individual characteristics. Indeed, the cumulative results of research-based inquiry and parent-based initiatives continue to open our eyes and expand our knowledge of those who have Down syndrome.

Nonetheless, despite the broad scope of prior work, the perceptions that *the subjects* of the research and intervention have about themselves and their lives have been neglected. While new information continues to discredit the stereotypes that have constrained both our expectations and their potential, people with Down syndrome have rarely been allowed to speak for themselves. We read about them, but their voices have been absent.

In 1992, I attended a conference in which writer and teacher Norita Dittberner-Jax spoke about the process of teaching young people to write poetry. During her presentation, she read a poem that Eric Fox, a sixth-grader with Down syndrome, had written about his grandfather, who had died recently. Eric and his grandfather had been devoted to each other, and the poem's immediacy drew me into Eric's experience in a powerful way.

> *A Portrait of Grandpa*
>
> My grandpa was in World War II.
> He came up to my house and visited
> for a little bit. Then he went back to
> Missouri and my Uncle Steve picked him
> up at the airport and brought him to
> McDonald's and he went to the bathroom
> and had a heart attack. My uncle went in
> to help him. He tried CPR on him.
> He brought him to the hospital and in
> 15 minutes he died. My Uncle Mark
> contacted us. He told my mom
> the whole story and then we went down
> to Missouri to his funeral. I got
> the flag that was on his casket.
> Also got his dog tags. My grandpa
> was a big giant.[1]

Norita related that after she had read all of the poems written by the students in Eric's general education class, she had asked Eric's classroom teacher to point out who had written *A Portrait of Grandpa*. She had been impressed by the poem on its own merits. It was only later that she learned that Eric has Down syndrome. She described her response to the poem:

> [The poem] has such power in the details and in the final lines. His grandpa's death and funeral were powerful events for Eric. But to be able to get it down on the page is something else. It's as if he was ready to write this—he had been working on this poem and probably didn't even know it.[2]

When the EDGE participants were born with Down syndrome in the late 1960s and early 1970s, their parents bucked the conventional wisdom of the era, which was to "put the baby in an institution before you get attached to it." Support systems and educational intervention programs were rare in those days, and all of us felt very fortunate to be involved in Project EDGE. It provided essential services that are now quite widely available. But we didn't know what lay ahead for our children. What was their social, emotional, and functional potential? What did they need to keep developing?

An EDGE parent recalled how vitally important reading *The World of Nigel Hunt,*[3] written by a young man with Down syndrome, had been for her. The book was published in 1967—a few years before her own son was born with Down syndrome. As this mother thought about the impact of the chapter you are now reading, she commented:

> I am going to enjoy seeing the [EDGE] children as they are now and their opinions. The only thing that I have ever read that [took this approach] is *The World of Nigel Hunt.* It made an impression on me. I always remember Nigel's observations and the feelings he expressed. [That book] was one thing that spurred me on. What everyone wants to know is how [these children feel]. The antiquated things that are said [about people with Down syndrome] just aren't true!

*Count Us In: Growing Up With Down Syndrome,*[4] written by Jason Kingsley and Mitchell Levitz, both of whom have Down syndrome, was published in early 1994. It makes an important contribution to our understanding of the complex process of growing up with Down syndrome. *Count Us In* and this chapter challenge readers to confront the question: What does it mean to hear the voice of people with Down syndrome? It means we:

- Become listeners.
- Accept the validity of their views and learn how to interpret them. In most instances, their views are as reliable and as consistent as our own. In response to questions such as, "If we ask Joan (a person with Down syndrome) about this topic next week, would she give us the same answer she gave today?" One can only answer, "Would any of us?"
- Perceive them as individuals who are neither victims nor heroes.

# ETHODOLOGY

All of the EDGE participants with Down syndrome were interviewed individually. Prior to the interviews parents talked with their adult child with Down syndrome about the purpose of the interview and helped them select a range of items to bring to and discuss at the interview. These items were to reflect the EDGE participants' interests, hobbies, talents, favorite activities, accomplishments, job or schooling, and other important aspects of their lives. All were asked the same set of questions; however, the interviews sometimes took the form of a dialogue. Interviews lasted one to two hours. One parent and occasionally both parents came to the interview with their son or daughter. Sometimes parents helped interpret phrases, added detail, or followed up on questions the interviewer asked. Interviews were recorded on audiotape and then transcribed. Direct quotes are used in this text; sometimes excerpts from long discussions are used. Pseudonyms have been used.

## ℘CHOOL YEARS: LEARNING, PEERS, AND SOCIAL LIFE

The EDGE adults have many memories, most of them pleasant, about their school days, including favorite subjects (such as math, computers, reading), things they enjoyed learning and doing, friends and socializing, teachers, special events and school activities, participating in Special Olympics, and graduation. Like most students, they found some things difficult to learn and experienced some unpleasant situations, such as being tardy. A few spoke of being teased, bothered, or pushed around by students without disabilities. As they spoke, some carefully distinguished between grade school ("early school") and secondary school ("late school").

Bruce described how his mother played with him and helped him learn to talk when he was young. He told a story about his mother taking him to a playground and demonstrated how she had used words to describe his actions:

> I was going up to the school, and I was [on] swing set. Yes, I was. And she [points to his mother], she take me there. And she says, "OK, Bruce. Time [for] swing set."

As he spoke, Bruce altered his voice to imitate his mother's higher, calm, precise tone.

Ben liked "going to different classes such as reading and computers." He also remembers his scuba diving class: "[My coach] would pull my ankle and tease me." Schoolwork "was sometimes hard" for him, especially math. Although he understood math concepts, he had difficulty extending the process he used for solving math problems to encompass more complex operations:

> I can't figure out the math. I don't have all the marks down, so I can't count them up. I say, "1 plus 1 is 2; 3 plus 3 is 6. 4 and 4 is 5." And like that. It's hard to figure out.

Joe spoke of the help and encouragement he received from teachers:

> My teachers in school understand about math, writing, time, and reading, and [they] brought me to the situation the way it is [taught me these things].... I did reading, writing, and math. That's a long time [ago]. Caroline used to

be one of [my] teachers. She taught me how to read. That's what she want me to do. And she so thrilled and excited because she knows I'm going to do [it].

Matt liked theater class. As he described it, "[I'd get] a few A's and B's like to get my mom and dad's eyeballs dancing." One year he was the master of ceremonies (MC) for the high school talent show: "There were four guys and the teachers banging their heads [to put] on a talent show. And I put my talent clothes on to be the MC." Matt has continued to work in amateur theater.

Jane liked "everything"—all of her subjects: "I like to study hard, and they told me I do a good job doing that. That's why I pass all these course[s]. I pass classes because I am an A and B student." She was a cheerleader and participated in Special Olympics. "I started saying 'Oh, jeez' in 1988. And then everybody was saying it because of me [i.e., it was a fad]. I'm the one who started it."

Allen said he liked learning, especially reading: "I read comics—Marvel comics, detective comics." He received an "award from the Vector program [for being the student of the year] and the Brian Fund award for being the outstanding special education student" at his high school.

Dale's favorite years were junior high because "I had a lot of friends. But I don't have a lot of friends now." In contrast, Roger felt relieved to be out of school: "The thing I like about school is that I'm done! Oh boy, other kids [without disabilities] gave me a hard time. 'Roger do this, and Roger do that!' Finally I'm done! Peace and quiet. Working is better."

Some of the other young men and women also recalled instances when peers without disabilities treated them badly.

> I am [was] really getting tired of being push me around. [Sometimes other students would say], "You retarded kid." And [I say back to them], "Who are you? You are a couple of Nerds." I not put up with that! There is one student named Jacob. He drove me nuts. And I say, "Go away from me. [You] push me around and you say bad names."

> [Sometimes] in my school, people treat me *bad*. One time some of my friends didn't like me and hurt [my feelings] bad. Somebody turned the lights off [when I was in the bathroom].

---

*In 1987, when he was in tenth grade, Alex Lindblad delivered a speech to the Down Syndrome Association of Minnesota about his life and interests. His address, presented below, succinctly captures a moment in time.*

My name is Alex Lindblad. I am 17 years old. I go to St. Louis Park Senior High. I'm in the 10th grade. I live with my parents and I have one brother and two sisters. My brother, Steve, lives in Lexington, Kentucky. Molly moved to St. Thomas College, and Beth lives at the University of Minnesota. I feel happy when they come [home] for Christmas.

I like to play Atari, read Super Hero comics, and listen to tapes. My favorite singers are Bruce Springsteen, Michael Jackson, and the Monkees. I like to go to my friend George's house to sleep over Sat[urday] until Sunday.

I had a job last summer at Oak Terrace Nursing Home. I did janitor work. I put my money in the bank and bought a new boom box.

A long time ago I was 8 years old, and I started Special Olympics. In Special Olympics, I have done basketball, bowling, swimming, cross-country skiing, track and field, [floor] hockey, softball, and soccer.

In swimming I can't dive because there is something wrong with my neck. My favorite sport is bowling. I go bowling every Saturday at Golden Valley Lanes in a bowling league. My best friend, George, goes bowling every Saturday with me. Last summer I went to the International [Special Olympics] Games. I flew on a private jet. We had some food and drinks, and there were bathrooms on the plane. I wasn't scared because I flew on a plane once before. International Games were in South Bend, Indiana. I bowled with Dan, Julie, Casey, and Sam. Betty was the coach. My best game was 102. I won 7th place in mixed doubles and bronze in team bowling.

A lot of my friends from St. Louis Park were on the soccer team. They beat Brazil. The whole Minnesota team had a pizza party. I'll never forget the International Games.

# $\mathcal{T}$HE PRESENT

The EDGE adults' reflections on the present are organized into five sections: Interests and Accomplishments, which includes popular culture, athletics, and other interests and activities; Dating and Marriage; Limitations; The Experience of Living Away From Home; and Dream Jobs (their response to the question, "If you could have any job in the whole wide world, what would you choose?").

## INTERESTS AND ACCOMPLISHMENTS

**Popular culture.** All EDGE adults are knowledgeable about basic aspects of popular culture, and they can discuss specific topics in considerable detail. Everyone has a collection of favorite movies on videotape, and several have compact discs (CDs) or cassettes of their favorite singers and musical groups. Their interest in popular music runs the gamut, with tastes ranging from country music to the Beach Boys to heavy metal and movie soundtracks. Some have microphones they use to sing along with tapes or CDs. A few have joined fan clubs and written to pop stars. One young man treasures a letter singer Wynonna Judd wrote to him. Films, specific television shows, sports, comics, and books about films or TV series and stars are also important to EDGE adults. Some collect animated Disney films. One person has tapes of all of the films that her favorite male actors have appeared in, several collect their favorite films, and others collect tapes of sports events. All enjoy going to movies and attending live concerts and plays, as well as other types of performances. One EDGE adult excitedly told the interviewer, "I can't wait until the 17th. My mom, and my brother, my sister-in-law, my sister, and my brother-in-law, and myself are going to see a play, *Miss Saigon.*" Another said, "I went to Robert Plant's concert in Austin. The next week [I] went to Oklahoma to see him with my brother."

Sally talked about her video collection of favorite films—*Home Alone [1 and 2]* and *Honey I Blew Up the Kid*—and the TV programs she likes best. She also showed the interviewer books about them which she buys at bookstores and garage sales.

> My favorite TV show [is "Beverly Hills 90210"]. This is my favorite actress, this one, Shannon Doherty. She's on "Beverly Hills 90210." This is my favorite actor, Brandon; he is Jason Preistley [on "Beverly Hills 90210"]. I [watch it] every Wednesday. It starts at 7:00; ends at 8:00. Sometimes [on the show] they talk about drugs, graduation, school stuff. It's very interesting. About drugs, you should not take drugs. She took drugs and she had to help her. [Sally points to characters in pictures.] She is depressed and feels sick. So she has to help her. It's very interesting.

Def Leppard, a heavy metal band, is Daniel's favorite group:

> I have two Def Leppard videos at home. I went to Minnesota State Fair and saw all five Def Leppard [musicians] play at the State Fair. I like [the] one-handed drummer. His name is Rick Allen. I went with Julie, Paul, and Mike. I stay[ed] up late. [There] were two shows. Number 1 is Ugly Kid Joe [the warm-up band with] four men on stage. [Then came] Def Leppard.

Most EDGE adults are very comfortable using technology. They learned to use computers during their school years, and some continue to use them for writing, drawing, learning, and playing games (see Figure 8). Many play electronic games, such as Nintendo and Sega. The EDGE adults find it easy to operate cassette tape and CD players. They also record off air, use video playback features, and cue up videos in order to watch their favorite parts of movies, home videos, and performances. Two adults have their own video

## FIGURE 8

Computer drawing of Randy Quaid by Amy Fletcher

cameras. Jane saved her paychecks for an entire year to buy a camcorder and is now "the family photographer." Roger paid for part of the purchase, and his parents contributed the rest as a present. He enjoys taking his camcorder on vacation. When Roger was on a recent trip to visit his brother Sam in San Diego, Sam took "shots of [me] swimming and [learning to] surfboard." Roger commented: "It's hard to learn. [I had] on a wet suit and the whole bit."

**Athletics.** EDGE adults began playing individual and team sports in grade school and through Special Olympics. Everyone brought Special Olympics medals, ribbons, snapshots, or trophies with them to the interview and spoke of their accomplishments over the years. During their high school days, half of the group participated in International Special Olympics team or individual sports. Now as adults, almost all continue to take part in Special Olympics sports such as bowling, power lifting, softball, basketball, floor hockey, soccer, skating, swimming, skiing, and tennis. Joe said he was "nervous about losing 5 pound[s]" for an upcoming Special Olympics power lifting event.

Roger plays softball on an inclusive Special Olympics team that includes adults with and without disabilities. In the interview he proudly commented, "My dad is one of the players. He's great!" Several EDGE adults who participate in the Wild Angels (a Special Olympics team for young adult women and men) brought their personalized team jackets and photos of teammates to the interview. Ann was among them. As she showed a team photo to the interviewer, she said: "This is my team from Wild Angels. I play softball."

All of the men follow at least one professional sport (baseball, basketball, football, hockey) and have their own views about which teams and which players are the best. Many of them keep score and maintain win-loss records on their favorite teams. They attend sports events, often with friends or family members, and they invite friends over to watch games or other events on TV. During his interview, Daniel read the sports news and looked up the weekly schedule of games in the local newspaper.

Daniel:     Tonight is sports. Minnesota Gophers against UMD [University of Minnesota Duluth], Midwest Sports Channel. [It] is on cable. Minnesota Timber Wolves is playing tomorrow at 5 o'clock. And at 1:05 tomorrow Gophers against UMD Minnesota. The Timber Wolves is playing Dallas Tuesday. Dallas Mavericks will win. Saturday, Gophers Hockey against North Dakota at 7:30 p.m., live on cable, MSC, Sports Channel 12.

Interviewer: Are you going to watch any of those games?

Daniel:     Yeah. Friday the 11th.

Interviewer: Who's playing that night?

Daniel:     North Dakota. I will miss Wednesday Gophers [because] I got the downhill skiing [that night].

Mike talked about his devotion to the Denver Broncos. He described the Broncos' gear he brought to the interview—gloves, jacket, sweatpants, shirt, hat, scarf, posters, and a tape of the Broncos playing the Bears, which he had recorded himself. John Elway is his favorite player. Last year Mike and his brother flew to Denver to see a Broncos game. As he showed a photo of the team, Mike said:

> This is John Elway. I've seen him once. I saw the game Sunday, November 20th, 1993, in Denver [at] Mile High Stadium. And I saw John Elway. He's the best guy! [He] throws from the shotgun. Score is 23 to 26; [it] is a close game! Close! Monday, I saw the Colorado mountains!

A number of the men are avid World Wrestling Federation (WWF) and World Championship Wrestling (WCW) fans. They attend matches with friends or invite them over to watch televised wrestling specials. Most of the fans have collections of often-watched videotapes of special matches, such as

Summer Slam, which are aired periodically on cable TV in addition to the regular weekly wrestling programs. Joe likes "all the different [kinds of] matches." He explained, "Some people are bad and they are going to beat up the [good guys]. And so, all the good guys are going to beat the bad guys up." He began collecting miniature WWF wrestling figures ten years ago and now has nearly 200 figures. Joe enjoys setting up matches between specific figures in his miniature wrestling rings.

**Other interests and activities.** All of the EDGE adults brought photo albums with pictures capturing moments of their lives—family events, vacation activities (such as visits to Universal Studios), special events (graduation, siblings' weddings, high school proms, playing on sports teams, dance recitals, scouting events, summer camp experiences)—as well as pictures of friends and people they were dating. A number of the adults talked about attending dances, working out at health clubs, and learning new skills in sports or other pursuits. Several, like Sally, said that they love to travel.

Sally: That's my [pay]check. [She shows interviewer her pay stub.] That's my tax. [I get paid] every second week.

Interviewer: What do you do with this check?
Sally: Save it. Saving for Mexico, Canada, Hawaii. [I] like to travel.
Interviewer: Are you planning a trip now?
Sally: Dad and I are going to Mexico, Cancun, C-A-N-C-U-N, on the 21st and coming back on the 28th. We'll fly down, stay in hotel, [and] take side trips.

Some EDGE adults said they liked "to organize things." Such activities included making lists of things to purchase or of favorite things (for example, Christmas songs), making lists of guests who appear on Friday's late night TV shows, maintaining win-loss records on sports teams, noting upcoming events on the calendar, arranging videotapes and CDs in a predetermined order, and organizing games for younger nieces and nephews to play. During their interviews, two young men presented notes they had written to organize and remind their mothers of things they urgently needed: headphones and money. Matt's succinct note read:

> Mom.
> Remember. Last worning [warning]. By [buy] some headphones. Please.
> Sign[ed] your son, Matt

Daniel's note requested that his mother leave a blank check that he could cash at the nearby grocery store. He needed money for the movie he was going to attend with a friend a few days hence.

> Friday, February 4
> BMM [Bryn Mar Market, grocery store] for movie.
> For money for Sunday.

Several of the EDGE adults are proud of their abilities to cook specialty foods, for example, French toast and Karen Burgers. One young man likes to draw wild cats—lions, pumas, panthers—and a young woman enjoys making computer drawings of her favorite actors (see Figure 8). Sally, who takes well-deserved pride in her excellent printing, commented that the interviewer's writing was "pretty good; but your 'Y' is not good." Then she added, "I'm [also] a name expert." She likes to read before she goes to bed: "I underline word[s] I don't know. After I read the whole thing, I talk about the hard words I don't understand. I [say I] don't know what that means, and [staff or parents] help me with the meanings."

## DATING AND MARRIAGE

Almost all of the EDGE adults want to have, already have, or have had a boyfriend or girlfriend. As one person put it, "I [don't] have a girlfriend yet. It will take a while. I will have one pretty soon." Some are dating or have dated in the past. Two-thirds said they would like to get married someday, approximately one-third didn't want to marry, and two were undecided. Bill wanted to get married for "companionship" and to have someone "to share [his] life with." He told the interviewer, "[My girlfriend and I] were talking about getting married and everything. But things wasn't going so well. We just hated to break up." A young woman who wants to get married in the future said teasingly, "First I have to find the right guy." One young man felt "upset" because he wasn't married.

Six adults knew who they wanted to marry. In two instances it was a popular singer or movie star on whom they had a crush. The others wanted to marry the man or woman they were currently going out with (or, in one instance, planned to date). Two people were dating others with Down syndrome. Sam, who wants to marry Joann, spoke of saying "I love you" to her, described the engagement process, what he would wear to the wedding, and the wedding cake. Dale would also like to marry his girlfriend but is concerned that she is "boy crazy":

> Well, my girlfriend is Down syndrome. We have been [dating], but I get disgusted [by] the way she acts. She's really boy crazy. And her mom and her sister says [she's] not supposed to be boy crazy. It's not my problem; it's her parents' problem. I'd like to help her a lot.

## LIMITATIONS

Not being able to drive a car was a disappointing and sometimes frustrating situation for all but one of the adults. Some felt quite "upset" or "down, bored, [and] crummy" about not being able to drive or own a car. Both circumstances undercut the adults' age-related expectations and desire for independence.

> Bill: I want to be able to get a car.
> Interviewer: How do you feel about not being able to drive?
> Bill: I constantly have to rely on my dad, my brother, and my mom to give me rides—or other people. I'd like to be independent and just do things that I like to do. Sometimes when I go to a concert or something, I'd like to be able to drive there myself.

Three EDGE adults had unique responses to questions about things they would like to do but can't. One involved communication; two others focused on male-female companionship and independence.

> Dale: I'd like to be able to talk better.
> Sally: I'd get my own band with Jim [my boyfriend]. I dream about Jim all the time. I dream about my future with Jim. He and [I would] live together, work together, read and write, drive a car, have my own job and his own job, adopt a child. That kind of thing.
> Roger: I want to move by myself and find a real woman and be nice to her. [I'd] talk nice to her and tell her about love. [I'd] eat diet food, barbecue chicken, and no mashed potatoes. I want a driver's license. I want a new car.

## THE EXPERIENCE OF LIVING AWAY FROM HOME

Half of the EDGE adults with Down syndrome have made the transition from home to other living situations: Two live in foster homes; two in group homes; two in supervised apartment living; and one lives independently in her own apartment. All of them continue to maintain strong, ongoing relationships with their parents and siblings.

Ann talked about leaving home and was all set to move into an apartment the day after the interview. Her building has 30 one-bedroom apartments. She was clearly excited and eager to live independently. She works as a prep cook. As part of the transition to apartment living, she transferred from the Perkins restaurant where she'd been working to one near the apartment.

> Ann: I am moving tomorrow, and I'll [be] living by myself. My apartment is out in Bloomington, and the address is _____ and my [phone] number is _____. I'm on the second floor. My apartment is 204. On the second floor I have neighbors. Mark, he's in 202. John, I know, and Phil, [and] Mary. The new girl has to move in.
>
> Interviewer: What will life be like there?
>
> Ann: Different! [She laughs.] I'll have to cook and fix a meal. I always clean my apartment—vacuum, dusting, that kind of thing.
>
> Interviewer: How often does someone come in to check you?
>
> Ann: I don't, independent.
>
> Interviewer: I bet your parents will call. Even though you moved out they are still going to be interested in you.
>
> Ann: Yes, I know that. Because they need me! [Laughter] It's a joke!

Jane, who lives in a group home, spends two weekends a month with her family. During the interview her father described the conflicting feelings Jane sometimes experiences during these visits:

> When she comes home, she's confused with the real deep historical emotions of being around the house and being around us. So she'll usually say sometime that evening that she loves Mom and Dad, but she likes her new house better.

When the interviewer asked Jane if there was anything she didn't like about living in the group home she replied,

> "I like living there. And I like all my staff. I'm used to them now. But I'm not used to my Mom and Dad. I don't like to be away from my friends."

## DREAM JOBS

All of the EDGE adults are either working or attending a job preparation program. Those with jobs brought work-related items, such as listings of job responsibilities, pay stubs, and awards for outstanding performance to discuss at the interview. Figure 9 breaks out the sequence of responsibilities for an EDGE adult involved in a candle-making process.

## Monday

| | | |
|---|---|---|
| **Ball Molds** | ☐ | Take candles out of molds and put into boxes |
| | ☐ | Repaper tables |
| | ☐ | Set up ball molds on both tables |
| | ☐ | Wipe out molds to remove wax pieces |
| | ☐ | Bring candles to driller's area |

## Break

| | | |
|---|---|---|
| **Sweeping** | ☐ | Mary's area |
| | ☐ | Wax room |
| **Trash** | ☐ | Mary's area—big box |
| | ☐ | Mary's area—small box |
| | ☐ | Store—under counter |
| | ☐ | Store—under counter |
| | ☐ | Store—under desk |
| | ☐ | Rob's desk |
| | ☐ | Pat's desk |
| | ☐ | Judy's desk |
| | ☐ | Joy's area |

## Lunchtime

| | | |
|---|---|---|
| **Empty Wax** | ☐ | Bring boxes to weigh area |
| | ☐ | Ask someone to weigh wax |
| | ☐ | Pour wax into large box |
| | ☐ | Bring empty boxes back to turners |

## Break

| | | |
|---|---|---|
| **Small Candles** | ☐ | Take candles out of molds and put into boxes |
| | ☐ | Take full boxes to driller's area |

**Time to go home!**

## FIGURE 9

Job task sheet

The EDGE adults were asked what job they would choose if they could do anything they wanted. Not surprisingly, their choices centered around leisure interests, promotion to higher-level jobs in their current workplace, or working for another company.

Their dream jobs often involved popular culture: I'd be "a disc jockey, singer, or make films," "work at Mister Movies," "play with Wynonna Judd's band," "have my own band," "be a cowboy star like on 'Bonanza,' or be a sheriff." Ben thought getting a job "watching wrestling tapes" would be ideal. When the interviewer asked, "Would you like to be a wrestler?" he quipped, "No! I don't want to be a wrestler," laughed, and reminded the interviewer that he wanted to watch wrestling tapes: "Stop, rewind, record, stop, rewind, record. And don't forget the pause button!"

Carol would like to sell candles at the shop where she currently assists in the candle manufacturing process. Daniel would like to be "a banquet server" in the hotel where he works and also wants his own band. Ann would like to switch from her food prep job at Perkins to a restaurant in the Mall of America, the largest shopping mall in the United States. Sam said, "I could work all day at Subway [fast food restaurant] and [wear] a new shirt with my name on it—SAM." Sally talked about playing in a band with her boyfriend and also working as a janitor: "I used to work at Super 8 Motel. I cleaned. Like vacuuming, dusting, make beds, wipe tables, wipe mirrors, pictures. It was peaceful and quiet."

# SELF-IMAGE

Having Down syndrome is one of the givens in EDGE adults' lives; it presents them with challenges others do not have. Each person with Down syndrome has his or her own deep, complex feelings about it. Yet EDGE adults appear to live as if they believe that having Down syndrome is *one* aspect of their life, not its defining feature. Such a view makes them neither victims or heroes, but simply individuals who lead productive, satisfying lives and are continuing to develop as human beings.

## HAVING DOWN SYNDROME

The EDGE adults know they have Down syndrome and that having it makes their lives different from others' in some ways. As one EDGE adult said, "[Having Down syndrome] "makes my life and myself [different]." It was hard for most to describe exactly how their lives were different from the lives of those who do not have Down syndrome. In the interviews, they talked about:

- *Being born "that way," that is, with Down syndrome*

  "That mean you have been, you have been born, that way. Like me."

  Down syndrome "is inside my body."

- *Difference in facial features between those with and without Down syndrome*

  People with Down syndrome are different—"their eyes, their face, their hair."

  One parent said that although "we've never really discussed [our daughter's] feelings about having Down syndrome, she knows from TV—she's always picking them out. Other people with Down syndrome see her and she sees them, and you can't miss the contact between them."

- *Not being able to do some of the things those who do not have Down syndrome can do*

  Interviewer: How does having Down syndrome make your life different from other people's?

  EDGE Adult: Oh, different. Really different. I don't know how to skate or ski.

But the EDGE adults were quick to point out that people who have Down syndrome are not all alike—they are individuals. As Ann described it: "We are different people; and some people have another kind of Down syndrome." Her father and the interviewer probed her observation:

Father: I don't understand quite what you mean.

Ann: I mean, if we [have] Down syndrome, the people in different ways have Down syndrome.

Interviewer: Do you mean they are all different? They are all individuals?

Ann: Yes.

Sally explained that her boyfriend and foster sister, Sue, also have Down syndrome but in "different" ways.

> About my Down syndrome, just like [my foster sister's], but different. I talk normal. She talks different than I do. That's why I help her. I understand what she is saying [and interpret for her]. What she is saying to me I say to [others]. Sometimes I don't understand. Sometimes I do. [When I don't, I ask her], "Are you talking about this?" [She might say], "No! I said plates!" [She means] set the table.

Sally is teaching her foster sister to read and write. As Sally put it, she's doing "pretty good. She usually write her name. It's not really hard. She practices sometimes, but sometimes not. It depends."

Learning to live with Down syndrome is not easy. The EDGE adults expressed strikingly different feelings about the experience of having Down syndrome. Some said they felt "OK"; others talked about feeling "good" or "happy" about it; and others expressed negative feelings. At one end of the spectrum was Dale:

Interviewer:  How does Down syndrome make you feel?
Dale:  Well, that really makes me feel wonderful.

One person redefined and reframed Down syndrome as "Up syndrome," a term she and her father use when they give presentations about it to groups. Others spoke of feeling "bad," "sad," "angry," or "downgraded." Comments by three EDGE adults follow:

> I don't really like being Down syndrome. It's like being downgraded.
>
> I have Down syndrome inside my body, but not outside. I don't like to see it out on the outside. It doesn't look good.
>
> [I feel] bad. I hate handicapped people with Down syndrome. I like regular people and regular females.

It is possible that a person's feelings about having Down syndrome may change over time. One parent noted that when her son was a teenager he felt angry and sad about it; now, as an adult, he says it feels "OK." A unique perspective on having Down syndrome was put forth by one young man: "It means, like, it doesn't matter what your [disability] is. It doesn't matter how disabled you are. It's how you get along with other people [that matters]."

Some adults who spoke about the negative aspects of having Down syndrome spent time explaining their feelings. It was with great emotion, sadness mixed with anger, that one man said, "I wish I didn't have it." In a conversation he made up between himself and his mother, he expressed the depth of his feelings and conveyed a sense of his personal struggle:

Interviewer:  How does it make you feel to know that you have Down syndrome?
Bruce:  I wish I not be. [He then created a conversational dialogue to express his feelings; he used two distinctly different voices for the speakers—himself and his mother.]

> "You are being retarded."
> "I not! I wish, I wish I not."
> And, my mom say, "Yes, you are."
> "No, I not!"
> "You?"

"I not be like, like, retarded, and I not be, like, physical handicapped. No I
not! No I not! I wish I didn't have it."

A high-functioning man explained why he doesn't want to have Down
syndrome. It is in part because he is aware of the differences between his
ability and that of others with Down syndrome:

> I just don't want to be Down syndrome. I'm not really part of the group,
> you know, with other friends [who have Down syndrome]. [I'm] not like
> these two here [points to pictures of adults with Down syndrome]. It's like
> being downgraded. You know of other people that [are] downgraded [be-
> cause they have Down syndrome]. I don't really like being Down syndrome.

He has told his mother that he wants to change his "Down's face" through
plastic surgery. According to his mother, "He's said a few times, 'I wish I
could change my face. I don't like this face. It's a Down's face.' " (See Chapters
2 and 10 for medical perspectives on plastic surgery.)

When she was fourteen, Jane became troubled by her Down syndrome
facial features and requested plastic surgery. Jane's concern was something
that her parents had not anticipated. In the interview she explained that although she was born with Down syndrome, as a result of the surgery she has
"Down syndrome inside [her] body, but not outside." She elaborated, "I don't
like to see it out on the outside. It doesn't look good." During the interview
her father encouraged her to talk about her feelings about having Down syndrome:

Jane: I have Down syndrome inside my body, but not outside.
Father: Why do you have it inside your body but not outside your body?
Jane: Because I don't like to see retarded people. I'm special. I'm a spe-
cial person. It doesn't show outside. That's why I [look attractive]. I
went to the doctor and I had plastic surgery. And this is what I look
like.
Father: It's one of those [things] we hadn't anticipated from her perspective.
Jane: That's why [after] I have plastic surgery, I'm cute.
Father: Not having it on the outside, just on the inside, where people can't
see it?
Jane: I like the inside better.
Father: So it's hidden.
Jane: It's inside your body. But I don't like to see it out on the outside. It
doesn't look good. Because I had it once, and I didn't look good
that way. But I had plastic surgery, and I look fine. Because they
put a bone in my nose, and bones up here by [my] cheeks. And my

tongue was long before, and now it's short. Because of surgery on it. And I like that the best.

## THE BEST THING ABOUT ME IS "BEING ME!"

All of the EDGE adults talked about what they like best about their lives; some also described the best things about them as a person and what makes them happy. Their views, sometimes stated in a few words, convey a positive sense of self. Some simply said, "It's great to be 22!" "Being young," or "Being me!" For one person the best thing is that "it's marriage time," meaning that he is dating and feels mature enough to get married.

A number of EDGE adults spoke of independence, although independence meant somewhat different things to each person:

> I plan my own life. It's fun to have a life. All of my activities make me happy. I look in the mirror [and] see that I look all right!

> Getting paychecks, [that's] when I get money. Living in a foster home with companions.

> Doin' stuff with my friends. Doin' stuff with my mother. And getting to be on my own. Living [in an apartment] and that kind of stuff. Going out and listening to music. [Going to] New Union. That's a good place. They have pool tables, too, games, video games and [live] bands that play there.

> The very best thing about me is [having] my own life. The family makes me happy, and I feel good. I appreciate what Mom and Dad do. My age is just fine, right now!

> I go to work every day, Monday through Friday. I [get up by myself] and listen to my tapes, watch the news. And I get dressed at 7:30 a.m. After KARE-11 [a local TV channel] Update at 7:45, I [go to work].

A young man with acting talent finds the best things about his life are being:

> involved with [an inclusive] theater company since 1991 or longer than that. And now I'm all grown up and I'm mature. When I'm on stage I ham it up in, like, a comedy sort of way. Two years [ago] right now the theater company had been on the road to Aberdeen, South Dakota, to perform. I had [to] talk like I was [from] Georgia. I might have a cigar in my mouth and I go [say], "How you like it?" [He blows out smoke from an imaginary cigar.]

Another young man spoke in some detail about the qualities he likes best in himself:

> I am a good person to be with, and I'm very energetic. That I'm very good with people. That I'm nice. Care-giving. And there's other things, too. The

list goes on and on. I really care about people. I care about females and their feelings.

Jane described the special things about her as having "a good sense of humor" and being both an "entertainer" and a "healer."

Interviewer: What are the best things about you as a person or friend?
    Father: Well, if somebody asked some other person, "What's special about Jane?" what would they say?
    Jane: I'm [an] entertainer who makes people laugh. An entertainer is singing, dancing, and [having] a sense of humor.
    Father: She will often describe herself as a healer, too.
    Jane: Healing with love.

Sometimes Jane writes healing prescriptions for people. One day, while working at Burger King, she overheard a customer talking with her manager about his wife's illness and hospitalization. Jane was concerned. When she got home she typed a letter of encouragement to the customer on her computer and gave it to him the next day.

    Jane: I wrote this because I heard one of my managers talk[ing] with somebody, and I heard [what they were talking about]. That's why I wrote this letter.
    Father: Maybe you could read it to her [the interviewer]? [The letter reproduced here uses Jane's original punctuation and spelling.]
    Jane: [Reads the letter.] I don't know your wifes' name. [Jane added, "I

didn't, but I do now."] I want you to show her this letter because I want her to see it ok. I heard this from you with somebody at Burger King I did. I hope your wife gets better ok. I'm so glad she loosing her weight I am. I know she eats healthy. Make her not eat the food, she can't have ok. Make her exzerise [exercise] everyday ok. Make her sleep alot [a lot] and drink lots fluted [fluid] ok. Give her a hug because how much you love her ok. And that makes her better it does. [I see the sunshine. It peps me up, it does. You're nice.[5]] When she gets better I want her to walk like a teddy bear ok. The teddy bear has no knees [needs]; but she does. I feel sorry that she is in the hospital I am. I think she is a wonderful nice atractive [attractive] woman and you [are] ok.

Sincerely, JANE

# BSERVATIONS

The central message of this chapter is extremely important but is one that is often neglected. That message is that young adults with Down syndrome:

- Have in-depth perspectives on their lives
- Are able to express their perspectives and opinions in an insightful manner, though not always in words alone
- Express their views with refreshing candor

Although it is not always easy to decipher or understand what adults with Down syndrome are saying, expending the effort to do so is rewarding for both the speaker and the listener. The person who is struggling to communicate a complex idea with limited expressive language is both affirmed and empowered when we engage ourselves in the process of understanding what she or he means. Once we do understand, we have gained rich knowledge about that person's ideas, thoughts, and opinions, as well as clues about how to communicate more effectively with that person in the future.

The self-image and perspectives of adults with Down syndrome have been shaped by the experiences and values they encountered in the developmental process of growing up. Parents, siblings, and extended families, as well as teachers, therapists, employers, friends, recreation program staff, and many others, have contributed immeasurably to their development. In many ways families, schools, and communities have been partners in shaping the growing-up and adult years of EDGE adults.

# 𝒫ORTRAITS OF EDGE PARTICIPANTS AS YOUNG ADULTS

In this final section of the chapter, photographs of each EDGE adult are accompanied by excerpts from that person's interview. This pairing allows readers to catch glimpses of what makes each adult's life meaningful and satisfying. The diverse nature of these portraits engages us in the process of seeing each person with Down syndrome as an individual. Pseudonyms are not used.

### DAVID BAUMAN

Athletics is an important aspect of David's life. He participates in sports and maintains win-loss records on his favorite professional teams. Among the items David brought to the interview were a number of trophies and medals he has earned over the years in Special Olympics floor hockey, bowling, and power lifting. He began the interview by talking about bowling.

> I get spares and strikes...[And here is] my Athlete of the Year Award for 1989–90 Special Olympics.

David talked about playing on the 1989 International Special Olympics Minnesota Floor Hockey Team. He commented, "[My] jersey was number 18. And I got this medal, right here [which says] 'sharing, courage, joy

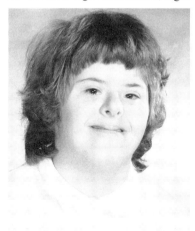

and skill.' " Some fellow EDGE adults who were on the same team recalled that David was the only member who didn't get sick! David continues to participate in Special Olympics on the Wild Angels team. In professional basketball, David's favorite player was "Larry Bird, number 33, [for the] Boston Celtics. I liked him for the swish. Over the glass. [He] retired."

### KAREN BYLAND

"I like to write things down 'cause I want to buy stuff with the list, take it out, and use it. It's a good hobby. Everybody makes lists. I write them right out of my head." Karen likes to make salads. Her dad says: "Each one looks just like a picture. She makes really good salads." She is also known for her "Karen Burger." As Karen describes it, "It's a bacon cheeseburger. It's a specialty with onions and fries. I just made up the name."

## HOLLY COLWELL

The first thing Holly talked about in the interview was figure skating, which she has devoted several years to learning.

> Well, first we have a picture of me and my [skating] coach, Kathleen. And a tape called 'Stars and Stripes Forever.' [I skated to that music] at Target Center [in Minneapolis]. I also brought the [silver] medal I won in skating at the 1989 International Special Olympics in Reno.

She showed the interviewer a photograph of the congratulatory sign displayed in front of her high school, which read: "Holly Colwell, Silver Medalist at Special Olympics Skating." But her "favorite thing is the picture of Patrick Swayze and me [taken at the International Games]. [Patrick Swayze] picked me from the waist, spins me around, and kissed me on the cheek. I told him [that I] liked the way he dances in the movie *Dirty Dancing*." Holly added, "I want to [dance] just like him sometime. And I want Patrick Swayze to teach me how to do that dance!"

## TIM FINNERTY

Tim takes the city bus to and from work. The second time he took the bus by himself he got confused about which bus to take to get home. Tim ended up "all the way downtown." He described what happened next:

[And there] I am downtown. [I said]: "Are you out of your mind? I'm going to 66th and Portland. How can I get off on [this] street when I have to go on

[to my stop]?" I got off the bus and the police put me on [the right bus]. It [was] scary for me. I think, [it is] just like [in the movie] *Home Alone 2*.

After Tim got off the first bus, he walked over to City Center, where he found a security guard, who called the police. "I [said] to the police, 'I'd like to go on another bus, please.' It worked out fine." That's the only time Tim has gotten lost.

## RICK FLEMING

Rick works part-time preparing food for cooking and "wiping off tables" at a local restaurant. The three things he likes best about his job are "[that] you can be the boss," "getting the food ready to cook," and "making more money and big bucks." Rick's leisure activities include riding his "green Kawasaki motorcycle" and mountain bike and participating in sports. He rides his mountain bike "on trails" located a few blocks from his home and "to the gym." At the gym he swims and works out "to get heavy muscles." In his teens, Rick did bodybuilding and competed professionally. As he described

a portrait taken at a competition, "[This is a] picture of my body. I got fifth place," he commented on the hard work bodybuilding requires. "Doing weights [for bodybuilding] was hard work. [I did] it almost every day. Oh boy!" When Rick looked at a picture of himself, his sister Kris, and her husband on a fishing boat, he laughed and quipped, "[We] went out on the ocean [to fish] and I [caught] a bird with my pole!"

## AMY FLETCHER

Amy Fletcher has worked at a fast food restaurant for three years. She described her duties to the interviewer:

> I wipe tables and I bring back trays. After I bring back the trays, I do the garbage,

Yuck! But I sweep before I do the garbage. That's not my favorite thing to do, the garbage. After I do the garbage, I wipe off the service area. And after that—this is my most favorite thing—I do the bathrooms. My boss tells me I'm one of his best workers—one of his best, fastest workers, who works the hardest [of] anybody.

During the interview, Amy said she was "tired of the work," and plans were under way to find a new job. She'd like to "work with computers." Some of Amy's comments included playful observations. Referring to a picture of herself in a small bus, Amy quipped, "[I'm in] that little vertically challenged bus." As she looked at a picture of her sister, Amy noted: "I'm older than her. And she always teases me about my age."

## WAYNE KRIPPNER

Among the things Wayne likes best about his life are living in an apartment, "hanging out with" his roommate, and "bowling on Saturdays." He described his household responsibilities: "[I take out the] garbage, make my bed. Yesterday, I sposed to cook. I [did] my laundry last night. It's all gone [done] now. And I clean my room." Wayne likes "Mexican and Italian food." He also likes to cook.

Mother: One of the first things he asked for when he moved out was recipes. So he has quite a few of my recipes.

Wayne: The first recipe is a casserole. Chicken. One's from noodles; one's from stuffing.

## ALEX LINDBLAD

Alex enjoyed talking about the experience of participating in the 1987 International Special Olympics Games as a member of the Minnesota Bowling Team. During his interview Alex showed photographs of several International Olympics events and described them. These were photos of the send-off party for the athletes, of his family attending events, and of him bowling and relaxing. During the opening ceremony it was hot—"105 degrees!" to quote Alex. His mother said, "it felt like that," and his father agreed that it was "almost that hot." Alex explained his bowling techniques: "I got [a bronze

medal] from the International Special Olympics, South Bend Indiana, in bowling. [The best way to get strikes is to] drop the ball in the middle [of the lane]." As he looked at a photo of himself resting on a blanket, he quipped, "Bowling! That's how I got really tired!" Alex enjoyed the stars who performed at the events, especially John Denver. He read the interviewer part of a story from the local community newspaper, the *St. Louis Park Sailor*, about the bowling team's return from the International Games. Alex concluded his 1987 address to the Down Syndrome Association of Minnesota by saying, "I'll never forget the International Games!" (The entire text of Alex's address appears earlier in this chapter.)

## ANDREW NIGHTENGALE

Andy is gaining broad-based work experience by participating in a job training program. When he completes the program, he'd like a job working with computers. In the interview Andy described the scope of the program, which includes classes as well as practical experience.

On Mondays I work for different companies that gave us different types of jobs, like running wires for computers, for disc drives, or [other assembly]. Sometimes we ticket clothing [or] do packaging. Monday afternoons I work in the [Center] mailroom and deliver mail to the offices

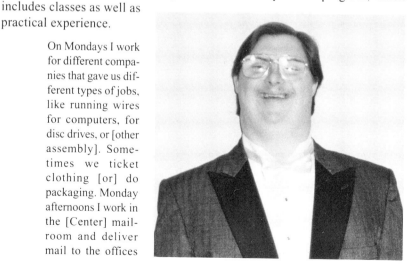

there. And then on Tuesdays I volunteer at a group home for elder people [nursing home]. We help them with bingo, picture bingo—they get coins for prizes. We [also] bring them [to other activities]. After that we go back to the library, back to the [Center] for lunch, and to the behavior in the workplace [class]. On Wednesdays, I have a YMCA work-out class and a canoe-making class. Right now we are making a canoe for [a local TV news anchor]. Thursdays, I have outside job training at different sites. I'm presently going to a bakery. Friday, I have the work-floor again in the morning; then afternoons I have computer class. We don't really get down into it, we just play games. If one of the people [in the class] leaves early, then I have a chance to work on my typing and that's on my schedule.

## TOM OPAT

One of the interview questions—"What makes you nervous or scared?"—provided Tom with an opportunity to talk about his experience working in a spook house "scaring people" during the Halloween season. The telling was animated, engaging, dramatic, and illustrated with dialogue.

> Back in October I [got] scared before going in the Spook House. Joe [his brother] was in there. And Joe [says], "I'll scare you, Tom!" And [I say], "No! You better not!" And so I back[ed] out, and didn't go in. All the years I worked in the Spook House. Twenty years I worked [there] with Sharon, my mom's friend. Sharon [asked] me, "Say, Tom, want to be in the Spook House?"—"Oh sure, Sharon." And I worked every week [during Halloween time]. Every Sunday. And so I dressed up in a mask and go "Hayes!" and scare them people out of the [Spook] House.
>
> Interviewer: But you weren't scared, they were!
>
> Tom: No, I working there. [He laughs.]

## ERIC SHERARTS

Eric and his brother, Teddy, who is two years younger, have a close relationship. Several of the items Eric brought to the interview centered around their relationship and included photos of them together, of Teddy, and of Eric's trips to visit his brother, an airline ticket for an upcoming visit; and a cassette of his brother's band. Eric said:

I called my brother in Austin, Texas, today. I am [going to] pay the [phone] bill. After 6 [p.m.] it's cheap. I'm going to [visit him soon]. [We'll] go out to eat—me, my brother, and [his girlfriend]. I [visited] my brother [last year] June 6. [We saw] California Angels against Red Socks in Los Angeles baseball stadium. My brother [took me to the game] and bought me snacks for my birthday—nachos, hot dogs, and pop. And after the game I saw the fireworks.

Eric then commented about the cassette: "That's my brother in the band on the cover. I got a free [band] T-shirt." He pointed out his name, which appears on the "special thanks to" list. "Oh, here. My name [is] on the list. Special guest [i.e., thanks to], me." Eric talked about watching the group with his friends. During the 1993 floods Eric heard the band in Iowa, where he also watched President Bill Clinton's visit to the disaster area "on TV in the hotel."

In the future, Eric would like to be promoted to a banquet server and live in an apartment with his best friend, who is also an EDGE participant.

## BRIAN THOMES

Brian Thomes has a hearing impairment. He communicates through signing, demonstrating, role playing, miming, and words. His verbal language is clearer when he signs. For the last four years Brian has been an altar server at the Catholic church he attends. It is a labor of love that brings him great satisfaction, and he is proud of the masterful way he executes his responsibilities. In the interview, Brian explained his duties through carefully orchestrated role-playing. He recruited his father to play the role of the parish priest. By combining

gestures, words, and actions, Brian described the garments he wears as well as the details and sequence of his responsibilities in the Mass.

Brian's mother commented that "[Brian] was the first one in our parish with developmental disabilities to serve [as altar server]. He works well at the altar. People like to see him there."

Brian commutes by van from Buffalo to his job at a conference center in a community nearby. At the conference center he makes beds and cleans rooms. His goal is to make seven beds each day. He likes to bowl, attend sports events, listen to music, travel, and be with people.

## ERIC WHEELER

Eric Wheeler has been actively involved in theater for several years. Acting is the love of his life. It all began when he auditioned for and got a part in an inclusive play entitled, "We're All in This Together." The group that mounted the production has since evolved into Interact Theater. The company is currently preparing an original play, "Bubba Nielson: The Endangered Species," for a three-week run in a professional theater. Eric has contributed to the process of creating this play and stars in its title role.

Eric took great delight in vividly, and often humorously, describing a number of the snapshots he brought to the interview. Photographs of Eric and his older brother provide irrefutable evidence that Arnie is taller than Eric. As he looked at these snapshots Eric observed:

These [photos] are [were taken] in my lifetime. Me and my brother here were kind of comparing muscles. I have short legs and he has stilt legs. My dad has bird [legs] and my mom has tree trunks for legs. My brother got tall here because he was drinking lots of milk and exercising. And I was trying to get close to him [i.e., his height], but I can't. I wasn't that short a long time ago. I'm trying to grow up [i.e., get taller] now. Like they always say, "Milk makes a body good." It doesn't matter how fat you are!

## BOBBY WOODARD

The first thing Bobby talked about in the interview was a coat hanger/shelf with "MOM" wood-burned into it that he made for his mother as a Christmas gift. He described some of the steps involved in making the gift. Bobby also talked about the deep meaning the gift holds for him and his mother. His only brother died a few years ago.

I make [this] for her. This is cedar wood. And I am sanding, sand it down. And, now you feel this wood. [It's] smooth, like your face, and I am smooth this down. Back here [he turns the shelf over to show where the screws for attaching it to the wall fit], I screw this in. [Then, he points out the holes he drilled for pegs.] One, two, three, four, and I made this hole [and put the pegs in]. And that say "Mom." And there her name on there. And I give her that for Merry Christmas gift. And [when] she open [the gift], her eyes, her eyes turn to tears. And I [said, "I made] it for you [to put] on your wall." Then [whether] I am dead or alive, she will remember me. When I am gone and is not. Can't speak or walk. I can now, right now. And I made it for her. [Bobby points to his mother.] I love her.

## LILLIANNE ZOLTAI

Lilli told an almost magical story about one of her Christmas presents, which was like a dream come true. She began the story with a telling comment: "Christmas is my favorite season." One of her favorite songs is Dolly Parton's rendition of "White Limousine." Last year around Christmas time Lilli said, "I wish I had my own white limousine!"

> So mom bought me [a ride in] a white limousine for a Christmas present. She rode in it. [So did] my roommate, my foster mother, my boyfriend, and myself. [I got] dressed up [for the ride] and wore a corsage. [The limousine was] big and beautiful inside [and] outside.

**OTES**

1. Used with permission of the author, Eric Fox. This poem appears in *If You Praise a Word, It Turns Into a Poem,* edited by Dana Jensen. St. Paul, MN: COMPAS, Writers and Artists in the Schools, 1992.
2. "Young Poets' Society." *Nineteenth Avenue,* Vol. 2, No. 5, April 1993. Published by the Humphrey Forum, Hubert H. Humphrey Institute of Public Affairs, University of Minnesota, Minneapolis.
3. Hunt, N. (1967). *The World of Nigel Hunt.* New York: Taplinger Publishing.
4. Kingsley, J., and Levitz, M. (1994). *Count Us In: Growing Up With Down Syndrome.* New York: Harcourt & Brace & Company.
5. As she read the letter, Jane added these three lines. They were not in the original letter she wrote and gave to the interviewer to include in this chapter.

---

*Karon Sherarts* is an independent consultant for diverse communities, schools, and institutions, focusing on research, media, arts, creativity, and education. She has a master's in American studies, is an adjunct instructor at Hamline University, and has conducted ethnographic research on media in Australia and New Zealand. Her son Eric, who has Down syndrome, has taught her many things.

The impetus for this chapter grew out of Ms. Sherarts' concern that the voices of adults with Down syndrome be heard, loud and clear. Her background in ethnographic research combined with the experience of parenting a son with Down syndrome (who was an EDGE participant) gives her a unique perspective and an opportunity to facilitate a broader understanding of the potential of people with Down syndrome. Ms. Sherarts designed the research methodology, analyzed the findings from the interviews, and shaped them into this chapter.

# $\mathscr{P}$HERARTS FAMILY

Mom: Karon
Brother: Teddy Morgan
Grandmother: Marion (Modisett)
Brother with Down
    syndrome: Eric

Fish for grandmother.

I want to be a cat.

Eric and Teddy.

## $\mathcal{S}$HERARTS FAMILY (continued)

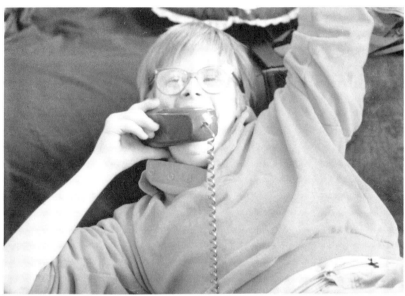

With friends on the phone.

Dressed for high school prom.

A new look at life.

# $\mathcal{E}$PILOGUE
# JOURNEYING INTO THE 21ST CENTURY

$\mathcal{L}$ ooking back on the 20th century, especially on the last 25 years, it is obvious that persons with Down syndrome have generally prospered. For instance, today an increasing number of educators are willing to entertain the possibility that children with Down syndrome can profit from academic instruction and substantial inclusion with nondisabled peers, given proper environmental supports. Similarly, recreational professionals have been gratified to see more young people with Down syndrome participate successfully in adapted, and even standard, sporting and recreation events. And an increasing number of employers are finding that adults with Down syndrome can become topnotch employees when they have adequate training and guidance. Through these accomplishments individuals with Down syndrome have earned the right to a promising place for themselves in the next century.

Nevertheless, each one of us needs to make certain that all elements of our society continue to appreciate the contribution of its citizens who have Down syndrome because society's decision-makers often reveal a tendency to view citizen contributions in terms of markers such as college entrance exam scores earned, positions held, and wealth accumulated. They need to have their viewpoints adjusted continually. They need to see that people who have Down syndrome not only become good students, teammates, employees, and neighbors, but bring a unique *humanizing* quality to all aspects of community life. They need to see that people with Down syndrome bring a rare kind of earthiness, freshness, and unpretentiousness to their community, a quality that can renew the spirits of nondisabled peers and citizens alike. They need to see that employees who have Down syndrome nearly always labor with a full measure of earnestness in their endeavors, showing a degree of industriousness that can occasionally make nondisabled workers' efforts look pale by comparison. Most of all, they need to see that communities become better places—more productive, energized, and compassionate places—as nondisabled members of the community learn to accommodate and appreciate those who have Down syndrome.

For these reasons (and many others) parents who have a child with Down syndrome never need to feel apologetic about pressing society to become more accommodating. Society *benefits* from having people with Down syndrome at the center of its community life rather than placed in an institution located in a remote area of the state, as was common up until the 1970s. Indeed, challenging our society to be more accommodating is exactly the kind of "stretching" experience that our form of democracy needs to thrive. Growth and development of an individual come about by the dual process of nurturance combined with challenge. Society is no different. Challenged by the legitimate rights and needs of people with Down syndrome, and nurtured by the experience of trying to meet these needs and rights successfully, every citizen, both disabled and nondisabled, becomes a more valued and valuable member of society. With the promise of new joint accomplishments and shared confidences, everyone in a community can look forward to sharing each family's journey into the 21st century as they learn and grow with individuals who have Down syndrome.

# APPENDIX

## RESOURCES

*Compiled by Shannon Matson*

# NATIONAL ORGANIZATIONS ON DOWN SYNDROME FOR PARENTS AND PROFESSIONALS

*Association for Children with Down Syndrome*
2616 Martin Avenue
Bellmore, NY 11710
(516) 221–4700
FAX (516) 221–4311

*Canadian Down Syndrome Society*
12837-76th Avenue, Suite 206
Surrey, BC, Canada V3W 2V3
(604) 599–6009
FAX (604) 599–6165

*Caring Inc.*
P.O. Box 400
Milton, WA 98354
(206) 922–8607

*National Down Syndrome Congress*
1605 Chantilly Drive, Suite 250
Atlanta, GA 30324
(800) 232–6372 or (404) 633–1555
FAX (404) 633–2817

*National Down Syndrome Society*
666 Broadway, Suite 810
New York, NY 10012
(800) 221–4602 or (212) 460–9330
FAX (212) 979–2873

# COMMUNICATION/TECHNOLOGY

## ASSISTIVE TECHNOLOGY RESOURCES

*Council for Exceptional Children*
1920 Association Drive
Reston, VA 22091
(703) 620–3660

*National Easter Seal Society*
70 E. Lake Street
Chicago, IL 60601
(800) 221–6827 or (312) 726–6200
TTY (312) 726–4258

## ASSISTIVE TECHNOLOGY DATA SOURCES

*SOLUTIONS and Macintosh*
*Disabilities Resources*
Apple Computer
20525 Mariani Avenue
Cupertino, CA 94510
(800) 732–3131 ext. 950 or (408)
974–7910

*IBM Special Needs and*
*Referral Center*
4111 Northside Parkway
Internal Code H06R1
Atlanta, GA 30327
(800) IBM–2132
TTY (800) 284–9482

## ASSISTANCE ON COMMUNICATION AIDS

*St. Luke's Hospital*
Department of Speech Pathology
and Audiology
1026 A Avenue NE
Cedar Rapids, IA 53402
(319) 369–7491

*Communication Enhancement*
*Center*
Children's Hospital
300 Longwood Avenue
Boston, MA 02115
(617) 735–6000

*Courage Center*
3915 Golden Valley Road
Golden Valley, MN 55422
(612) 588–0811

*Gillette Children's Hospital*
200 W. University Avenue
St. Paul, MN 55101
(612) 229–3800

*International Society for*
*Augmentative and Alternative*
*Communication (ISAAC)*
P.O. Box 1762, Station R
Toronto, ON
Canada M4G 4A3
(416) 737–9308

## COMMUNICATION AIDS*

*Handy Speech Communication*
CCT, 508 Bellevue Terrace
Pittsburgh, PA 15202
(412) 761–6062

Affordable, state-of-the-art augmentative communication device and related hardware products; IBM-compatible.

*Palmer DeYoung: Buddy Boards*
10424 Aquila Circle
Bloomington, MN 55438
(612) 942–9300
FAX (612) 942–7919

Facilitated communication board designed to take everywhere—playground to restaurant. Qwerty-style keyboard and back side has 22 word/phrases. Retractable key chain for easy use. Jr. 4 × 7, Sr. 5½ × 8½.

---

* Annotations found in *Exceptional Parent*, Sept. 1993, Market Place p. 89.

# OMPUTERS/TECHNOLOGY

## RESOURCE CENTERS

*Alliance for Technology Access
(formerly National Special
Education Alliance)*

*National Offices*
1307 Salono Avenue
Albany, CA 94706–1888
(415) 528–0747
FAX (415) 528–0746

217 Massachusetts Avenue
Lexington, MA 02173
(617) 863–9966
FAX (617) 863–9932

*Team of Advocates for Special Kids*
100 W. Cerritos
Anaheim, CA 92805
(714) 533–TASK

*Access Ability Resource Center*
1056 East 19th Avenue, B–410
Denver, CO 80218–1088
(303) 861–6250

*Technology Resources for
Special People*
3023 Canterbury
Salina, KS 67401
(913) 827–0301

*PACER Center*
4826 Chicago Avenue S.
Minneapolis, MN 55417–1055
(612) 827–2966 [Voice/TTY]

*Parents, Let's Unite for Kids*
1500 N. 30th Street
Billings, MT 59101–0298
(406) 657–2055

## SOFTWARE*

*Access Unlimited*
3535 Brairpark Drive, Suite 102
Houston, TX 77042–5235
(800) 848–0311
FAX (713) 781–3550

Nonprofit assisting educators, health care providers, and parents discover how personal computers help children with disabilities compensate through technology. Free video and information on Apple, Macintosh, IBM special access devices/software.

*Kidsview Software*
P.O. Box 98
Warner, NH 03278
(800) 542–7501

Apple II and Commodore software with large characters on screen and printout for students with learning disabilities and low vision.

---

* Annotations found in *Exceptional Parent*, Sept. 1993, Market Place p. 89.

## LEKOTEK CENTERS

*National Center*
National Lekotek Center
2100 Ridge Avenue
Evanston, IL 60201
(708) 328–0001

*Easter Seal Lekotek of
Southern Arizona*
5740 East 22nd Street
Tucson, AZ 85711
(602) 745–5222

*Lekotek–YWCA*
318 Fifth Street, SE
Cedar Rapids, IA 52401
(319) 365–1458

# ℛECREATION

## RESOURCES

*Special Olympics*
1350 New York Avenue NW
Suite 500
Washington, DC 20005
(202) 628–3630

*Aquatics:*

*Beach Wheels*
1555 Shadowlawn Drive
Naples, FL 33942
(813) 775–1078

*Baseball:*

*Challenger Baseball*
Little League Baseball Headquarters
P.O. Box 3485
Williamsport, PA 17701
(717) 326–1921

*Camping:*

*Wilderness Inquiry*
1313 Fifth Avenue SE
Box 84
Minneapolis, MN 55414
(612) 379–3858

*Access: Camping*
P.O. Box 356
Malverne, NY 11565–0356
(516) 887–5684

*Canoeing:*

*Canadian Recreational
Canoeing Association*
1029 Hyde Park Road, Suite 5
Hyde Park, ON
Canada NOM 1ZO
(519) 473–2109

*S'PLORE (Special Populations
Learning Outdoor Recreation and
Education)*
27 West 3300 South
Salt Lake City, UT 84115
(801) 5484–4128

*Fishing:*

*Adaptive Physical Education &
Recreation*
Frederico Ceccoti
P.O. Box 269
Alfred I. duPont Institute
Wilmington, DE 19899
(302) 651–4000

*Gardening:*

*American Horticultural Therapy
Association*
362A Christopher Avenue
Githersburg, MD 20879
(301) 948–3010

*General Recreation:*

*International Center on Special
Recreation*
362 Koster Avenue
Iowa City, IA 52246–3038
(319) 337–7578

*Horseback Riding:*

*North American Riding for
the Handicapped Association*
P.O. Box 33150
Denver, CO 80233
(800) 452–RIDE

*Skiing:*

*Ski for Light International*
Old Highway Eight
Roseville, MN 55113
(612) 633–9250

 **OOKS** _____

## INTEGRATED RECREATION AND LEISURE PROGRAMMING

Rynders, J. E., and S. J. Schleien, *Together Successfully: Creating Recreational
and Educational Programs That Integrate People with and without
Disabilities*, National Office of 4-H and Youth Development, Research
and Training Center on Community Living, University of Minnesota
Institute on Community Integration (UAP), University of Minnesota
(Arlington, TX: Association for Retarded Citizens of the United States,
1991).

Schleien, S., and M. T. Ray, *Community Recreation and Persons with Disabilities: Strategies for Integration* (Baltimore: Paul H. Brookes Publishing, 1988).

Special Olympics International, *Unified Sports Handbook* (Washington, DC:
Special Olympics, 1989).

Wilcox, B., and G. T. Bellamy, *The Activities Catalog: An Alternative Curriculum for Youth and Adults with Severe Disabilities* (Baltimore: Paul
H. Brookes Publishing, 1987).

## TRANSITION TO POSTSCHOOL PERIOD

Buckley, S., and B. Sacks, *The Adolescent with Down's Syndrome* (Ontario, Canada: Down's Syndrome Association of Ontario, 1987).

Pueschel, Siegfried, editor, *The Young Person with Down Syndrome: Transition from Adolescence to Adulthood* (Baltimore: Paul H. Brookes Publishing, 1988).

## INDEPENDENT LIVING

Close, D. W., and A. S. Halpern, "Transition to Supported Living," in *Community Residences for Persons with Developmental Disabilities: Here to Stay*, edited by M. P. Janieki, M. W. Krauss, and M. M. Seltzer (Baltimore: Paul H. Brookes Publishing, 1988).

Halpren, A. S., D. W. Close, and D. J. Nelson, *On My Own: The Impact of Semi-Independent Living Programs for Adults with Mental Retardation* (Baltimore: Paul H. Brookes Publishing, 1986).

## VOCATIONAL/EMPLOYMENT

Bellamy, G. T., L. Rhodes, and J. M. Albin, "Supported Employment," in *Pathways to Employment for Adults with Developmental Disabilities*, edited by W. Kiernan and J. Stark (Baltimore: Paul H. Brookes Publishing, 1986), pp. 129–138.

Rusch, F. R., editor, *Competitive Employment: Issues and Strategies* (Baltimore: Paul H. Brookes Publishing, 1986).

## SEXUALITY

Edwards, J. P., *Being Me: A Social-Sexual Training Guidebook* (Austin, TX: Pro-Ed, 1979).

Edwards, J. P., "Sexuality, Marriage, and Parenting for Persons with Down Syndrome," in *The Young Person with Down Syndrome*, edited by S. M. Pueschel (Baltimore: Paul H. Brookes Publishing, 1988), pp. 187–204.

Edwards, J. P., and T. E. Elkins, *Just Between Us: A Social Sexual Guide for Parents and Professionals with Concerns for Persons with Developmental Disabilities* (Austin, TX: Pro-Ed, 1988).

## FAMILY*

Dougan, Terrel, Lyn Isbell, and Patricia Vyas, *We Have Been There* (Nashville, TN: Abingdon Press, 1988).
Deals with the fears, tears, courage, and ability to laugh at ourselves that keeps families going.

* Supplemented with annotations by the National Organization of Parents and Professionals.

Meyer, D., P. Valdasy, and R. Fewell, *Living with a Brother or Sister with Special Needs* (Seattle: University of Washington Press, 1985).
Written especially for siblings to discover how other siblings of a brother or sister with a disability share much of the same questions and emotions.

Pueschel, S., *A Parent's Guide to Down Syndrome: Toward a Brighter Future* (Baltimore: Paul H. Brookes Publishing, 1990).

Simons, R., *After the Tears* (San Diego: Harcourt, Brace, & Jovanovich, 1987).
Subtitled "Parents Talk About Raising a Child with a Disability" it is beautifully edited, illustrated, and designed. Parental experiences are integrated into short, readable chapters. Suggestions of simple, constructive things to do follow each chapter.

Tingey, Carol, *Down Syndrome* (Boston: College Hill Press, 1988).

Trainer, M., *Differences in Common. Straight Talk on Mental Retardation, Down Syndrome and Life* (Rockville, MD: Woodbine House, 1991).

## EARLY INTERVENTION

Cunningham, C., *Down's Syndrome: An Introduction for Parents* (Cambridge, MA: Brookline Books).
Provides some answers to immediate questions parents ask; excellent basic book.

Hanson, M., *Teaching the Infant with Down Syndrome: A Guide for Parents and Professionals* (Austin, TX: Pro-Ed, 1987).
A manual for parents with step-by-step instructions for teaching skills to infants with Down syndrome.

Stray-Gunderson, K., editor, *Babies with Down Syndrome: A New Parent's Guide* (Rockville, MD: Woodbine House, 1986).
Comprehensive guide for new parents and interested others concerning how to help a child with Down syndrome reach his/her potential.

Tingey, C., *Implementing Early Intervention* (Baltimore: Paul H. Brookes Publishing, 1989).

## BIOGRAPHIES*

Bakely, Donald C., *Bethy and the Mouse—God's Gifts in Special Packages* (Newton, KS: Faith & Life Press, 1985).
An almost poetic father's account of his special children—Bethy with Down syndrome and "the Mouse," who was born with microcephaly. A tender, rugged, earnest, honest narrative expressing a father's love, fear, and gratitude.

---

*Supplemented with annotations by the National Organization of Parents and Professionals.

Edwards, Jean, and David Dawson, *My Friend David: A Source Book About Down's Syndrome and a Personal Story About Friendship* (Austin, TX: Pro-Ed, 1983).

This story of a special friendship is co-authored by David, a man who has Down syndrome, and Jean Edwards, who has worked for many years with her friends who have developmental disabilities. Special sections are devoted to new parents and "breaking the news," as well as issues involving the adult.

## SELF ADVOCACY

Kingsley, Jason, and Mitchell Levitz, *Count Us In: Growing Up with Down Syndrome* (New York: Harcourt Brace, 1994).

# JOURNALS*

*Down Syndrome News*

Publication for parents and professionals concerned with Down syndrome, it includes articles on medical, educational, recreational, residential, and legislative matters, as well as a variety of other current topics affecting people with Down syndrome and their families. 10 issues per year. National Down Syndrome Congress, 1800 Dempster Street, Park Ridge, IL 60068–1146.

*Sharing Our Caring*

Journal for parents of children with Down syndrome. Contains parents' personal stories and articles by professionals. Vehicle for parent/professional exchange of problem-solving techniques and information on various programs. 5 issues per year. *Caring*, Box 400, Milton, WA 98354.

*Exceptional Parent*

Bimonthly publication dealing with many issues affecting exceptional children and their families. 6 issues per year. 605 Commonwealth Avenue, Boston, MA 02215.

*Exceptional Grandparents*

Quarterly newsletter written for and about grandparents of children with special needs. King County Advocates for Retarded Citizens, 2230 Eighth Avenue, Seattle, WA 98121.

*Sibling Information Network*

Newsletter providing information for and about siblings of individuals with handicaps. Published four times a year. Sibling Information Network, Connecticut's UAP, 991 Main Street, Suite 3A, East Hartford, CT 06108.

---

* Supplemented with annotations by the National Organization of Parents and Professionals.

# READING SKILL DEVELOPMENT SEQUENCE FOR STUDENTS CLASSIFIED AS EDUCABLE

## $\mathscr{S}$TAGE I

"This is the stage in which children engage in a program of experience designed to develop mental, physical, emotional, and social readiness for reading" (Anderson).

    A. Gross motor development and visual-motor skills
        1. Body image
        2. Visual-motor training
        3. Perceptual motor match
        4. Laterality
        5. Spatial relationships
    B. Language development (Mainord and Love, pp. 91–92)
        1. Listening skills
            a. Auditory attending (pay attention by listening)
            b. Responding to own name
            c. Recognizing sounds in the inside and outside environment
        2. Oral expression
            a. Nursery rhymes
            b. Telling experiences

## $\mathscr{S}$TAGE II

"This is the stage in which the children are taught to read material based on their current group experiences. The simple content involved may be that of science or events of daily living. Charts or booklists made by the teacher are used. It is important at this stage that children come to realize that their reading

---

This scope and sequence combines the material of J. C. Mainord and H. D. Love, *Teaching Educable Mentally Retarded Children: Methods and Materials* (Springfield, IL: Charles C Thomas, 1973), and Paul S. Anderson, *Language Skills in Elementary Education* (New York: Macmillan, 1964). This sequence is helpful particularly at the early stages of reading instruction.

yields information useful to them in their activities and to feel that reading is fun. Habits of reading from left to right and from line to line are begun. Some practice in locating sentences is provided. Children are encouraged to note the distinctive configuration of words of special interest or of unique form and to compare words with like beginnings. At this stage, a basic reading vocabulary is established upon which to build as progress is made" (Anderson).

A. Visual abilities
   1. Visual discrimination
      a. Likenesses
      b. Differences
      c. Color
      d. Form
      e. Size
      f. Position
      g. Detail
      h. Shape
      i. Letter configuration
   2. Visual memory
B. Auditory abilities
   1. Listening and developing the habit of following one simple direction, two simple directions, etc.
   2. Listening to stories, records, or nursery rhymes
   3. Developing an awareness of rhythmic patterns in sounds and words
   4. Beginning sounds
   5. Ending sounds
   6. Recognizing words that have similar sounds
   7. Blending sounds
   8. Developing ideas in logical sequence (Mainord and Love, p. 92)

# $\mathscr{S}$TAGE III

"During this stage a child increases his sight vocabulary and develops ability to recognize new words by content, by association, by known parts or by more detailed analysis. He forms the habit of reading independently for information and for pleasure. He develops the desire to share pleasant reading experiences with others and sees some of the possibilities of using reading in problem-solving activities" (Anderson).

A. Core of sight vocabulary (Dolch word list)
   1. Child's name (nouns)
   2. Color words

      3. Action words

      4. Verbs

      5. Connecting words

      6. Prepositions

      7. Pronouns

B. Context skills

C. Phonetic analysis

      1. Beginning consonant sounds and digraphs—wh, th, sh, ch

      2. Ending consonant sounds

      3. Short vowel sounds

      4. Consonant blends—bl, br, cl, cr, fl, fr, st, tr, spr, scr, dr, gl, pl, pr, sc, sk, sl, sm, sn, sp

      5. Long vowel sounds

D. Structural analysis

      1. Reviewing configuration clues, if needed

      2. Word endings and suffixes—s, es, ing, ed, er, ly

      3. Compound words

E. Dictionary skills

      1. Alphabetizing

      2. Definitions (Mainord and Love, pp. 93–94)

# TIPS FOR ADAPTING COMMON RECREATION ACTIVITIES FOR YOUNG ADULTS

## EWING ADAPTATIONS

- If the person has finger dexterity and coordinated movement difficulties, use paper of a heavier weight to make pattern pieces. Contact a company that supplies patterns for people with visual impairment. If you make patterns yourself, use heavy-weight wrapping paper.
- To facilitate measuring, adapt a regular tape measure by inserting a staple to mark each inch and two staples to mark every foot.
- To help an individual thread a needle, poke the point of the needle into a cork to secure the needle and hold it erect. Help him or her to place the thumb and finger of one hand near the eye of the needle. Using a wire needle threader, have the person pass it through the needle eye as far as possible and draw the thread through, or use a self-threading needle.
- If the participant has difficulty using scissors to cut fabric, let him or her practice by snipping off bits of coiled clay. Then try paper. Once these are mastered, move to fabric. Make sure scissors are sharp. Don't stay too long at the clay- or paper-cutting activity, as it is essentially nonfunctional. Cutting fabric is what you want the person to do. Also, adapted scissors are available commercially for individuals with poor manual dexterity (for example, double-handed scissors available through Developmental Learning Materials).
- Mark patterns to guide participants. Draw cutting lines on patterns. Put red X's on the patterns to show where pins go. In the beginning,

---

Some ideas in this appendix are based in part on two excellent 4-H publications: *Together—A Leader/Agent Workbook for 4-H Programming to Include Youths with Disabilities*, by Patricia Kraal (distributed by National 4-H Council) and *Adaptive Methodology*, an unpublished paper that comes from Insights-Arts in Special Education, Art Education of New Jersey, 445 Wyoming Avenue, Millburn, NJ 07041. The authors wish to thank Drs. Marie Knowlton and Susan Rose, University of Minnesota, for their helpful suggestions in the areas of vision and hearing adaptations.

mark the seam line for the person. Let him or her hand-baste the seams with long running stitches.

- If the participant has little or no movement impairment in the upper body and has a reasonable level of intellectual ability, he or she often can master basic use of a sewing machine. To begin using a sewing machine, the person must learn how to thread the machine and needle, prepare the bobbin, and set the seam gauge accurately. Review the sequence of these tasks with him or her until the skills have been mastered. Provide assistance as needed, but not more than is absolutely necessary.
- With beginners, try sewing operations that do not require precise small muscle use, such as rug hooking.

# $\mathcal{W}$OODWORKING ADAPTATIONS

- Begin the task of learning to hammer by using shingle nails and prepunching a hole for the nail point to be inserted. In beginning to hammer a nail, shorten the person's grip on the handle of the hammer. Have him or her position the index finger along the hammer shaft, pointing toward the hammer head. Keep the wrist as close as possible to the nailing plane. When necessary, use needle-nose pliers to position and hold the nail. Encourage him or her to begin tapping the nail into the wood gently. After the nail is started, remove the pliers (if used) and ask person to take fuller swings. Allow the hammer to bounce on the nail between strokes.
- To saw across a board, modify the task in one of three ways: use a miter box, a saw guide (a narrow board held in place with C-clamps), or cut a beginning line in the board with the saw. Always clamp the object to be cut, preferably in a bench vise.
- Select clear, soft, straight-grain wood for projects. Pre-cut, pre-drill, and pre-route project components that are difficult, because they require the use of machine tools that are potentially dangerous.
- Use jigs to reduce the chance of error. Templates can help to position a footstool surface for drilling holes to receive the legs. A doweling jig will help position the drill bit so dowels fit properly, etc.
- For gluing wood, use carpenter's glue, because it comes in a squeeze bottle and washes off with water. It is similar to the familiar white glue but is much stronger for bonding wood. It dries faster than white glue, though, so be sure to "dry-fit" pieces of a project, have clamps ready if they will be needed, and have a damp cloth handy to wipe

up excess glue. Even when removed quickly and thoroughly, glue will seal the wood surface so stain will not penetrate, leaving a light spot on the wood's surface. Therefore, stain pieces before gluing them together.

- Stain the wood with an oil-based stain because it is much more "forgiving" than water-based stain, which streaks and shows fingerprints if it is not wiped off quickly and skillfully. This is especially important if participants have severe cognitive and movement disabilities.
- Allow the use of relatively "safe" machine tools only after proper instruction, and always with good supervision. Safety first!

## CREATIVE ARTS ADAPTATIONS

- During weaving, when an individual cannot identify individual warp lines and confuses "over" and "under," identify every other line with a colored marker. For example: row 1 = white threads over and red threads under; row 2 = white threads under and red threads over.
- Huck weaving, if patterns are not too complicated, can be a rewarding project. Choose loosely woven fabrics, and use small portions of a large piece in the beginning, so the space will fill up quickly. A needle with a fairly wide and long eye will be easier to thread.
- Sometimes the color, odor, and coldness of the wheat paste used for papier maché upsets stomachs. If this happens, use warm water and add a drop of vanilla extract and a drop of food coloring to change the feel, color, and odor. For those who do not like the feel of cold clay, try adding warm water to powdered clay or have them use rubber gloves.
- Demonstrate handicraft operations, if needed, by standing behind the person, letting his or her hands rest on yours as you do the task.
- Some overly timid participants who "work small" and seldom finish a picture may feel threatened by a large piece of paper. Have the participant work with a small piece of paper until he or she fills the paper and develops self-confidence. Slowly enlarge the size of the paper until the participant is working full-scale.
- When introducing painting, limit the palette to one to three colors. A more extensive color choice may confuse some participants. As painting skills increase, gradually add colors to the palette. Provide one brush for each color and use long-handled brushes because they are easier to manipulate.
- For participants with "grip control" problems, cover handles of brushes

with cotton batting and masking tape. This method works with other drawing tools, too.

- Be creative with paint applicators. They can be paintbrushes, palette knives, sponges attached to "clip" clothespins, tongue depressors, cotton swabs, and roll-on deodorant bottles.
- For individuals who have difficulty putting on a smock, lay the smock flat on a table or the floor. Have the person pick up the top of the smock, place arms in the sleeves, and let the rest of the smock fall into place. If a smock has buttons, have the person put it on backward to avoid buttoning it if this is a difficult step.
- When learning to paint, participants do not always understand the progression of painting routines or brush manipulation—dipping brush into paint, applying brush to paper, and manipulating brush back and forth to cover an area of the paper. If so, demonstrate this sequence and have the person practice it several times. Some participants will need assistance holding and manipulating the brush.
- For participants with poor muscle control, use C-clamps or a vise to help secure an embroidery hoop or a sculpture project. Wood frames with the fabric attached also are useful for stabilizing stitching projects.
- For participants who cannot exert enough downward pressure to draw with "hard" materials (pencil or chalk), make lines in soft materials such as clay or with soft-tip watercolor pens. Avoid markers with toxic ink.
- If participants need to strengthen hands and fingers, have them work with clay, tear paper for making papier-maché projects, and arrange mosaic pieces. If a person's fingers or hand muscles tighten, massage the area above the wrists gently to reduce tension and relax the hand.
- Place an object with physical boundaries, such as a shallow box lid, under a project.
- To avoid scattering, spills, and smudges, fasten water containers, paper, paint containers, etc., to the table with masking tape. Place strips of wood or cardboard around work areas.
- For participants who can't squeeze a standard plastic glue bottle, pour glue into a soft plastic bottle with a spout for easier squeezing. Cut the spout to enlarge the hole if necessary. Hairdressing containers, plastic dye bottles, and plastic paint containers with pouring spouts work well. Glue also can be applied with brushes, cotton swabs, and sponges attached to clothespins.

# COOKING

- To adjust dials, the participant or instructor can mark critical settings with small pieces of colored tape. Set a kitchen timer to signal when foods are done.
- Participants should always place pans on the burner and center them before turning on the heat. Never place a pan handle so it protrudes over the front of the stove where it may be hit or pushed off the stove. Point the handle toward the back of the range.
- To cool a hot pan in a safe area on a hot pad, participants should carry the hot pan across the room with one oven mitt on the carrying hand and another oven mitt on the free hand. Have them hold the free hand in front of the pan like a "bumper" to be used as a guide if necessary. No portion of the hot pan should be exposed enough to touch any person who might be in the path.
- Instruct participants that large, sharp knives should be carried by the handle in a vertical position, blade down. The handle should be held loosely by the thumb and fingertip, never grasping it in a tight fist. The non-carrying hand should be used in front of the knife as a "bumper" guard. Smaller knives can be carried by the blade in a closed-fist position. If the other hand, the "bumper" hand, is not free for any reason, the wrist of the carrying hand should lead.
- A sharp knife should never be left in the sink, but should be washed and dried immediately after use, and put away. Sharp knives should be kept apart from other utensils, and not be loose in a drawer.
- If an individual cannot follow a written recipe, attach drawings or photographs to recipes. A photo album, each page containing one photograph illustrating the individual performing a step of the cooking activity, can be helpful and enjoyable.
- When teaching how to measure liquids, use colored water. It's easier to see.
- Select kitchen tools with large, easy-to-grip handles that do not conduct heat.
- When cutting meats or vegetables, have participants use a cutting board that has stainless steel nails protruding from its top surface to stabilize the food.

# ASSESSMENT INSTRUMENTS

## Interest Tests

*Career Assessment Inventory*
Charles B. Johnsson
National Computer Systems
P.O. Box 1294
Minneapolis, MN 55440

*Kuder General Interest Survey*
Science Research Associates, Inc.
259 East Erie Street
Chicago, IL 60611

*Minnesota Importance Questionnaire*
Vocational Psychology Research
Elliot Hall
75 East River Road
Minneapolis, MN 55455

*Minnesota Vocational Interest
    Inventory*
The Psychological Corporation
304 East 45th Street
New York, NY 10017

*Reading-Free Vocational
    Interest Inventory*
Elbern Publications
P.O. Box 09497
Columbus, OH 43209

*Strong-Campbell Vocational
    Interest Test*
Stanford University Press
Stanford, CA 94305

## Achievement Tests

*California Achievement Test*
CTB/McGraw Hill
Del Monte Research Park
Monterey, CA 93940

*Gates-MacGinitie Reading
    (Forms A, B, D, and E) Test*
Teachers College Press
1234 Amsterdam Avenue
Columbia University
New York, NY 10027

*Nelson-Denny Reading Test*
Houghton Mifflin Company
One Beacon Street
Boston, MA 02108

*Peabody Picture Vocabulary Test*
American Guidance Service, Inc.
Publishers' Building
Circle Pines, MN 55014

*Wide Range Achievement
    Test (WRAT)*
Jastak Associates, Inc.
1526 Gilpin Avenue
Wilmington, DE 19806

## Dexterity Tests

*Bennett Hand Tool Dexterity* and
*Crawford Small Parts Dexterity*
The Psychological Corporation
Order Service Center
P.O. Box 839954
San Antonio, TX 78283-3954

*Purdue Pegboard Dexterity*
London House
9701 W. Higgins Road
Rosemount, IL 60018

## Aptitude Tests

*Bennett Mechanical
  Comprehension,
Differential Aptitude Test (DAT),* and
*Revised Minnesota Paper Form
  Board*
The Psychological Corporation
Order Service Center
P.O. Box 839954
San Antonio, TX 78283-3954

*General Aptitude Test Battery
  (GATB)*
National Computer Systems
5605 Green Circle Drive
Minnetonka, MN 55343

*SRA Computer Operator/
  Programmer Aptitude Test
  Batteries* and
*SRA Short Tests of Clerical Ability*
London House
9701 W. Higgins Road
Rosemount, IL 60018

# INDEX